In Search of
Deep
Throat

In Search of
Deep
Throat

*The Greatest
Political Mystery of
Our Time*

LEONARD GARMENT

BASIC
BOOKS

A Member of the Perseus Books Group

Published by Basic Books,
A Member of the Perseus Books Group

ISBN 0-465-02613-3

First Edition

A CIP catalog record for this book is available from the Library of Congress.

The paper used in this publication meets the requirements of the American
National Standard for Permanence of Paper for Printed Library Materials
Z39.48-1984.

00 01 02 03 / 10 9 8 7 6 5 4 3 2 1

Contents

Acknowledgments

Suzanne Garment and Ross Davies picked me up off the floor halfway through the writing of this book and carried me across the finish line. I am indebted to them as collaborators in every sense of the word except for the selection of Deep Throat, which is my sole responsibility. Suzanne was for years an associate editor of the *Wall Street Journal* and is the author of *Scandal: The Culture of Mistrust in American Politics*. Ross is editor-in-chief of *The Green Bag: An Entertaining Journal of Law*, which demonstrates that legal writing can be both sophisticated and engaging. He also practices law in Washington with the firm of Shea & Gardner.

Matthew Warner, my assistant, performed all kinds of herculean deeds of research.

Ron Goldfarb, my agent and friend, made all this happen efficiently and painlessly.

Introduction

In ancient Brittany, after a burial, when everyone else had left to partake of the funeral banquet, some of the old men would remain behind in the graveyard to ask each other riddles. Sir Frazer described this strange ritual in *The Golden Bough* but said he did not know its origin. He speculated that solving riddles was considered a kind of training for solving the greater mysteries of life and death.

One winter day early this year, I was sitting around with my old friend and law partner Harry McPherson, whose memoir of his years in Lyndon Johnson's White House, *A Political Education*, is perhaps the best personal account that exists of postwar American politics. Harry and I were talking about the lead science article in that morning's *New York Times*. Its headline read, "Maybe We Are Alone in the Universe, After All." Over the headline, covering the top third of the page, was a photo of a piece of the black, star-clotted universe. The picture was composed of millions of galaxies and solar systems, only a tiny part of what is known to be out there in possibly infinite, eternal space.

Yet despite these innumerable stars and planets in the universe, the *New York Times* article said, two prominent scientists had announced that we humans are probably the only sentient beings inhabiting it. The conditions necessary to create and sustain life, the scientists argued, seem not to be duplicated or duplicable anywhere else in the cosmos. As a gambler would put it, the odds of life's happening anywhere else are off the books.

Well, McPherson mused, maybe yes and maybe no; but there's nothing like an intriguingly beautiful puzzle. Before long we were immersed in discussion of other puzzles—like the one that Einstein successfully solved ($E = mc^2$), the one he did not (his quest for a unified theory of physics), and the irreducible puzzle to which Wittgenstein concluded that the only response is silence. In other words, for a moment, we talked about everything except clients.

Compared to deep space and eternity, the identity of Deep Throat is just a minor-league mystery. But for a quarter century, it has been a durable source of wonder. People have sensed that somewhere out there is a living, breathing answer to this puzzle and that if we find him, we will experience the very particular sort of satisfaction we feel when we have tied up one of the loose ends of the universe.

I think I have solved this particular puzzle. It is my conviction that Deep Throat, Bob Woodward's mysterious source in *All the President's Men*, was John Sears.

At the time of Watergate, Sears was an obscure political operative who had worked in the 1968 Nixon presidential campaign and, briefly, in the Nixon White House. After Watergate, Sears became more prominent. He gained national attention when he served as campaign manager for

Ronald Reagan in 1976 and 1980. Sears's name is well known and respected among those who participate in or write about national politics but unknown to most of those who have puzzled over the identity of Deep Throat.

There is no point to being told that Sears is Deep Throat, however, without an opportunity to evaluate the evidence behind the claim and to consider the importance of the idea of Deep Throat in post-Watergate American politics. Providing that opportunity is the aim of this book.

*   *   *

By the late spring of 1974, with the Watergate scandal approaching its end, virtually all political observers in Washington, except for those of us still thrashing around in Richard Nixon's White House, knew that his presidency was doomed. Indeed, politically sentient individuals could not take their eyes off the slow-motion train wreck that Watergate had become. While people were thus occupied, Simon & Schuster published *All the President's Men*.

The book was written by Bob Woodward and Carl Bernstein, two journalists who had reported on Watergate for the *Washington Post* beginning with their June, 1972 accounts of the Watergate break-in. Woodward and Bernstein's news stories had been instrumental in keeping the Watergate scandal alive during the months after the break-in when other media had ignored the issue or minimized its importance. *All the President's Men* told the behind-the-scenes story of the two reporters' news gathering during that pregnant time. The book included descriptions of Woodward's encounters with the source whom the authors called Deep Throat.

Soon after the book appeared, it was reviewed by Christopher Lehmann-Haupt in the *New York Times*. Lehmann-Haupt speculated that Woodward and Bernstein's tale of their reporting exploits might be overshadowed by the very success of those exploits. Reality had overtaken art: Nixon's political crack-up, then in progress, was proving to be a spectacle far more vivid than the story told in *All the President's Men* about the journalistic efforts that brought about the destruction.

The *New York Times* need not have worried. *All the President's Men* sold briskly from the start, launching its authors into the journalistic stratosphere. Moreover, the national fascination with Watergate proved to be more than a case of collective rubbernecking at the scene of a disaster. Though the events of Watergate are long past, its story, characters, and themes have spawned an endless, Niagara-like outpouring of essays, cartoons, voodoo dolls, books of argument, works of fiction, major motion pictures, and made-for-TV movies.

This incessant return to Watergate is as pronounced in recent years as it was immediately after the episode. Even today, otherwise sane and responsible people openly declare themselves to be Watergate buffs, reading everything they can get their hands on that is related to the disaster. It is not so long ago that Oliver Stone—who had previously given us the movie *JFK*, based on a CIA-linked conspiracy theory of President Kennedy's assassination—released his film *Nixon*, which drew a surprisingly sympathetic portrait of its subject and his Watergate trauma. (Some things, however, do not change. *Nixon*, too, included a conspiracy theory. This time the culprits were rich Texas oilmen instead of the CIA.)

In short, Watergate has survived in the public imagination to become an enduring element of the national culture.

The meaning of Watergate, however, changes from one generation to the next. In the early post-Watergate years, those who talked and wrote most obsessively about Watergate were anti-Nixon partisans. They wanted to relive, in satisfying detail, what they saw as their triumphal battle against political evil. This impulse persists. Anti-Nixonites still seek, by repeating the details of Watergate, to insure that people will not forget who the bad guys are in American politics. The practice is reminiscent of the annual Jewish holiday of Passover, in which Jews retell the story of our divinely decreed exodus from Egypt. Part of this retelling is a reminder that God, by His acts, did not merely aid our ancestors: "It is . . . what the Almighty did for *me*," we are told to say. Some Watergate stories are like that.

Yet most people's absorption in things Watergate stems more straightforwardly from the endlessly fascinating, endlessly complicated character of Richard Nixon. Indeed, the appeal of Nixon's multifaceted psyche increases with the years because it stands in such sharp contrast to the flat and shallow temperaments of most American politicians who have followed him. To put it another way, the continuing interest in both Nixon and Watergate reflects the awe traditionally inspired by the fall of kings. In Nixon's case, the awe we feel is heightened by the fact that—since the presidency is no longer kingly—we can no longer experience such a feeling at first hand.

Along with the enduring interest in Watergate has come an equally enduring interest in the question of who was the real-life individual behind Deep Throat, the dark star of *All the President's Men.*

Deep Throat, as Woodward and Bernstein explained in *All the President's Men*, was not a conventional journalistic source. Only occasionally did he supply the reporters with new facts. Instead, he gave them confirmation, usually cryptic, of information they had gathered elsewhere. More important, Deep Throat provided Woodward and Bernstein with a general "perspective," to use his word, on the disparate pieces of information that the two journalists were uncovering. He was the reporters' guide through the confusion of Watergate.

This general guidance was more important to the reporters than any specific fact that Deep Throat could have provided. During most of the period in which Deep Throat spoke to Woodward, the Watergate scandal was still being successfully covered up. The things that the reporters were being told by their other sources seemed not only unfamiliar but actually bizarre, difficult to fit into any familiar notions of how politics worked. In addition, much of this information consisted of accusations—accompanied by scant evidence or no evidence at all—against very powerful political figures.

Either of these features might have been enough to deter Woodward and Bernstein from printing what they had learned. The reporters needed added confidence to write their stories and to persuade their editors to print them. Deep Throat, because of his acumen and "insider" status, provided this confidence.

Deep Throat, as presented in *All the President's Men*, was a vivid and dramatic character. He was the perfect protagonist in a book filled with villains—an insider who dared to do dangerous things, a man mysteriously yet concretely present at times and places of his own designation. The movie version of the book, which appeared in 1976, gave Deep Throat a fleshly existence in the person of the handsome but haunted-looking Hal Holbrook. Deep Throat now had everything except a real-life name.

By providing only the most elliptical clues about Deep Throat's identity in *All the President's Men*, the authors heightened the speculation about him. The descriptions of Deep Throat in the book were usually ambiguous on the questions of his identity and motivation. Deep Throat could have been moved by a desire to unmask political evil and destroy the Nixon presidency in the process. On the other hand, he could have been trying to save Nixon, by forcing him to take action, rather than scheming to destroy him: That was the lesson that Woodward and Bernstein took from Deep Throat's repeated insistence, "I have to do this my way."

On the third hand, Woodward said in *All the President's Men* that he and Deep Throat were friends. Therefore Deep Throat's motive in providing information could have been to help out an old pal. Finally, the elaborate signals and deceptions that Deep Throat devised for making contact with Woodward suggested that Deep Throat was stirred to action in part by the thrill of a great, secret game.

The book's seemingly specific clues to Deep Throat's identity preserved this ambiguity. For instance, one meeting between Deep Throat and Woodward—as usual in an underground parking garage—took place after Woodward and Bernstein had made an error in a story they had written in the *Post* about Nixon's chief of staff, H. R. "Bob" Haldeman. The mistake had enabled the White House to issue a triumphant denial. A few more such mistakes, Woodward and Bernstein thought, might irreparably damage their credibility. The book described Deep Throat's reaction to the error: "'Well,

Haldeman slipped away from you,'" Deep Throat said in the garage, "making no attempt to hide his disappointment." Did the show of disappointment mean that Deep Throat had some kind of special personal resentment of Haldeman? Was that among Deep Throat's motives? Or was it that Deep Throat thought, or even knew, that Haldeman was at the center of the intrigues destroying the Nixon presidency?

People's abiding curiosity about Deep Throat is, however, more than just the product of such tantalizing clues to a mystery, because the Deep Throat puzzle is not just a mystery but a secret. That is, it is not merely something unknown in the sense that the meaning of the universe is unknown. Instead, it is something unknown to most people but very much known by someone—or, in this case, someones. Even more interesting, the knowledgeable someones have kept Deep Throat's identity secret even though the fields of endeavor in which they operate—journalism and politics—almost never keep secrets.

Journalists protect their sources, of course, as a matter of professional ethics and in order to preserve their access to information. Yet the purpose of journalism is to disclose, not to conceal. Moreover, within political journalism, as in politics generally, information is not just food for entertainment and gossip. It is the official and unofficial coin of the realm, the universal matter out of which individuals create their status, power, and wealth. Information can benefit the holder in these ways only when it is told to someone else. Therefore it virtually never stays hidden for long.

Yet four individuals from the worlds of journalism and politics are conceded to know Deep Throat's identity—Woodward, Bernstein, their *Washington Post* editor, Ben Bradlee, and Deep Throat himself. This is not a negligible number. Yet the four have safeguarded their information for more than twenty-five years.

Woodward and Bernstein have said that they will reveal Deep Throat's identity only when he dies. Of the four secret-holders, only Woodward has departed from the strict rule of "no comment" on all things Deep Throat. On those few occasions, he has said that a given individual is *not* Deep Throat. Woodward has made these pronouncements in order to "clear" the individual in question and thus keep him from some impending professional harm (sort of like a "compassionate use" exception for controlled drugs). Apart from these departures there has been silence.

The persistence of the secret has led to two predictable reactions. Some people claim that they know the secret, while others insist that the secret does not exist.

Claims of knowing the secret began almost as soon as *All the President's Men* was published in 1974. Richard Whalen, a distinguished historian and journalist and a former Nixon campaign staffer, led the way in a review in—of course—the *Washington Post*. Whalen speculated that Deep Throat must be a staffer in the Nixon White House—someone like Robert Finch, a disappointed liberal, or Harry Dent, a Southern conservative with a reputation for integrity. Each of these men, Whalen said, was the type of principled individual who might have thought it his patriotic duty to help Woodward expose the Watergate cover-up. And each was a man who, in a complex piece of rationalizing, might have reasoned that exposure would force Nixon to save his presidency and himself.

Whalen's suggestions were off the mark (and therefore unusual among his writings, which were typically very much on the mark). The error did not stem from particular discrepancies—such as who was in Washington on what date or who had direct knowledge of what piece of Watergate information, details of the type that came to dominate the obsessive writings of later hunters after Deep Throat. Instead, the problem with Finch and Dent as Deep Throat candidates was, ultimately, that neither man had anything like the character or temperament necessary to produce the eccentricities attributed to Deep Throat in *All the President's Men*. Neither man, for instance, would participate in extravagant duplicities like the signaling system with which Deep Throat arranged meetings with Woodward. You simply would not find Finch or Dent on the floor of a Washington parking garage from late at night until six the next morning gabbing about senior White House staff intrigue with a young reporter. Not on your life, as you knew if you were acquainted with them.

This type of jarring anomaly—between the voice, style, and personality of the Deep Throat of *All the President's Men* and the characteristics of Finch and Dent—was premonitory. The same problem has dogged all subsequent efforts to attach a real name to the literary Deep Throat. The characterological pieces of the candidates never seemed to fit the figure fully or credibly. In the words of political analyst Fats Waller, their feets too big. That is a major reason why the Deep Throat secret has remained intact for more than a quarter century.

This problem of a lack of "fit" has led many respectable commentators to claim either that Deep Throat did not exist at all or that he was, at most, merely a composite of several sources. Those who view Deep Throat as a pure fiction say that he was simply a gimmick, beginning to end, invented to make Woodward and Bernstein's story more dramatic. Those who make the "composite" version of the argument contend that Deep Throat was a combination of sources whom the authors blended into a one-man Greek chorus. The chorus had to take the form of one man, in this view, because only a single voice would give the needed narrative structure and pace to the story of a news-gathering process that was otherwise fragmentary, desultory, and dull, like most good journalistic investigations.

The composite version of the argument is especially plausible. Telling a complex story like the one in *All the President's Men* wholly through a number of unremarkable sources, some named and some anonymous, would have been chaotically confusing and boring at the same time. I have read through all the *Washington Post* articles on which the book was based, with the aid of gallons of coffee, and can testify personally to this proposition.

People who argued that Deep Throat was a literary device also contended, as a corollary, that the identifying characteristics attributed by the book to Deep Throat, the ones that made him so singular, were more or less fake. Either they were merely camouflage or worse, deliberately designed to be false leads that would lure investigators away from the solution to the puzzle.

Like the more general theories of Deep Throat as a literary device, the argument for the book's description of Deep Throat as a type of fakery was plausible. What could be less likely or more unnecessary, for instance, than the idea that Deep Throat would choose an underground parking garage as the site of his middle-of-the-night meetings with Woodward? Even more improbable were the details of the signaling system by which Deep Throat and Woodward arranged meetings. According to *All the President's Men,* when Woodward wanted to meet with Deep Throat, the reporter would move a flowerpot to a certain position on the balcony of his apartment. When Deep Throat wanted to meet with Woodward, Woodward had only to pick up his morning *New York Times* (delivered to his apartment building by 7:00 A.M.), and turn to page 20, where Deep Throat would have drawn a clock face with hands pointing to the time of the proposed meeting.

Woodward said in the book that he did not know how Deep Throat managed the logistics of this tortured mode of communication via the *New York Times.* For reasons unknown, the investigative reporter seems never to have asked.

Some people arguing for a fictional or composite Deep Throat have had a political agenda. *All the President's Men* pictured a Nixon administration so corrupt that even a Nixon insider like Deep Throat was repelled by it. In the years after Watergate, other Nixon insiders came forward to challenge this picture of thoroughgoing corruption. They argued that in spite of the excessive nasty tricks, lawlessness was not so pervasive in the administration so as to produce a Deep Throat.

Similarly, many people disapproved of the type of secret-source investigative journalism that emerged after Watergate and claimed Woodward and Bernstein as a model. (I sympathized with the disapproval.) If there was no real Deep Throat, then Woodward, Bernstein, and perhaps Bradlee had perpetrated a hoax on the public, the worst of journalistic sins. If so, the journalism symbolized by Deep Throat stood massively discredited.

But not all the doubters had identifiable political agendas. For instance, some of the best detective work on the Deep Throat mystery appeared in the 1982 book *Lost Honor*, written by Nixon's White House counsel, John Dean, whose public testimony during Watergate played a major role in exposing the scandal. Dean set out to find Deep Throat. Dean had the advantages of his position at the center of the Watergate events and his remarkable recall of the details of those days. He came up with a list of more than a dozen final candidates and subjected them to painstaking analysis.

Of his candidates, Dean concluded—wrongly, as he later allowed—that the best bet was Nixon's chief of staff during the last phase of Watergate, General Alexander M. Haig. But Dean made his pick only hesitantly. In *Lost Honor* he explained the reason for his tentativeness. It stemmed from the fact that Alice Mayhew, editor of Dean's first book, *Blind Ambition*, had also been Woodward and Bernstein's editor in the preparation of *All the President's Men*. Mayhew told Dean that she was the one who had invented the detective story structure for the reporters' book. Mayhew also told Dean that she did not believe there was a single source for Deep Throat. "She," Dean noted laconically in *Lost Honor*, "should know."

Yet Deep Throat cannot have been merely a creature of the demands of the book-writing process. The name Deep Throat, used to identify a source of Woodward's, came into existence well before Alice Mayhew entered the reporters' lives. By the fall of 1972, months before they sat down to outline a proposed book, Deep Throat was Deep Throat.

During the time when Woodward and Bernstein were engaged in the Watergate reporting that would later become the basis for *All the President's Men*, their day-to-day managing editor at the *Washington Post* was a formidable journalist and a humane, witty man named Howard Simons. The reporters would sometimes talk to Simons about a friend of Woodward's who was a source for their stories. It was Simons who named the source Deep Throat, after the then-notorious pornographic movie of the same title.

So Deep Throat was more than a literary device. Almost everything beyond that, however, remained the secret of the four men who held it.

There was one remaining set of factors in Deep Throat's magnetic pull, consisting of the varied connections between the idea of Deep Throat and the politics that followed Watergate. The first such connection was Deep Throat's importance in publicizing the role of the whistleblower in politics. Deep Throat was no conventional whistleblower. True, like other whistleblowers, he held a position inside an organization and told outsiders about wrongdoing within it. Most whistleblowers, however, give the outside world concrete information about the bad acts taking place in their organizations; indeed, such information is all the power they have. Deep Throat, by contrast, did not deliver concrete details. Instead, his power was greater: It lay in the general picture he communicated to Woodward and Bernstein of what was really going on in the Nixon inner circle. That is why Deep Throat was able to exert an influence over the psychology of the *Washington Post* as no ordinary whistleblower could have wielded.

Despite this crucial difference, the picture of Deep Throat in *All the President's Men* publicly dignified the phenomenon of whistleblowing. Deep Throat became a model for whistleblowers who followed him, just as Woodward and Bernstein's Watergate journalism became a model for investigative reporters who followed them. Deep Throat also became a justification for a series of legislative and administrative actions designed to protect and encourage more conventional whistleblowers. These attempts at protection have not succeeded, largely because the well-meaning reformers who launched them failed to appreciate how different ordinary whistleblowers are from their model, Deep Throat.

Deep Throat's second connection to post-Watergate politics lay in a political phenomenon that Deep Throat himself identified for Woodward and Bernstein. Deep Throat, portrayed in the book as no stranger to political operations, had told Woodward that critical numbers of people in the White House evinced a "switchblade mentality" and were practicing a newly unpleasant, winner-take-all type of politics. In the years since Deep Throat's complaint, this political style has become even more marked. American politics since Watergate has presented an uncomfortable irony. After Watergate, the country enacted reforms, one after another, designed to make politics and government more upright. Deep Throat had told Woodward—the phrase was from the movie version of *All the President's Men*, but the message permeated the book as well—to "follow the money." In response, Congress tightened limits on campaign contributions and on the lobbying that a former government employee could do in his or her old agency. Congress also required more disclosure of information about campaign finance and the financial situation of government officials.

Yet politics after Watergate has grown not cleaner but meaner, increasingly marked by the undue influence, obsession with money, and switchblade mentality that seemed so shocking when people learned of its prevalence in the Nixon

White House. Deep Throat's complaint was thus more than just a description of the Nixon administration. It was, we can see in retrospect, oddly premonitory of the nature of American politics in the post-Watergate years. Deep Throat's most important act was to blow the whistle not on particular crimes but on the rising tide of a repugnant style of politics. Somehow, this act brought about the opposite of what he intended. For this reason, too, Deep Throat's identity and the circumstances surrounding his actions have remained a matter of perennial interest.

*   *   *

When *All the President's Men* appeared in 1974, during the final days of the Nixon administration, I was one of the least curious people in Washington about the identity of Deep Throat. At the time, I was serving as acting counsel to the president. I was trying, with marked lack of success, to pick up the Watergate pieces left to me by my predecessor in the job, John Dean, and to put them back together again. The pressures of reality had driven out any capacity I might otherwise have had for speculating about who and what had produced that reality. My colleagues remaining in the Nixon White House generally reacted in the same way.

This state of oblivious indifference to Deep Throat's identity lasted, in my case, for twenty years, until the time in the 1990s when I began to supplement my day job in the practice of law with work on a memoir that focused heavily on my years in the Nixon White House. I began to think once again about the Nixon administration. This thinking led inexorably to reconsidering Watergate and its aftermath, which in turn required recognition of the important role that Deep Throat had played in the scandal.

In the end, the memoir itself—titled *Crazy Rhythm* and published by Times Books in 1997—referred only briefly and tangentially to Deep Throat. But my thinking about him continued. I had finally joined the ranks of those who were hooked on the mystery.

I first read through the large Deep Throat *oeuvre*, in which various authors advanced arguments for one candidate or another, many candidates, or no candidate at all. After this reading, I was inclined to the "composite" theory of Deep Throat.

I had learned that in the book proposal prepared by Woodward and Bernstein for *All the President's Men*, there was no reference to Deep Throat and no dominant reliance on a single source. Instead, there were many sources, most of them anonymous, some more important than others. The final, published version of the book retained many of these anonymous sources, not dignified by pseudonyms like Deep Throat's. Woodward and Bernstein's sources included law enforcement officials, lower-level officials at the Committee for the Re-election of the President (CRP), knowledgeable outsiders, and perhaps even someone like White House Chief of Staff Al Haig or National Security Adviser Henry Kissinger, acting in person or through an intermediary, dispensing morsels of information as he thought useful to the White House, himself, or both.

According to the voluminous diaries of Bob Haldeman, Nixon and Haldeman knew during the early days of Watergate that some White House staffers were talking to Woodward and Bernstein. Nixon approved of these contacts. I was one of the approved leakers; there must have been others.

Deep Throat could have been a collage pasted together out of pieces of information from these sources. Alternatively, he could have been based mainly on one such source but amplified and elaborated into a colorful presence, appearing in the end relatively more important than he actually was.

In sum, Woodward and Bernstein had plenty of actual sources from whom to draw. The composite theory would have been easy to stick with on a permanent basis.

But that, as the man said, would have been wrong. I was uncomfortable with the composite idea for several reasons. For one thing, in the years since Nixon's resignation, Woodward and Bernstein had been clear and adamant in insisting that Deep Throat really existed and that he was really a single person. Woodward had told John Dean, during one of those interminable book tours that throw together authors of the most incongruous stripes, that Deep Throat had been publicly identified but had denied being Deep Throat. Woodward's reference to Deep Throat's denial did not really narrow the field much. For example, in 1976 *Time* magazine published an article by Hays Gorey presenting no less than fourteen serious Deep Throat candidates, complete with photos. In the wake of the article, journalists asked all of them (including me) whether they were Deep Throat. Everyone denied it. But at least Woodward's comment to Dean was an affirmation of Deep Throat's identity as a single soul.

In addition to Woodward's general comments over the years, he gave me particular reason to believe that Deep Throat existed in the flesh. I have known Woodward since my time in the Nixon administration. After Nixon's resignation, I, like a number of other individuals who remained in the Nixon White House until the bitter end, gave Woodward and Bernstein substantial help in their writing of their second book, *The Final Days*, describing—well, the Nixon administration's final days. By that time, the battles were over; we wanted to be sure that our side of the story became part of the event's history.

Woodward is a firm believer in the honorable journalist's principle of quid pro quo. As a result, when I began to pester him on various occasions for clues to Deep Throat's identity, he did not summon the police. Instead, he relied on his skill at opaque conversation, of which he is a master, to keep him safe from Deep Throat entanglements. But Woodward did affirm repeatedly that Deep Throat was one person and that the descriptive details about him in *All the President's Men* were accurate and genuine.

At a lunch with Woodward while I was writing *Crazy Rhythm*, I asked him why Deep Throat, after all these years, would not be willing or even eager to have his identity known. After all, large portions of the politically sentient populace considered him a hero for the risks he had taken to do what he did. Surely only the small number of remaining die-hard Nixon loyalists would bear him any ill will. Woodward answered that, in 1972 and early 1973, Deep Throat had been, if not wholly unknown, at least relatively anonymous. In the years since then, Deep Throat's "public persona"—Woodward's exact words—had changed. His "public persona" after Watergate was inconsistent with his actions during Watergate days.

From Woodward's comment I surmised that some people among Deep Throat's post-Watergate audience or clients or constituents would think less of him for having consorted so notoriously in secret places with a journalist for the liberal *Washington Post*, even in the increasingly distant past.

Thus it appeared increasingly likely to me that Deep Throat was indeed a real-life individual. If that was the case, I would have to figure out which one. This would not be a wholly new type of enterprise for me. Before jumping into the swamps of politics, I had for years been a trial lawyer; hunting Deep Throat looked to me like a more interesting version of innumerable puzzles I had faced in the course of litigating. There were lists to be made, logistics to be arranged, background facts to be assimilated and winnowed, and witnesses to be questioned. This was home ground.

In all these activities I had an advantage over most other Deep Throat searchers whose works I had read: Almost invariably, I knew these candidates personally. In many cases, I had worked with them very closely or even hired them in the first place. This level of personal acquaintance meant, first of all, that I would not have to rely as much as other researchers had on secondhand information and surmise. I could usually contact a candidate directly and talk to him face to face, or at least voice to voice.

An even more important advantage derived from my personal knowledge was something I understood only retrospectively. Such knowledge gave me, with some brushing up, a natural sense of whether a particular candidate "fit" the description of Deep Throat in *All the President's Men*. In the absence of such an informed intuition, a researcher could come up with a plausible-sounding argument in favor of one candidate or another who met all the criteria present in the published information—but who was nevertheless clearly, wildly wrong, because of some anomalous characteristic in the candidate that the researcher could have no way of knowing from the literature and secondhand reports. To a substantial degree I could avoid this pitfall.

Take, for instance, the question of whether Leonard Garment was Deep Throat. Some people have pointed out that I fit the most likely mold of Deep Throat characteristics. I was a Nixon loyalist, having been with him from the beginning of his comeback in 1963. On the other hand, I was known as a liberal in the White House, constantly worried about blacks or Jews or Indians or the arts or some other do-good area of endeavor. These concerns, the argument went, put me at odds with the hard-nosed politics of Bob Haldeman and his henchpersons. The same concerns gave me wide and favorable contacts in the liberal Washington press corps. Voilà.

Except for one thing, which is that I am a congenital blabbermouth—not an instrumental gossip like Deep Throat but a talker in general. This characteristic gave me good press and makes me a good intermediary, but it also made it— makes it—impossible for me to keep a secret unless there is a specific reason to do so. I have lost quasi-friends for saying things that they forgot they told me I could say and that, once given permission, I would of course say. I was kicked out of my monthly poker game for describing it to the newspapers. I am, in short, utterly impossible as a candidate for Deep Throat. Yet this conclusion, though correct, might be hard to reach in the absence of contextual knowledge.

In addition to the advantage of this contextual knowledge, I had a more serendipitous advantage in the work of another researcher. Toward the end of 1996, with my memoir done, I met Jim Hougan, author of the well-respected book *Secret*

Agenda, a solid rock of Watergate research around which less persuasive Watergate books have flowed and ebbed over the years. Hougan and I, pondering the exponentially expanding mystifications of the Deep Throat saga, considered collaborating on a book about the figure. We abandoned the idea because at the time we could not settle on which of the plausible candidates was the likeliest—and because Hougan, a successful author of fiction as well as a writer about intelligence matters, had a novel in the works. But as we parted, Hougan deposited with me a huge amount of useful information to add to my accumulation of clues and theories.

Thus armed, I began gathering fresh information in the prototypical Washington ways—through talk in general and lunch and dinner in particular. The journey was full of wrong turns. Indeed, until the very end they were virtually all wrong turns. This was true partly by definition: If you always find your keys in the last place you look for them, then all the preceding places you looked had to be dry holes. But there was a more specific reason for the many false starts. Though I finally came to understand the importance of contextual knowledge and intuition in a quest like this one, I did not understand it for a long time. Therefore I spent a lot of time talking with candidates and about candidates who looked good on paper, only to discard them when good sense finally kicked in.

Nevertheless, most of the wrong turns became stories, of which I tell a few later in this book. That was almost reward enough. More important, even the conversations that did not add anything specific to the Deep Throat dossier helped in the end to explain him, the political climate that produced him, and the modern politics that he unintentionally helped bring into being.

For instance, I had occasion to talk several times about Watergate and Deep Throat with former Nixon White House counsel and chief domestic policy adviser John Ehrlichman before he died last year. One of the chief villains of endless numbers of television and film documentaries about Watergate, Ehrlichman had recently produced a Watergate documentary of his own, narrated by the novelist Tom Clancy, one of the many people who came to admire Ehrlichman during the post-Watergate years.

Ehrlichman did not have anything specific to contribute to my Deep Throat research. He gave me the benefit, however, of his formidable intelligence and wit—the same intelligence and wit he displayed, along with his many decent impulses, when he served in the White House. It struck me that had Watergate not put Ehrlichman's character under such extreme pressure, he would probably be remembered as one of those presidential aides, tough but respectful of good policymaking, who have accompanied most of the country's postwar presidents to the White House. Instead, history threw him in with the knife wielders whom Deep Throat immortalized.

Richard Helms, who headed the Central Intelligence Agency at the time of Watergate, offered as few clues as Ehrlichman did to Deep Throat's identity. I began lunching with Helms at a time when I was pursuing the theory—a beguiling one for many Watergate researchers—that the CIA was somehow at the center of the Watergate scandal. As I look back on it, I am mystified as to why I thought that Helms, after a lifetime of training in keeping his mouth shut, would suddenly spill some long-held secret to me upon imbibing a single martini. He did not spill anything, of course; and my CIA theory was as wrong as everyone else's. But in learning something from Helms about the depth of the shock that coursed through the permanent government as a result of the political turmoil of the Watergate years, I got a better sense of the seismic character of the dislocations in American politics that made Vietnam, Watergate, and Deep Throat possible.

Thus false starts that did not directly lead to an identification of Deep Throat nevertheless told me things I needed to know about him. Conversely, when I finally concluded that John Sears was Deep Throat, I realized that I had discovered not just the answer to one particular puzzle but something more general—sobering and a little bit saddening—about American politics of the past twenty-five years.

My opinion is that Sears took the actions he did because of mixed motives, as is the case with all humans; but if there was a dominant political impulse moving him, it was a sense that the marriage of realism and idealism in our politics, a delicate union to begin with, was on the rocks. The political arena, he thought, was in danger of becoming just a war between the knife-wielders and the moralists. Sears was right, of course; he could not have known that the drama of which he was a part was about to drive the wedge between the two camps even deeper.

*   *   *

During times when hunting for Deep Throat seemed not just futile but idiotic, an occasional happy accident would restore my enthusiasm. The spring of 1998, for instance, was a particularly dark time for the Deep Throat search. Among other things, I had a hip that had suddenly collapsed within a

period of just three months. It was going to have to be
replaced, and in the meantime I was hobbling around with a
cane. The lameness made it physically more difficult to go
running after Deep Throat, and an attack of self-pity made
my disability seem symbolic (unfortunately for symbolism,
but not for me, the new titanium hip is terrific).

Just then, Caspar and Jane Weinberger, friends since the
days when Cap headed the Office of Management and Budget
in the Nixon administration, invited my wife and me to spend
a few days navigating the Panama Canal on a yacht owned
by *Forbes* magazine, of which Cap was chairman. This was
not a bad prospect, and the reality proved even better. Our
fellow guests were a cosmopolitan group. Among them was
an Air Force general who had been an aide to Cap in Weinberger's post-Nixon incarnation as President Ronald Reagan's
Secretary of Defense. The general was accompanied by his
wife, a warm and articulate woman who had traveled all over
the world.

At our last dinner on the boat, I explained why I was looking for Deep Throat and offered up my latest candidate. I
spun out my theory in colorful detail. My fellow dinner guests
listened with, it was clear, more than politeness. The general's
wife, in particular, seemed rapt. At the end of the account, she
said, "I am so grateful to you." This remark, while flattering,
was not self-explanatory, so I asked why the gratitude. "One
of my major worries," she said, "was that I would die without
knowing who Deep Throat is."

That night's theory turned out to be wrong. But I kept
going back at the puzzle, mainly for the inexplicable hell of it.

There can be no absolute certainty in the results of such an
inquiry. Woodward and Bernstein will not give up Deep Throat,

whether because of journalists' ethics or self-protectiveness or a combination of both. Deep Throat himself, having kept his silence for more than a quarter century, is unlikely to produce a confession now. Nevertheless, I am convinced that this time I have got it right.

1

Before Watergate

This book is not a history of Watergate or the events that led up to it. Yet it is impossible to understand Deep Throat's behavior, in life or in literature, without recalling certain features of the Nixon comeback and of the Nixon White House that emerged from the process.

I first laid eyes on Richard Nixon in 1963, when he moved to New York to join the law firm in which I was a partner. In 1960, he had suffered a defeat at the hands of John F. Kennedy in a close presidential election. The thin margin by which Nixon lost did not make the experience less humiliating for him. A mere two years later, Nixon lost his race for the governorship of California. On the morning after his California defeat, Nixon told a group of assembled journalists that they would not have him to kick around anymore. Many people believed him. Nixon had finally decided, they said, that enough was enough: He would make a new professional life for himself as a lawyer in the private sector.

In 1963 the Nixons moved to New York, far from Nixon's political roots. The Nixon family even established itself in an apartment on Fifth Avenue in the same building as Nixon's old political nemesis, Nelson Rockefeller. The choice seemed a sign of both Nixon's new affluence and his banked fires. In honor of Nixon's arrival, my law firm renamed itself, becoming Nixon, Mudge, Rose, Guthrie & Alexander. Nixon did his part for the firm, meeting with clients and discussing legal strategy. I even recruited him to make an argument to the Supreme Court, which he did with undisputed distinction.

The press, lulled by the idea that Nixon had been defanged, cooperated in sounding the theme of his transformation. Journalists claimed to have discerned the emergence of a "new Nixon," a term by which they referred to their discovery that Nixon did not have cloven hooves and a tail and in fact could be a rather pleasant fellow.

But the notion that Nixon had left politics was quite wrong. From Nixon's conversation during our first meeting in 1963, it was clear to me that he intended to return as soon as possible to the political life from which he had been ejected. Nixon's main activity in New York was the building of a foundation for his re-emergence as a Republican Party leader and presidential candidate.

Veterans of Nixon's previous campaigns began helping him. Trusted friends like Maurice Stans and Peter Flanigan, both comfortably ensconced by 1963 in the upper reaches of New York's financial community, started building a fundraising infrastructure and making preliminary logistical arrangements for a presidential campaign. On the West Coast, Bob Finch, Nixon's close friend and his manager in the 1960 and 1962 campaigns, stood ready. Finch's two energetic and talented assistants from these campaigns, advertising executive Bob Haldeman and attorney John Ehrlichman, were also waiting, though they had not yet made up their minds about whether to join the campaign and would not do so until after the 1968 primaries.

At the beginning, in 1963, Nixon's New York political headquarters consisted of his offices at our law firm. There, I became the first of his new recruits. His other helpers were of long standing. One was his wife, Pat, who sometimes appeared at the office to help with the mail. The other was Nixon's secretary, Rose Woods. Rose was lovely, with red hair and creamy skin, and maternal, though she never had children of her own. In those early days, she was much more than Nixon's secretary. She also functioned as his administrative assistant and access controller. She loved the Nixon family with constancy, and they reciprocated.

Rose came from a political family; her brother, Joe Woods, was then sheriff of Cook County, Illinois. She also had her own political sophistication and shrewdness, as well as a long memory. In 1973, during the worst of Watergate, when I was acting White House counsel and the press had just discovered the 18 $\frac{1}{2}$-minute gap in Nixon's tapes, I sent Rose a cheery note advising her to get her own lawyer. "Love, Len," I stupidly signed it. She never fully forgave me.

It did not take long after my self-recruitment to the Nixon campaign before I was joined by other new recruits, because Nixon knew that one of his major jobs in building his new political foundation would be to recruit an enlarged political staff. It is important that while doing this recruiting, Nixon was ensconced in a type of organization—a large, white-shoe Wall Street law firm—that was very different from those he had known before. It cared more about polish and intellectual sophistication, less about ideological and historical loyalties. Partly as a consequence of this new environment, some of the people drawn into Nixon's 1968 campaign were different from those who had staffed his political campaigns in the past and often different from one another.

Thus Nixon's years in New York turned out to be more than a fueling stop. They brought people into his entourage who made his campaign even more diverse than is usual in such enterprises. Because of the diversity, the 1968 campaign was riven by special kinds of internal clashes and tensions. Once the Nixon administration took office in 1969, the clashes and tensions worsened. These struggles were the breeding ground out of which Deep Throat emerged.

The polyglot nature of Nixon's new crew suited him very well. First, he wanted competence and was smart enough to know it came in all political colorations. Indeed, though Nixon later became known for his opposition to the counterculture, as a personal matter he was quite ready to deal with people who differed widely by ideology, religion, race, ethnicity, sexual preference, you name it. The readiness stopped abruptly when he received any sign that such people disliked him; but his 1968 campaign reflected his initially open attitude.

Nixon was also after the "fresh" look that a varied staff connoted. Perhaps the most important advantage of the campaign's early diversity, however, stemmed from the fact that Nixon was not a happy campaign camper. Most of the time he preferred to be left alone to make his own decisions about strategy and issues. These decisions emanated from a coherent view of the world but not an ideologically consistent one. So Nixon did not want a staff that would lock him in ideologically. A politically fragmented group, he calculated, would not be able to apply enough pressure in any one direction to cause him serious discomfort.

Nixon also wanted to preserve his freedom to alter a particular opinion or position if it was politically expedient for him to do so. He wanted aides who were loyal to him, not to some ideology, and who would stick with him through his shifting policy stances.

If diversity was what he wanted, diversity was what he got. When it came to Nixon's speechwriters, his balancing act worked pretty well. One of the first staffers to join the group was Pat Buchanan, who arrived shortly after Nixon settled into the firm's offices at 20 Broad Street. Buchanan joined Rose Woods in the small office adjoining Nixon's and started to do all of the nascent campaign's routine political writing—letters, speeches, articles, memos to possible political allies. He was to become one-third of the presidential speechwriting team.

Buchanan hailed from a Father Coughlin–style, America First family in Washington, D.C. He had been an editorial writer before joining the campaign and could talk about one subject while simultaneously writing about another, pausing in conversation only to rip pages of perfect copy out of his machine. He was quick-tempered and sometimes a bully but a cheerful and witty one.

As the campaign rolled on, Buchanan became Nixon's one-man right wing. Having done so, Pat never changed—not in the campaign or the White House, not as a columnist and TV personality after Nixon's resignation, and not as a candidate for president (as I write this, it seems that Pat will be the Reform Party's candidate for president in the 2000 election). Most of the large policies that emerged from the Nixon White House, whether on détente, China, desegregation, affirmative action, or welfare, were anathema to Pat's ideology. Buchanan's opposition to recognizing the Communist regime in China was so implacable that Nixon at one point considered cutting him loose over the issue. Yet on one of the Sunday TV shows recently, Buchanan said, with unalloyed, unembarrassed affection, that Richard Nixon was "like a father" to him.

Ray Price, the second member of Nixon's speechwriting troika in the campaign and the White House, had been editorial page editor of the *New York Herald Tribune* and the author, in 1964, of the first editorial in the *Herald*'s history that supported the Democratic rather than the Republican candidate for president. This did not make Ray a liberal; he was a sensible, humane Republican. But such details did not matter at the early stage of the campaign. Ray was fresh, moderate, and extremely talented, all those things that spoke well to the press of the "new Nixon."

It was a telling fact about Nixon that Ray, of all his White House staffers, was the one who became closest to him and most a part of the Nixons' small extended family. Ray was quietly sick about the worst parts of Watergate, but he had also seen a great deal of Nixon at his best. Price wrote Nixon's resignation speech in 1974 and, after Nixon had resigned, continued writing for the former president. He truly remained "with Nixon"—the title of Price's fine memoir—until Nixon's death.

Bill Safire, the final major member of Nixon's speechwriting team, had floated in and out of Nixon's professional life since the day in 1959 when Safire, working as a public relations man, got then-Vice President Nixon and Soviet premier Nikita Khrushchev together at a display of a "typical" American house in Moscow. The ensuing "kitchen debate" almost won Nixon the presidency in 1960.

Safire was in those days a connoisseur of technique, not ideology; he could scribble to his political right or left (or both at once) with ease and had an easy back-and-forth relationship with the press. Under Bill's wisecracking manner, however, lay immense self-discipline. During the campaign and in the White House, he would walk into a meeting, take off his watch, and lay it on the table; if the meeting ran longer than it was worth, he would simply walk out. When he stayed, it was often to take notes for his book on the Nixon administration, which he was writing while on the White House staff. The book, titled *Before the Fall*, would become a major contribution to the Nixon canon.

The speechwriters managed to work together, well if not always harmoniously, all through the campaign and most of the way through the White House years. With the political operatives, however, the planned creative tension was not so successful.

I helped create the divided Nixon political staff by becoming one of his major recruiters. In contrast with Haldeman and Ehrlichman, who were experienced and therefore cautious about joining the campaign, I was wholly without experience of Nixon past (before meeting him, I was a conventional liberal Democratic Nixon-hater, and not even much of that), and therefore had no qualms about throwing myself into the project of Nixon's future.

As a long-time trial lawyer, I had acquired the skill of locating expert talent. As a long-time political agnostic, I did not much care about the ideological coloration of that talent. I ran around visiting with everyone from Edward Teller to Dick Gregory, and my recruits were a very mixed ideological bag. In the beginning, this diversity was an advantage, reinforcing the notion of a Nixon who had entered a fresh, nontroglodytic phase.

A few of the people I unearthed in my political star search were distinguished policy types, such as Martin Anderson and the now-fabled Alan Greenspan. Alan and I first met when we were both jazz musicians playing with Henry Jerome's band. After those early musical days, however, we could not have diverged more sharply. I stayed a jazz musician—always riffing, verbally if not musically. Alan, always mostly silent, with a slight smile on his face, proceeded to direct his attention inward, to the ordering of numbers and economies. I am immensely proud to have been the occasion for his entering public life.

Mostly, however, I recruited nuts-and-bolts political operators. In this endeavor, one of my greatest small claims to fame was bringing Nixon the young John Sears. Actually, Sears just turned up at my office one day in 1964. He had attended Notre Dame University and Georgetown Law School. His early ambition had been to become a psychiatrist; but during his college years he entered politics, as a partisan of John F. Kennedy. When I met Sears, he was clerking for Judge Adrian Burke of the New York Court of Appeals, the state's highest court, and making the rounds of Manhattan law firms looking for a postclerkship job. He clearly wanted a place where he could not just practice law but engage in politics as well.

Then barely twenty-five, Sears was very good looking—tanned, brown-haired, hazel-eyed, glistening like a baby seal.

He was also poised and strikingly articulate, one of those young men who seem to know too much for their age. He was impressive enough in that first meeting so that even before it was over, the next step seemed obvious: "Let me introduce you to Mr. Nixon, John." They talked. When Sears and I left Nixon's office, Sears worried about whether he had made a good impression. But shortly afterwards, the candidate phoned me to say, "Get me Sears."

Sears thereupon joined Nixon Mudge. He worked for me on a variety of legal matters and performed skillfully. But soon Nixon clasped the young man to the bosom of his political family and commandeered his time. Nixon polished Sears's natural political skills, then turned the young man loose to persuade and organize delegates to the Republican convention.

Sears was also a talented political writer. I saw as much when he worked with me and Bill Safire on the speech Nixon gave at the University of Rochester on academic freedom. Sears would also help me in the development of the campaign's advertising, an enterprise I managed along with Roger Ailes, Frank Shakespeare, and Harry Treleaven.

In the main, however, I did not see much of Sears during working hours. I did, however, see him many nights. After a day's politicking, he would come to my office at the law firm, where I kept a bottle of Scotch. We drank it straight and smoked cigarette after cigarette. We talked for hours about politics and theology.

Sears was widely read, from Aristotle to current politics, and full of Catholic metaphysics and Irish charm. He had an intensely psychological approach to political operations. He could also talk about the relationship between the nature of the

Triune and the tripartite structure of American government and make it seem both plausible and poetic. Amid our clouds of smoke and Scotch, we plotted and dreamed about winning the presidency. We would go until two in the morning.

Sears was my favorite among the new Nixon recruits. He was also the favorite of Nixon himself, who gave him a wide variety of jobs to do. Nixon, who had campaigned hard for Republican candidates in 1966, spent election night that year at the Drake Hotel in New York watching the news of Republican victories roll in. Sears, along with Buchanan and Nixon himself, phoned each winning Republican with congratulations. Much later, when Nixon was at home in his apartment, he phoned Sears, still at the Drake, to have the young man read the happy results to him again.

In 1967, with Nixon still not officially in the race, Sears was one of the two Nixon agents who attended the Republican governors' conference to keep the governors from jumping to other candidates. Sears also spent a large amount of time with the press, especially since the campaign, until June of 1968, did not have a full-time press secretary. Sears quickly acquired friends and admirers among these journalists, who recognized a gifted political analyst when they saw one.

Sears was also a favorite of Rose Woods. He was often in Rose's office, talking with her and with her office mate, Pat Buchanan. He remained friends with both of them long after the 1968 campaign. In becoming Rose's friend, Sears also became, in due course, the friend of Jack Caulfield. Caulfield was a former New York City policeman who had belonged to the elite unit that protected visiting dignitaries during their visits to the city. In this capacity he met then–Vice President Nixon during the presidential campaign of 1960. Caulfield kept in touch with the Nixon camp during the 1960s and grew especially close to Rose Woods.

When the 1968 Nixon campaign took shape, Caulfield moved into a security job within the organization. He was a cheering presence within the campaign—New York-tough and a decent, friendly human being. After the election, in April of 1969, Caulfield went to work for John Ehrlichman in the White House. Sears remained friends with Caulfield, too.

The fact that Sears was a favorite of Nixon and Rose Woods did not, however, make him a favorite of John Mitchell; quite the opposite. Mitchell was another one of my recruits to the campaign. For better or worse, I have the letter to prove it—from President Richard Nixon, thanking me for my suggestion to him in 1968 that Mitchell become his campaign manager. At the time, Mitchell was Nixon's law partner and mine, having merged his law firm into ours.

Mitchell's old firm had specialized in arranging the bond financing by which states and municipalities build their schools, their bridges, and the political reputations of their governors and mayors. As a result of this specialty, Mitchell knew a vast amount of detail about state and local politics and was heavily involved in political issues. I have always suspected that when he agreed to the merger, he did so partly with an eye to becoming involved in the Nixon campaign.

Mitchell was his own man from the start, seemingly confident and in command. Indeed, that was a major reason why Nixon chose him as campaign manager. Nixon knew that in his previous two campaigns, he had functioned largely as his own campaign manager and that the blurring of roles between manager and candidate had been one source of the misjudgments that had cost him these elections. Nixon thought that with Mitchell at the head of the campaign organization, there would be no question about who was in charge. In this Nixon was right. Throughout the 1968 campaign, Mitchell managed the organization and the candidate with pipe-smoking imperturbability.

Mitchell was certainly not a bad man, as the cliché machine painted him during and after Watergate. But Mitchell, in contrast to Sears, knew less about politics than he was thought to know and, more important, considerably less than he should have known. Mitchell was the master of a narrow piece of the political world, municipal financing. From this fact he made the faulty generalization that he was similarly the master of all of politics.

After the 1968 campaign, Mitchell strode with his over-confidence into his post as attorney general—and into a jungle. Even during the campaign, Mitchell had never opposed Nixon outright, instead trying to divert him and muttering a lot. After the election, Mitchell no longer managed Nixon. Instead, Mitchell was in thrall to Nixon like any other aide, beset by the pervasive anxieties about power that afflict all political subordinates and afflicted Nixon's inner circle with special intensity.

Mitchell had to compete for Nixon's favor with Haldeman, Ehrlichman, Kissinger, and much less savory characters in the White House. Yet Mitchell, because he was attorney general, had managerial responsibilities at the Department of Justice and thus had to make his bids in the White House power game from a base half a city away.

In the process, Mitchell lost his footing long before he fell.

Intimations of Mitchell's future troubles appeared in the 1968 campaign, where the most pervasive internal battle was between those who believed in political technique above all and those who insisted on the value, intrinsic and instrumental, of ideas in politics. Mitchell's laconic tough-guy stance put him habitually in the camp of the former. More, underneath Mitchell's confident exterior lay a deep unsureness about himself. Therefore he would not brook disagreement. If I had not enjoyed such senior status in the campaign, he would have treated me as a major antagonist. As it was, Mitchell's insecurity led to flare-ups between him and what must have seemed to the older man like an impossibly self-assured Sears.

Nixon had a special affection for Sears—as he did for the other young men I recruited to his campaign, like Tom Evans and Bob Ellsworth, later U.S. ambassador to NATO. Because of Sears's particular closeness to Nixon, Mitchell was unable to act brutally enough toward the young man to force him out of the campaign altogether. Mitchell was also unable to keep Sears from building his own relationships with fellow politicians and the press.

However, Mitchell did what he could. He placed Sears in the noncentral location of the Nixon campaign's Washington office. After the convention, Mitchell assigned Sears the less-than-enviable job of traveling with vice presidential candidate Spiro T. Agnew. The original plan was for Sears to shuttle back and forth between the Nixon and Agnew campaigns, keeping track of Agnew's mouth and maintaining communication between the two operations. But he ended up traveling with Agnew full time.

Mitchell usually acted in the campaign in alliance with Haldeman and Ehrlichman. It was not that the three men were fond of one another; instead, they were in competition with each other to see who was the toughest, most effective manager.

In the early, pre-convention days of the 1968 campaign, while we New York–based recruits ran around without much adult supervision, Haldeman and Ehrlichman watched expectantly and apprehensively from the sidelines. The two men still bore wounds from the ill-fated, excruciating Nixon campaigns of 1960 and 1962; they were watching to see how Nixon fared in New York and handled himself in the primaries. They would make their own judgments about whether Nixon could make it. If they decided to join the campaign, they would further determine the terms on which they would get aboard. They intended to run things—and, with the help of Mitchell exercising his campaign manager's prerogatives to keep the candidate in line, they did.

Haldeman and Ehrlichman must have known going in that despite the good early omens, there remained a major obstacle to their ability to control matters around Nixon; and that was Nixon himself. The portents for 1968 may have been favorable, but Nixon's personality had not fundamentally changed. He would always be tempted to take the controls himself and, in grabbing the reins, perhaps do things dangerous to himself and those close to him. From conversations with Haldeman and Ehrlichman in later years, I have come to think that the two men were quite aware of this danger. They assessed its size and decided to risk it. They were, after all, political men.

Haldeman, once he decided to join the campaign, became and remained the undisputed top manager in the Nixon entourage. One of those he displaced was Rose Woods, whom he moved outside the advisory circle and tried to assign exclusively to writing letters. Rose responded with a cordial and lasting dislike of Haldeman.

Haldeman maintained his dominant position, however, because of his intelligence, skill, and thoroughgoing identification with his boss. More accurately, Haldeman identified, as perfectly as any staffer I have known, with the tough exterior that Nixon presented to most of the world. Haldeman's own toughness, in turn, encouraged Nixon to act consistently with this tough self.

Nixon also had a profoundly emotional, thoughtful interior to which Haldeman did not speak. (Haldeman had his own interior complexity, but never the twain did meet.) It was the walled garden of Nixon's soul, harboring the "goodness" he had taken from his mother, Hannah Milhous Nixon, and other sensitivities. I saw some of this side of Nixon during the 1968 campaign, when Nixon would call me late at night, after all the campaign stops were over, and talk himself to sleep, worrying and meandering in free association.

Haldeman, convinced that the emotional part of Nixon was dangerously vulnerable, led the men around him in trying to keep the sad, soft side first of the candidate and then of the president under control and to keep Nixon himself talking the cold-blooded language of political instrumentalism. In the 1968 campaign, Haldeman succeeded—barely.

Ehrlichman was different from Haldeman, more so than the press treatment of the two men recognized. Ehrlichman did not have any personal or political connection of his own to Nixon that placed him in the inner ring of power. Instead, Ehrlichman was, at first, at the center of events simply through his friendship and old school ties with Haldeman. Thus Ehrlichman, as opposed to Haldeman, had to cling to his place in the inner circle by will, wit (which was famously coruscating), and bulk.

Ehrlichman sustained his morale amidst all this clawing by daring to be decent in small things—not small in policy importance but small in the daily calculus of White House power. Thus Ehrlichman played major and essential roles in creating the Environmental Protection Agency, endowing the arts, helping desegregate the public schools of the Deep South without violence, and creating a new regime under which American Indians, for the first time in this country's sorry history with them, were given the legal means and resources to begin, finally, a course of self-determination.

None of this, however, made him a powerful independent voice when it came to the political activities that were ultimately to bring about Nixon's downfall.

Some of the individuals that Haldeman and Ehrlichman brought with them to the campaign and the White House achieved measures of independence in indirect ways. The most interesting of them was Ron Ziegler, the fulcrum of Haldeman's communications system, lifted out of Disneyland—yes—into Republican politics via the J. Walter Thompson advertising agency. (After all, as Ziegler had to endure hearing myriad times, how far was it from Fantasyland to briefing the White House press corps?) But Ron was not your average advertising apparatchik; for instance, he not only could repeat verbatim the jungle tour spiel he had given when he was a guide at Disneyland but could deliver it backwards. Forget the memory skills thus revealed; undertaking to learn the thing in the first place illuminated a corner of Ziegler's mind that was demented in the best sense.

Briefing the press is an art form. Ron was very good at it.

But part of the art form is obfuscation. Another part consists of a stubborn refusal to follow lines of logic where they lead, at least publicly. Therefore outsiders did not know how smart Ziegler was. By the end of Watergate, from which he emerged unscathed, it was clear that he was very smart indeed.

Another kind of independence was the route chosen by Richard Whalen, who was later to speculate about the identity of Deep Throat in the *Washington Post*. Whalen was a respected journalist by the time he joined the Nixon campaign. Before the nomination, he worked with the speechwriters to produce some of Nixon's most memorable early lines. Whalen was also close to Sears. It was foreordained that once Haldeman and Ehrlichman appeared, the chunky, grouchy Whalen would sooner or later run up against the tough new Nixon campaign regime.

Whalen's first collision with the new order occurred at the Republican convention in Miami. Haldeman and Ehrlichman had arrived. Whalen tried to get to the hotel floor where Nixon's suite was located. Ehrlichman would not allow it: Whalen did not have a badge of the proper color, and the new management refused to issue him one.

Whalen finally got his badge, but the next run-in was worse. Just after the primaries, the campaign staff gathered at Mission Bay in San Diego to plan for the general election campaign. One evening John Mitchell, slightly in his cups, let loose at Whalen with a mess of invective about writers, their inflated notion of their importance to political campaigns, and the need to keep them in their place.

Whalen told me about Mitchell's abuse later that night and was out of the campaign the next morning—literally— trudging away from the hotel carrying his suitcases. He was prescient. But while Whalen left, the rest of us avatars of the "new Nixon" stayed, thinking that we could make our own independent way among the "realpoliticians."

The only reason that there were not more of these fractures is that Nixon tried to keep the various parts of his campaign organization working in separate, parallel political universes. For instance, I recently reread Jules Witcover's excellent book *The Resurrection of Richard Nixon* and was reminded that shortly after President John F. Kennedy's assassination in 1963, Nixon convened a large meeting of veterans of his previous campaigns at the Waldorf-Astoria to weigh Nixon's future as a party leader and possible presidential candidate.

At the time the meeting took place, Nixon had long since recruited me to his fledgling campaign. More specifically, the invitations had already gone out for a reception to be held in Nixon's honor at my home in Brooklyn Heights for the purpose of introducing him to the overwhelmingly Democratic Brooklyn bench and bar (the reception, when it finally took place, was a great success). But I did not know about the conclave of Nixon old-timers, and they certainly did not know what I was doing.

I can see the logic of the compartmentalization: I had no experience of Nixon to bring to the question of whether he should run again, while not many of the Nixon veterans could possibly have known or cared about a bunch of Democratic lawyers in Brooklyn. Nixon was extremely talented at inventing and maintaining such divisions, which so suited his temperament. For instance, I do not remember ever having seen Mitchell and Sears in the same meeting with the candidate.

Nixon wanted everyone around him to know that he was the only one with all the information necessary to make proper decisions. Indeed, during the 1968 campaign he employed a private pollster—Joe Batchelder, Senior, the father of a law partner of mine—who reported to Nixon alone. Nixon used him as a check on the information that came to him from his regular campaign polling apparatus.

Nixon was always juggling his self-created separate constituencies. Sometimes he nearly dropped the ball. Once during the campaign, forgetting that he was now the new Nixon, the old Nixon remarked publicly that the DuBois Clubs, a network of Communist front organizations, had chosen their name in order to mislead people into thinking they were Boys Clubs. Sears was shaken. I was shaken. Nixon told us to relax. He said the press would forget about the remark in a week. He was right.

However, this same insistence on proceeding in parallel or even contradictory tracks was to play a role in creating both Watergate and Deep Throat. I remember the day in 1969, for instance, when I heard that one Charles Colson, who had been raising money for Nixon in another part of the campaign swamp, had been named special counsel to the president. "Who the hell is *that?*" I asked.

It was a mark of the fragmentation of the Nixon campaign that I hadn't known of Colson's existence, let alone his closeness to the president. Colson was in those days the man who declared that he would walk (or was it drive? or roll?) over his grandmother for Richard Nixon. If Haldeman habitually shored up Nixon's tough side, Colson whipped that toughness into a caricature of itself. Colson became the man who most vigorously stirred up the demons that had accompanied Nixon to the presidency.

Colson is a very different man today from the one he was then. The same force of personality that he brought to his White House job is now deployed in the salutary service of prison reform.

*   *   *

We almost didn't make it in the general election. The country in 1968 was reeling with bitterness and violence that almost cost Nixon his victory, just as they would later help to end his presidency.

The 1968 presidential campaign took place against a background made up of Vietnam, student unrest, urban riots, and general cultural chaos. At first, Hubert Humphrey, Lyndon Johnson's vice president and the Democratic presidential candidate, was associated in the public mind with all this unpleasant tumult. By contrast, negative memories of the Nixon of the 1950s had faded, in part because of the media's focus on the story of the Nixon comeback. Nixon, endlessly reviled and endlessly a loser in the media, had by virtue of this very endlessness become a familiar, durable, even comforting figure, a model of stability in a time of rock-and-roll anxiety. Nixon took the lead.

In the last weeks of the campaign, however, the lead evaporated. Johnson boosted Humphrey by announcing a bombing halt and a proposal for peace talks in Paris. Antiwar voters, who hated Humphrey because of the Johnson administration's Vietnam policies, finally remembered that they hated Nixon even more. Labor came home. The national

Democratic majority gradually clarified, like a Polaroid photo.

In the end, Nixon outmaneuvered the Democrats on Vietnam and squeaked through, but only just.

Once the campaign was over, the internal tensions among Nixon staffers grew worse. The high-stakes war of a presidential race exerts a powerful cohesive force on each side. But then the race is over, won or lost; and internal competition moves to the fore. The campaign was, in microcosm, what Nixon's first term in office was to become. Both enterprises began well, harboring decent impulses. Then they soured even as they succeeded, turning increasingly rancid with poisonous struggles that were passively indulged by Nixon and that, to some extent, mimicked his own internal tug-of-war. In the case of the presidential campaign, Nixon was saved from the natural consequences of this process by the gun. Time ran out on Humphrey before the votes ran out on Nixon. The Nixon presidency, by contrast, had enough time to self-destruct, generously aided by the many enemies that wanted it dead.

*   *   *

By the day after the election, we had already forgotten those ominous last weeks. We were relieved, euphoric, transformed. Nixon arrived in Washington smiling, waving, and brandishing his "Bring Us Together" motto. He had a good beginning. My most vivid public memory from this period is of the birthday party and mammoth jam session I helped organize for Duke Ellington at the White House in April, 1969. At evening's end, Nixon and Earl Hines were upstairs in the private quarters at the White House, discussing the role that piano practice played in their respective careers. The magnolias were in bloom. I thought the honeymoon would last forever.

Nixon began his time in office with large plans and lofty visions, perhaps even more than most American presidents. He intended to end the American involvement in Vietnam, to engage the Soviet Union and China, to bring order, progress, and broader opportunity at home, and to do so with all deliberate speed. Nixon was also, however, very good at making enemies. It was in part because of this talent that his initial honeymoon in office was fragile to begin with and its aftermath was disastrous, despite his impressive capacities and the undisputed policy accomplishments they produced.

Nixon inherited the extraordinary hatreds spawned by the 1960s. Chief among them was the virulence of Vietnam, which killed not only the Nixon presidency but the presidency of Lyndon Johnson before him and poisoned the institution of the presidency itself. This was a rage so enveloping that it remade not only the political present and future around it but the political past as well—because, as Ward Just has said, it persuaded so many people that they did not know the truths they thought they knew. Watergate was umbilically connected to this anger.

That said, there cannot have been an individual less equipped than Nixon to respond rationally to such hatred.

Nixon was the most successful American Cold War politician, not an unmixed blessing. After World War II, political reputations were made and broken over real or manipulated issues of Communism, anti-Communism, and eventually anti-anti-Communism. Nixon was in the thick of the battle. He became a major player in American politics by leading the momentous investigations of Alger Hiss, a man who came to represent the disappointed hopes of a generation of spirited liberals. Thus Nixon became the object of a focused and unforgiving hatred by a large part of the permanent, largely liberal intellectual and media establishment that helps shape public opinion. And Nixon fought back and hated back.

It is sufficient for our purposes to note that the wounds inflicted on both sides during these bitter ideological campaigns never really healed. Certainly they did not for Nixon. Each layer of scar tissue formed over the last, holding things together without healing them. In this state Nixon entered, exited, and re-entered national politics.

One result of Nixon's bedrock resentments was his treatment of the federal bureaucracy once he entered office. As Richard Nathan has recounted the story in his brilliant book, *The Plot That Failed: Nixon and the Administrative Presidency*, Nixon at first sought to achieve his policy goals by conventional means. For instance, at the beginning of his administration he formed and used his Cabinet in the traditional way. Apart from John Mitchell at the Department of Justice and Bob Finch at what was then the Department of Health, Education, and Welfare, the members of Nixon's first Cabinet were not close to him. Many were picked to represent external constituencies. Three of Nixon's initial Cabinet officers were former governors with their own political reputations—George Romney of Michigan, who had been Nixon's opponent for the 1968 Republican nomination and was chosen to head the Department of Housing and Urban Development; John Volpe of Massachusetts, who went to the Department of Transportation; and Walter Hickel of Alaska, who became secretary of the interior.

As in previous administrations, the Nixon White House did not routinely consult with Cabinet members, except for Mitchell, when making policy in their areas. George Shultz, Nixon's first secretary of labor, came to play an important role in domestic policy, particularly school desegregation; but his influence grew because of his individual talents, not his Cabinet position.

If Cabinet officers were not ordinarily heard at the White House, they were initially given a great deal of freedom in managing their departments, including substantial control over political appointments. This arrangement, too, was in accord with politics as usual. But it meant that the White House had given up patronage that it otherwise could have exercised in the Cabinet departments.

Nixon also began by trying to make his mark on history through much the same means as those used by John F. Kennedy and Lyndon Johnson. Nixon envisioned passing grand pieces of legislation like those that made up the New Frontier and the Great Society. To develop this legislation, Nixon formed task forces and working groups in the areas of welfare reform, revenue sharing, education, health, urban affairs, the environment, and labor-management relations— the same areas that had formed the core concerns of the earlier Democratic presidents.

In order to pass the proposals that these groups produced, Nixon would have to work with the Democratic Congress. Thus the White House would have to use some of the diminished amount of patronage it retained to form alliances with Congressional Democrats.

Both the delegation of patronage to the Cabinet secretaries and its use to mollify Democrats in Congress eroded the already precarious power of White House staffer John Sears.

Before the election, Nixon had told the younger man that Sears would be his political counselor, controlling the political aspects of patronage and serving as liaison between the White House and the Republican Party. Party leaders, who knew Sears from his delegate operations in the 1968 campaign, liked the idea. After the election, however, and before Nixon took office, Mitchell exercised his prerogative as victorious campaign manager and appointed his own man as chief of patronage. In addition, as part of the "Southern strategy," Mitchell made special arrangements for politics and patronage in the region, placing Harry Dent in charge.

When Nixon went to the White House in 1969, Sears went also, as deputy to then White House counsel John Ehrlichman. In reality, however, Sears was without a portfolio and without power. Sears had argued that the White House had to marshall its patronage and use it to build the Republican Party in the South. But Mitchell was more concerned with using this patronage to placate Democratic senator James Eastland, chairman of the Committee on the Judiciary. In this debate, Mitchell won.

The White House's early attempts to play conventional politics with Congressional Democrats did not work for Nixon as it had for Kennedy and Johnson. The difference should have come as no surprise. Nixon's two predecessors were Democrats shepherding legislative proposals through a Democratic Congress. Nixon, by contrast, repeatedly struck out in trying to push his legislation through a Congress not controlled by his own party, patronage deals or no patronage deals. Nixon was not going to achieve his place in presidential history via the legislative route.

By default, Nixon and his top aides decided to make policy through administrative action, using the discretion that many laws already gave the executive branch and the president. The White House first tried to implement this administrative approach through the relatively simple means of reorganizing itself so that it could exercise better control over the federal bureaucracy. But it soon became clear that trying to control the bureaucracy through old-fashioned threats and cajolery from above was a losing battle. Therefore Nixon and his lieutenants—both management experts and political operatives, led by John Ehrlichman—prepared a different strategy to be implemented after the 1972 election.

Nixon announced his intentions publicly, for those who cared to read the signs; and many in Washington did indeed care. In his 1971 State of the Union address and a subsequent message to Congress, Nixon argued that the bureaucracy was insufficiently responsive to elected officials and, therefore, to the American people. In response to this problem, Nixon proposed to reorganize the domestic Cabinet agencies into four new superagencies—for Natural Resources, Human Resources, Community Development, and Economic Affairs. Each superagency would be headed by a presidential appointee who would function as both a White House staffer and a manager of the various Cabinet departments making up the new superagency.

Thus appointees with primary allegiance to the White House and its goals would assume direct line control over Cabinet officers and bureaucrats.

Nixon and Ehrlichman aimed to carry out as much of this plan as possible without going to Congress for legislation. On the day after the president's 1972 election victory, Haldeman instructed all Cabinet officers to submit their resignations and to order the top political appointees in their departments to do likewise. Presidential press secretary Ron Ziegler announced that many of these resignations would be accepted. This brutal manner of proceeding was interesting chiefly as a mark of the embattled frustration animating the White House by that time. The main short-term effect of the announcement was to bring high-level Washington to a standstill—except for the gossip and rumor mill, which was running overtime.

The demand for resignations was not mere rhetoric. A group of Nixon aides moved out of the White House and into high-level posts in the Cabinet departments and the Office of Management and Budget. Three Cabinet secretaries received the additional title of counsel to the president, joining Secretary of the Treasury George Shultz, who held a comparable position. Each "Super Secretary" was to coordinate the Cabinet departments in his policy area, and report directly to a top White House aide.

The plan had barely gotten started in Nixon's second term, however, when the growing problems of Watergate stopped it dead. The scandal forced Ehrlichman, one of the chief architects of the administrative presidency, to resign in April of 1973. Shortly afterward, the "Super Secretaries" lost their special titles and functions. Nixon became too politically vulnerable to pick further fights with Cabinet departments and agencies regarding who was to hold power over them. The White House exercised less and less control.

Yet the White House plan to take control of the bureaucracy had meaning and consequences. It was fueled by the White House's profound mistrust of official Washington. In turn, as the plan gradually became known in Washington over the course of its development, it fueled the capital's mistrust of the Nixon administration. The plan, to those prone to view it so, looked like a White House plot to take over the government by means that were somehow improper. This suspicion was half-right. The means proposed were in fact not illegal or even improper. There is no doubt, however, that Nixon intended to get an unprecedented grip on the federal government and bypass Congress as much as possible in doing so.

Between the time of the Watergate break-in in June of 1972 and the decision in March of 1973 by Watergate burglar James McCord to tell what he knew about the involvement of higher-ups, the scandal was in gestation. During this period, official Washington was in a state of heightened anxiety and hostility towards the Nixon White House because of the plans for the administrative presidency. Thus the permanent government's hostility towards Nixon did not stem merely from general factors like Nixon's political history or the embittering Vietnam War. Something more concrete was at stake: the power and livelihood of many important people in the bureaucracy and those in and out of government who relied on it. When McCord began talking, his audience was quite ready to believe the worst version of events.

In addition, there were also people within and close to the White House who were suspicious of the shifts in power that Ehrlichman and some of Nixon's other lieutenants were trying to engineer. It was no accident that a major theme in Deep

Throat's utterances to Woodward was the idea that some men close to Nixon were trying to take the reins of power from the rest of the government.

The resentments that fueled plans for the administrative presidency also shaped both the administration's reaction to the continuing dilemma of Vietnam and its preparations for the electoral contests after 1968. These efforts became inextricably and destructively mixed up with one another.

In keeping with the multi-pronged plan that Nixon and Kissinger had developed to extricate the United States from the Vietnam War, the president publicly announced U.S. troop withdrawals in 1969, hoping thereby to dampen domestic antiwar activism. At the same time, he sought to bring increased pressure on the North Vietnamese to negotiate by launching air strikes at the Cambodian sanctuaries that the Communists were using as bases from which to launch murderous attacks on American and South Vietnamese troops in the Saigon region.

Nixon kept this bombing secret for two reasons: to prevent any possible interference with the plan by the U.S. antiwar movement and to provide cover for Cambodian President Sihanouk, who acquiesced in the bombings but who, Nixon and Kissinger thought, would feel obliged to protest the U.S. action if it became public.

In 1969, someone, somewhere, presumably in the White House or the State or Defense Department, leaked the fact of the bombings to William Beecher of the *New York Times*, which promptly ran the story. Not long afterwards the *Times* published information, similarly leaked to Beecher, about the U.S. fallback position in America's ongoing SALT nuclear disarmament talks with the Soviet Union.

Nixon was furious at the leaks. Part of the reason was substantive. The SALT leak, in particular, threatened a serious national security initiative. He was angrier, however, because of his suspicion that the leak might have come from people politically close to him.

Nixon was already primed for such suspicions of perfidy from within. Not long after the election, there appeared a book by Joe McGinniss called *The Selling of the President, 1968.* This book was my fault. McGinniss showed up one day, said he was writing some academic piece on campaign advertising, and asked to follow the advertising group around. I said sure. (McGinniss had previously approached the Humphrey people, I later learned. They had laughed him out of their offices.) We clasped him to our collective bosom, letting him in on virtually everything we did. And he, of course, bit.

I was especially annoyed: McGinniss's book reproduced a number of our confidential campaign memos. Someone, I discovered, had stolen them from my office. And if I was annoyed, Nixon was livid. Three years later, the White House tapes show him complaining to Haldeman about the McGinniss incident and the fact that the "kids" talked to the press too much.

After the McGinniss incident came the Beecher leaks, even more serious. Those leaks produced the moment, as much as any, when the hurts and habits of the past swept the "new Nixon" away.

In those days, before the Supreme Court had ruled otherwise, it was still plausible to argue that in matters of national security, the attorney general had authority to order a wiretap by the FBI without first obtaining a court order. The White House used this authority to try to find the leaker. In line with this intention, Nixon and Mitchell ordered fourteen FBI national security wiretaps.

However, three non–national security staffers were also wiretapped—Bill Safire and John Sears, both of whom were suspected of being significant leakers to the press, and James W. McLane, head of the White House's Committee on Aging, who worked in the White House for the liberal Bob Finch. John Mitchell, methodical as always, read through the wiretap results.

Sears was the recipient of even more special—nay, unique—attention. He was placed under twenty-four-hour surveillance for more than two months. This extraordinary treatment began, as author David Wise recounts, with a tap that had been placed at the direction of the White House on the phone of journalist Henry Brandon. Brandon, in one of his phone conversations, quoted a White House official, whom he did not name, as saying, "The President is weak. He has difficulty saying no. He wants to please all and he dislikes having to make a choice. . . . With a man like this, Henry Kissinger, of course, has great influence." Through the channel of Mitchell and Haldeman, Nixon learned about the quote. Perhaps because it was so trenchant, Nixon suspected Sears. Perhaps because he had felt such affection for Sears, Nixon turned on him with fury. Mitchell ordered the FBI to undertake the round-the-clock surveillance of Sears. He said it was the express direction of the president.

The surveillance began on July 23, 1969. It ended on the last day of September, after the FBI complained that the task required ten agents per day and had produced nothing except the not-exactly-secret information that Sears was a man given to nocturnal roamings.

But by that time, Nixon's attitude towards Sears had been permanently poisoned. Ehrlichman gave Sears less and less work to do. By October of 1969, the quantity of this work had dwindled to near nothing; someone even arranged to have Sears's name missing from White House personnel lists.

Sears left the White House—though he remained close to many people in it, including Rose, Pat Buchanan, and Jack Caulfield, and could often be seen in the halls of the Old Executive Office Building. Chuck Colson gradually took over the role of political counselor that many had assumed would be filled by Sears.

In the spring and summer of 1970, the suspicion that had produced the wiretaps of administration staffers turned outward and rose to a new level of self-destructiveness. By this time, the administration had been the target of a year and a half of antiwar demonstrations and of unremitting pressure from Congress to hasten the pace of U.S. disengagement from Vietnam. In response, Nixon and Kissinger increased military pressure on North Vietnam, launching a ground incursion into the North Vietnamese sanctuaries in Cambodia.

If Nixon had treated the incursion as a routine military operation, the domestic reaction to it might not have been so intense. (Before the incursion, Al Haig, then still working for Henry Kissinger, gave a briefing to the White House staff, complete with maps and pointers. As he talked, Donald Rumsfeld, then an assistant to the president, piped up, "Why are we making such a big deal of this? Why don't we just do it?") But Nixon acted otherwise: Once the invasion had been launched, he announced it in a televised speech to the nation. The demonstrators began demonstrating; the authorities began overreacting. There were killings of students at Kent

State and Jackson State universities. Outrage erupted. A nationwide campus shutdown began, and students thus liberated headed to Washington by the busload to continue their demonstrations. They created, briefly, a state of siege in the White House. It is easy to forget, unless you were there, the beleaguered quality of those days, when there were sandbags piled around the White House for protection.

That was the time when I, as well as others, first became anxious about the bizarre quality of some of Nixon's behavior. One evening, during what Nixon felt—not without some reason—to be the occupation of Washington, he made yet another televised speech in an effort to calm the nation. Later that night, at 4:00 A.M., he wandered out of the White House accompanied only by his valet, Manolo Sanchez, like a Don Quixote with his Sancho Panza, to joust verbally with a bunch of startled students who were camped out at the Lincoln Memorial.

The encounter at the Lincoln Memorial, however, was not the end of the president's nocturnal journey. He then took Manolo into the empty House of Representatives, where the president delivered a civics lesson to his valet. Next, Nixon rode to the Mayflower Hotel on Connecticut Avenue, near the White House, where he breakfasted on his favorite comfort food, corned beef hash and poached eggs.

In the summer of 1970, for reasons unrelated to Nixon's enchanted evening, the demonstrations petered out and the domestic anger over Vietnam abated somewhat. Nixon, however, remained in a state of siege. The demonstrations may have been over, but the off-year Congressional elections were now on the near horizon, reopening and aggravating yet another, more specific set of psychological scars and fears.

Nixon had been seared by his loss to Kennedy in the presidential race of 1960. It was not simply that Nixon lost the presidency in 1960, though that was bad enough; it was the *way* he lost. Nixon was beaten by a smarter, shrewder, and—hardest of all to take—tougher bunch of politicians, led by the Kennedy family itself, fed by the Kennedy fortune, and implemented by all the iron-headed Kennedy political professionals epitomized by Larry O'Brien, later to become chairman of the Democratic National Committee. The Kennedys ran roughshod over the Nixon team (and, it later came to light, the electoral rules), grinning all the way. "Nixon's just got no class," JFK patronizingly said of his opponent, adding to Nixon's pain.

True, all presidential election campaigns are bloody. I know personally, though, that Nixon took into the 1968 presidential campaign a boundless, almost inhuman determination to even the score—and that the overwhelming nature of this determination did not abate once Nixon was in the White House. In addition, this anger at the Kennedys over their past insults and injuries to him made Nixon fearful of the family's intentions towards the 1972 election. At some point, explicitly or not, Nixon must have taken a vow to leave no stone unturned, no money unspent, no trick untried in order to win the White House, govern, get re-elected, and do it in spades.

Nixon began planning for his 1972 re-election even before he took office in January, 1969. His pre-inauguration correspondence with Haldeman and Haldeman's diaries in the following weeks record Nixon's direction to Haldeman to get the 1972 campaign under way on all fronts—fundraising, personnel, all cylinders. Every politician, they say, is continually looking to the next election; even against this background, however, Nixon's directive is striking as a mark of the morbid intensity with which he approached his electoral future.

In 1970, fresh from the Cambodia demonstrations and with the off-year Congressional elections approaching, Nixon decided, in accord with the aggressive conservatives on his staff and against substantial opposition from more prudential staffers, to take a personal and leading role in the campaigns. Nixon's strategy was his own. He would run against what were then called the "radic-lib" elements in the country, meaning hippies, long-hairs, student demonstrators, anyone who looked left over from the 1960s.

Nixon proceeded to campaign on this provocative platform from coast to coast on behalf of Senate, House, and gubernatorial candidates. He delivered heated harangues about law and order, campus violence, and kindred subjects. The press concluded that the new Nixon of 1968 had fully disappeared. In his place stood the old Herblock caricature of a stubble-faced Nixon climbing out of a sewer.

On election eve, Nixon decided to deliver a televised summation, using a film of a speech he had given in Phoenix, Arizona during the campaign. It was one of his more unpleasant demonstrator-baiting addresses. Its topic was the decadence of substantial parts of the American culture; and apart from its acerbic content, it had technical problems that made it partly unintelligible. Nixon had the film televised on all three networks; as a result, the networks were obliged (and, no doubt, delighted) to allocate equal time to the Democratic Party, which chose Senator Edmund Muskie to make its presentation.

That evening, Muskie, from his home in Maine, gave a relaxed, warm, sensible-sounding fireside chat. On that particular night, Muskie, unlike Nixon, looked like a president and sounded like a president. According to the polls, Muskie also had an excellent chance of actually replacing Nixon as president when the 1972 election rolled around.

During the 1970 campaign itself, some of the Republican candidates for whom Nixon spoke expressed unhappiness with the tone of Nixon's rhetoric on their behalf. We got criticism as well from members of Nixon's core constituencies who were upset with the caliber of his performance on election eve. None of this, however, compared in impact to the results of the elections themselves. Republican candidates overall did not do well, especially in the races for governorships. Republican candidates began to see Nixon as more of a problem for them than for the Democrats.

Nixon's prospects for re-election now seemed shaky; and Nixon became not only angry, as he had been, but increasingly anxious, an aggravating factor. He began 1971 in a foul mood, determined to win by any means, conventional or otherwise—and he made sure his political staff knew it. "No more of that nice guy stuff," he repeatedly gave the message to his political aides.

In truth, Nixon's objective political situation was not bad: The efforts at winding down American participation in the war, though attended by various domestic upheavals, seemed to be succeeding. The Democrats could not make as much capital out of the issue as they once had done. This fact, however, did little to calm Nixon's fears.

While Nixon's political anxieties grew, his foreign policy was at a delicate stage. Because of these two simultaneous conditions, presidential attention in the spring of 1971 was highly labile, shifting back and forth from the low politics of campaign preparation to the high politics of foreign policy. The former had its distinct effect on the latter.

On the world stage, Nixon and Kissinger were moving step by step towards consummation of their complex "triple strategy." They would, according to their plan, create an opening to China. The opening, in turn, would create an incentive for the Soviet Union, because of its ever-active rivalry with China, to engage in summit talks. The Soviets, finally, would put pressure on North Vietnam to agree to a settlement that would give South Vietnam a fighting chance to survive as an independent nation. Nixon and Kissinger's immediate, specific goal, it should be noted, was not to realign the world geopolitically but to influence actions by the North Vietnamese; the geopolitical tail was wagging the dog. Such was the shadow that Vietnam cast over all of politics then.

As the moves of the triple strategy were being carefully plotted in the spring of 1971, Daniel Ellsberg, a former Department of Defense official, gave the *New York Times* the Pentagon Papers, which he had helped to prepare while in government. These Papers consisted of a large number of top-secret assessments by the Department of Defense of its conduct of the Vietnam War during the Johnson administration and its predecessors.

Nixon's first reaction to the news of the Pentagon Papers' impending publication was calmly pragmatic: Insofar as the documents revealed American bungling and duplicity, it was pre-1968 bungling and duplicity, mostly by Democratic administrations. Properly handled, Nixon said, the documents could become grist for the Republicans' mill.

Kissinger, on the other hand, was enraged. He considered both the leak and its publication to be treason. He warned

Nixon that administration passivity in the face of these events would send a message of presidential weakness and unreliability to both allies and adversaries. The grand strategy would dribble down the tubes.

Colson and Haldeman, too, stoked Nixon's anger at the leak. Nixon was persuaded; and, once persuaded, he became angrier than Kissinger had been. He instructed Mitchell, his attorney general, and Colson, his White House special counsel, to take every possible retaliatory step.

The administration tried to restrain publication of the Papers. Under the direction of Robert Mardian, then assistant attorney general in charge of national security matters and later to become political coordinator at the Committee for the Re-election of the President (CRP), the Justice Department went to federal court and obtained an injunction against publication. This Supreme Court, however, soon ruled against the government. The *New York Times* began publication of the Pentagon Papers on the same front page on which it reported the wedding of Nixon's daughter, Tricia, rubbing salt in the partly self-inflicted wounds.

The other major response by the White House to the Papers' publication was the establishment of the White House plumbers. Ellsberg's leak had reignited the administration's always-simmering rage to find and punish leakers within the government. But time had passed since the White House's original 1969 wiretaps. The law had changed. Moreover, J. Edgar Hoover, director of the FBI until his death in 1972, had grown nervous about the administration's use of national security wiretaps.

Even in the early days of the administration, Hoover refused the White House's request to bug the telephone of columnist Joseph Kraft, forcing Ehrlichman to give the job to Jack Caulfield to supervise. Then Hoover abruptly discontinued the administration's existing national security wiretaps in February of 1971. Thus the White House could no longer cite national security concerns to the FBI and expect it to bug suspected leakers without the benefit of a court order.

Therefore in the wake of the Pentagon Papers affair, Ehrlichman and, of course, Colson oversaw the formation of the secret, ad hoc Special Investigations Unit within the White House that later became known as the "plumbers." The ostensible mission of the plumbers was to prevent press leaks and identify leakers. The group was run by Egil Krogh, one of Ehrlichman's most highly regarded deputies. Krogh was a good man, a true Nixon believer, and much too young for the job given to him. Krogh's deputy was David Young, whom Kissinger had willingly seconded from his national security staff.

The plumbers' operational members were G. Gordon Liddy and E. Howard Hunt. Liddy, a lawyer and former FBI agent, was soon to become finance counsel and head of campaign intelligence at CRP. Hunt, a spy novelist and former CIA agent, was serving as a consultant to Charles Colson at the White House while simultaneously employed by the public relations firm of Robert R. Mullen & Co., a CIA front organization. When the plumbers were first established, Ehrlichman approached the CIA, then headed by Richard Helms, and asked that the agency cooperate with Hunt. The agency, true to its tradition of serving presidents, agreed.

The White House, after its failure to prevent publication of the Pentagon Papers, had shifted its battle plan to the launching of personal attacks on Ellsberg and his supporters in order to blunt the force of their criticism. Engineering these attacks was the first major assignment given to the White House plumbers.

Thus at the very outset, the plumbers deviated from their presumably core mission of finding and plugging leaks. This departure was not the last such detour. For instance, under Colson's guidance, the group hatched a fairly lunatic plan to retrieve—a useless task in the first place—a set of the Pentagon Papers that they believed was stored at the Brookings Institution. Here is how it was supposed to go: Plumbers operatives would set a fire at Brookings (just a small fire). Other plumbers operatives, impersonating D.C. firefighters, would respond to the fire. While on the scene, the operatives would retrieve the documents.

A number of people in the White House knew about the plumbers' activities. For instance, Colson told Jack Caulfield about the Brookings plan, seeking Caulfield's participation. Instead, Caulfield took the news to others in the administration, including John Dean, who had succeeded Ehrlichman as White House counsel. Dean became, reasonably enough, extremely alarmed. Indeed, Dean flew cross-country to meet Ehrlichman, then in California, and tell him what was up. Ehrlichman, reacting like a sane human being, vetoed the operation. (As Liddy would say contemptuously years later, after he had served his prison time but before he became a noted radio talk show host, the same high-level White House aides who had ordered the retrieval of the Pentagon Papers turned out to be "too cheap to pop for the $40,000 for the fire engine.")

Only slightly less loony was the plumbers' notorious attempted burglary of the office of Ellsberg's psychiatrist in

California. They were attempting to obtain derogatory information about Ellsberg for use in a psychological profile of him that they had requested from the CIA. To do so, they recruited some Cuban-American friends of Hunt, veterans of the Bay of Pigs invasion that Hunt had helped direct during his CIA days, to help them seize and photograph Ellsberg's medical records. The group failed, once again attracting negative attention from higher authorities.

This time it was Ehrlichman and Krogh who became alarmed, eventually terminating the plumbers altogether with what they thought was extreme prejudice. During the latter half of 1971, the group was largely relegated to mundane work; by the end of the year it was out of business.

Ehrlichman and Krogh's extreme prejudice was not, however, extreme enough. The end of Hunt and Liddy's employment by Ehrlichman did not put the two operatives out of work. By then, Liddy had transferred to CRP, where he was to become counsel to the campaign finance operation. He and Hunt proceeded to enter into a joint venture for the production of political intelligence.

2

Watergate

If the story of Nixon's comeback has been told before, the story of the Watergate break-in and its aftermath has been told even more often. But before we come to flowerpots and garages, I must remind readers, briefly, of what happened during Watergate and when. It is impossible to make sense of Woodward and Bernstein's role in the scandal, and the role of Deep Throat in Woodward and Bernstein's enterprise, without a clear contextual picture of the background against which they operated. Yet a clear picture is precisely what most published versions fail to deliver. Some histories of Watergate are untrustworthy because their authors have axes to grind. Others mindlessly recycle other people's errors.

One feature of the account I will give is especially relevant to the matter of Deep Throat. It is the fact that the early days of Watergate were utterly bewildering, with events roiling invisibly beneath the surface before they exploded into public view. That is why the guidance provided by Deep Throat was so important to Woodward and Bernstein and to the eventual exposure of the scandal.

When G. Gordon Liddy joined the Committee for the Re-election of the President (CRP) at the end of 1971, the organization was headed by Jeb Magruder, a Haldeman aide who was serving as acting director until John Mitchell could resign his post at the Justice Department and take over the campaign effort. Nixon, Haldeman, and Colson had already made clear that one of their top campaign priorities was the establishment of a political intelligence program. In response to this high-level mandate, Magruder asked Liddy to prepare a proposal for such a program. Liddy, in turn, enlisted Hunt, who was still working for Colson and for the Mullen & Co. PR firm. Liddy and Hunt, in keeping with their instructions, designed a plan whose first phase consisted of gathering and spreading negative gossip about the Democratic presidential hopefuls who, if nominated, would pose the strongest threats to Nixon in November.

In January, 1972, Liddy, accompanied by Magruder, met with John Mitchell, who was still attorney general, and White House Counsel John Dean in Mitchell's office at the Department of Justice. Liddy laid out the political intelligence and dirty tricks program that he and Hunt had designed. They had of course given their plan a code name: Gemstone. It included electronic eavesdropping, kidnapping political opponents, disrupting public gatherings sponsored by the opposition, and deploying prostitutes to compromise Democratic convention delegates. The budget was one million dollars, which in those days was real money.

Mitchell knew, of course, that Liddy's proposed actions

were not just illegal but incredibly so. The attorney general could not possibly have wanted or intended to approve the panoply of skullduggery that had been laid before him. On the other hand, there in his office sat John Dean, with a direct line to Haldeman, Ehrlichman, and Colson. They would soon hear about it if Mitchell were to make any lily-livered objections.

So Mitchell said the plan was not quite what he had in mind and told Liddy to prepare a scaled-down proposal. This Liddy proceeded to do, returning to Mitchell in February with a smaller Gemstone plan. Once again Mitchell declined to approve Liddy's presentation. Mitchell must have thought he was doing the smart thing by sending Liddy repeatedly back to the drawing board. He was doubtless confident that once he took over at CRP and began exercising full authority, he could keep Liddy's plots under control. Yet much of the subsequent mess of Watergate originated in Mitchell's cryptic and indecisive reactions to Liddy's proposals.

Mitchell grievously misjudged how much control the White House would continue to exercise over the campaign and how difficult it would be to stop an operation launched under such high auspices as this one was. He was not, however, without some slight apprehension. It was during this time that he remarked to me one day, as he was getting into his black limousine outside the Old Executive Office Building, "That fucking Colson is going to kill us all." I nodded knowingly, having not the slightest idea what he meant.

In March of 1972, Mitchell finally left his post as attorney general and took over at CRP. Jeb Magruder relinquished his post as acting director to become Mitchell's deputy. After this transfer of power, Liddy presented a third, still-smaller Gemstone proposal, as Mitchell had requested. This time, Mitchell authorized Liddy to spend $250,000 on his plans for disruption, espionage, and wiretapping. Some people have claimed that Magruder alone, not Mitchell, finally approved Gemstone. But no one familiar with Mitchell thinks that Magruder would have done such a thing without Mitchell's knowledge.

At the time when Mitchell and Magruder approved the shrunken Gemstone operation, the Nixon apparatus was engaged in a number of other unsavory activities. This fact would prove central to the way Watergate later unfolded. Liddy, in his capacity as finance counsel at CRP, was participating along with others in the substantial irregularities that marked the committee's fundraising efforts. Liddy was also in charge of a number of projects in addition to Gemstone that aimed at spying on Democrats and on Democratic candidates' campaigns. These additional intelligence activities naturally bore their own code names, like Sedan Chair and Ruby.

There were also dirty tricks operations begun well before Liddy joined CRP. These were supervised by aides to Bob Haldeman, including Jeb Magruder, Dwight Chapin, Gordon Strachan, and Bart Porter. These efforts consisted primarily of spying on Democratic candidates' campaigns but also included attempts at disruption.

Donald Segretti, who was hired by Dwight Chapin, was one of the disrupters; he would become the best-known of them once the Watergate scandal broke open. Segretti's tricks ranged from the trivial (ordering hundreds of pizzas for delivery to a Democratic campaign event) to the highly malicious and patently illegal (forging letters, purporting to be from Democratic candidates, that accused other Democratic candidates of sexual improprieties). He was paid out of slush funds left over from the 1968 and 1970 campaigns. The funds were controlled by Nixon's personal lawyer in California, Herb Kalmbach.

The scaled-down Gemstone, approved in late March or early April of 1972, became part of this array. In its shrunken version, it consisted mainly of organizing hecklers and counterdemonstrators at Democratic campaign events. However, it retained its plans for wiretapping Nixon's likely Democratic opponents and Democratic National Committee chairman Larry O'Brien. From the days when O'Brien had run Kennedy's 1960 presidential campaign, he had been a Nixon nemesis. O'Brien was also a consultant to billionaire Howard Hughes, with whom Nixon's personal and political connections were numerous and serpentine. Nixon wanted to know what Hughes had told O'Brien.

To help in the wiretapping, Liddy recruited James McCord. McCord was chief of security at CRP, hired partly on the recommendation of his friend in the White House, Jack Caulfield. McCord, like Liddy, had been an FBI agent. McCord had also served almost twenty years with the Central Intelligence Agency, where he was head of the agency's physical security division.

Hunt, too, recruited personnel to help with the wiretapping. In 1961, the CIA's Bay of Pigs operation, which Hunt had helped direct, had been a disaster. The U.S. government organized Cuban exiles for an invasion of Cuba, and these Cuban forces attempted a landing in Cuba at the Bay of Pigs. But the Cuban exiles were stranded on the beach when the Kennedy administration failed to provide them with promised air cover. The Cuban-Americans who participated in that campaign emerged with bitterness towards Democrats, especially towards Democratic presidential hopeful George McGovern, who was thought to be soft on Fidel Castro and who looked as if he might win his party's nomination. The Cuban-Americans also emerged with a sense of loyalty towards those Americans who they thought had showed loyalty to them—including Hunt, whom they affectionately called by his Bay of Pigs code name, Eduardo.

After the Bay of Pigs operation, Hunt and his Cuban-American friends remained in contact. When Hunt called on a group of them to serve their country once more by participating in a wiretapping of Democratic Party headquarters, they agreed to do so.

The presence of all these CIA-related individuals in the Watergate wiretap operation has given birth to a whole nursery of theories about the nature of the CIA's involvement in Watergate. Some of these theories claim that the break-ins at the Watergate—there were two of them—were directed by the CIA for Agency purposes. Others contend that the CIA-connected operatives in the wiretapping party were actually double agents who alerted the police to their activity or otherwise arranged for themselves to get caught, either to topple a president that the agency disliked or to provide distracting cover for past CIA crimes.

But in the years since Watergate, the CIA's possible role in the break-ins has been the subject of multiple congressional investigations and hearings and untold hours of investigative reporting. Not much has turned up. The agency probably did not direct the Watergate operations or their discovery, for motives either pro- or anti-Nixon. It is true that some people other than the Watergate burglars themselves heard before the break-ins that something of the sort was going to take place. It appears, however, that this knowledge was the result of random loose lips on the part of the burglars, almost surely including McCord, rather than of any deliberate efforts by the CIA.

The first Watergate break-in took place on May 28, 1972. Eugenio Martinez and Frank Sturgis, two of Hunt's Cuban-American recruits, made a middle-of-the-night entry into Democratic Party headquarters at the Watergate office complex. Once they had entered, they were joined by the other Cuban-Americans, Bernard Barker and Virgilio Gonzalez, and by Jim McCord. Liddy and Hunt, who had planned the break-in, did not enter the Watergate but were nearby, in communication with their troops via walkie-talkies.

Once inside Democratic headquarters, the operatives photographed several dozen documents from file cabinets near DNC chairman O'Brien's office. They also attached one wiretap to the phone of O'Brien's secretary and another to the phone of Spencer Oliver, director of the Association of State Democratic Chairmen. The O'Brien tap was explicable in light of Nixon's obsessions. But in the years since Watergate, no one has given a rationally persuasive reason why Oliver's phone should have been tapped.

In any event, the results of this first break-in were disappointing. The photographed documents did not contain any important information. In addition, only one of the wiretaps functioned properly, the one on Spencer Oliver's phone. McCord set up a listening post in the Howard Johnson's motel across the street from the Watergate to collect the information transmitted by the one functioning bug. To help him, McCord recruited Alfred Baldwin, a former FBI agent serving as bodyguard to John Mitchell's talkative loose-cannon wife, Martha.

McCord and Baldwin monitored, recorded, and transcribed the conversations held on Spencer Oliver's phone. This did not prove to be a fruitful exercise. Oliver was out of town for much of the time. His phone was used mainly by DNC staffers who were taking advantage of his absence to make personal calls from the phone in his private office. The information from the wiretap was useless.

McCord nevertheless sent the transcripts of these conversations to Liddy, who edited them and passed them on to Magruder. In at least one instance, Liddy also passed a transcript directly to Mitchell. While no one knows for sure whether Mitchell read the transcripts, I have reason to think he did. I know from personal experience that he read transcripts from taps on the phones of foreign embassies. Because I dealt with Mideast matters, I would often talk to people at the Israeli Embassy. One evening Mitchell, slightly in his cups, said to me cordially, "Chatty little bastard, aren't you? Why don't you let [Prime Minister Yitzhak] Rabin make his own mistakes?"

Magruder shared the Watergate transcripts he received from Liddy with Mitchell and with Gordon Strachan, Haldeman's White House liaison with CRP. There is no evidence that Nixon himself saw the material.

Liddy's superiors, disappointed with the results of the Watergate entry, told him to do better. At Liddy's behest, therefore, the five burglars went back into the Watergate on the night of June 16–17, 1972. This time they planned to bug O'Brien's office itself, the most likely source of information substantial enough to satisfy the appetites of the campaign's higher-ups.

In the course of this second entry, the burglars took the now-famous, still-inexplicable steps that got them caught. They taped the locks open in the Watergate parking garage and in a stairwell leading to the DNC offices. A security guard making his rounds noticed the tape on one of the locks and, perhaps thinking that maintenance men had placed it there while doing some work, simply removed it. The door locked again. In the course of the break-in, one of the burglars found the tape missing on the door—and re-taped it. The security guard, on his next round in the earliest hours of June 17, saw that the lock from which he had removed tape had been taped again. He drew the obvious conclusion and called the District of Columbia police.

When the police arrived at the DNC a few minutes later, it did not take them long to find the five men hiding in a secretary's cubicle, dressed in suits and ties, wearing rubber gloves, and equipped with wiretapping, lock-picking, and photographic gear.

The police were mystified by their haul of well-dressed burglars, but in retrospect there was not much mystery about it. The burglars were there because Nixon and the political men around him had an insatiable thirst for campaign intelligence, which they considered vital to pulverizing their political opponents. The results they demanded could be achieved only by breaking the law. In the environment of this particular campaign, such lawbreaking seemed not only necessary but natural.

The police carted the five burglars off to jail.

And where was I while all this was going on? As it happens, I have the world's best alibi. When Nixon became president, he appointed Frank Shakespeare, with whom I had worked on campaign advertising, as head of the United States Information Agency. In 1972, I took advantage of his position and mine to go with him on a—well, junket. We went to many countries. On the day of the Watergate break-in, as it happened, we were in a helicopter trying to get a glimpse of Mount Everest. There was fog. We never got our glimpse. We almost died. We journeyed on to Saigon and points east. It was only when we got to Hawaii that I learned from a newspaper that the break-in had taken place.

I have pictures to prove it.

Meanwhile, with the Watergate burglars arrested, Hunt went into hiding while Liddy began damage control. Two days of organizational chaos ensued. Its details are relevant mainly for the confusion they reveal.

On the morning of June 17, a few hours after the burglars were arrested, Liddy called Magruder in California, where Magruder, along with other prominent Nixon administration members, was attending various Republican Party functions. Magruder, after speaking with Liddy, quickly talked with Mitchell and with Mitchell's assistant and confidant Fred LaRue. The men conferred with Assistant Attorney General Robert Mardian.

After these conversations, Magruder phoned Liddy back and told him to track down Richard Kleindienst. Kleindienst was now the attorney general, having replaced Mitchell when Mitchell left the Justice Department to take over at CRP. Liddy, Magruder said, should get Kleindienst to arrange for the release of the burglars. It took Liddy an hour or two to track down Kleindienst, who probably did not want to be tracked down. Liddy finally found the attorney general enjoying a Saturday afternoon lunch at the Burning Tree Country Club. Liddy delivered Magruder's request. Kleindienst refused it. He later told the head of the Justice Department's Criminal Division, which was investigating the case, to treat it like any other. But the attorney general did not mention Liddy's revealing demand.

On June 17, when Magruder tried to push Kleindienst into action, he made other calls as well. Notably, he called his administrative assistant at CRP and told him to hide the Gemstone file and other documents relating to political espionage. Meanwhile, Mitchell ordered Mardian, an assistant attorney general of the United States, to take charge of damage control. But Haldeman countermanded that order, placing Magruder in charge. By Monday, the mantle of chief damage controller had passed yet again—this time to Ehrlichman, who in turn passed the project to John Dean. While these transfers of authority were taking place, Liddy, Magruder, Dean, and others were shredding, burning, burying, and otherwise disposing of incriminating evidence, ranging from U.S. currency to wiretapping equipment to Hunt's diaries to the Gemstone files to the hotel soap wrappers that Liddy compulsively collected in his travels.

In this vast confusion there was one certainty: Within hours of the arrest of the Watergate burglars, everyone connected with the campaign intelligence activities of which they were a part knew that there had been a disaster and began—unthinkingly, in the manner of most human beings—to try to cover up their mess.

Just as naturally, plans began for cash payments to Liddy, Hunt, and the Watergate burglars. On June 20, Liddy briefed Mardian and LaRue, who had returned to Washington, on Watergate and related campaign intelligence operations. Liddy also delivered a message: The burglars expected someone to pay the bill. "The bill" meant bail for the burglars, legal expenses, and living expenses for the burglars' families; this was the way things were done in clandestine operations. Liddy told Mardian and LaRue that high-ranking officials had promised as much in the event the burglars were caught, and that Liddy had passed these promises along.

Liddy did not say which high-ranking officials had made the promises. It did not matter. Even if no one had made such advance pledges, everyone knew that the burglars' needs would have to be met. Mardian and LaRue delivered Liddy's message to John Mitchell.

While these preliminaries were taking place, Nixon himself was not in Washington. He was in the Bahamas, vacationing for a few days on an island owned by his friend Robert Abplanalp, the aerosol tycoon. Nixon returned to the capital on Tuesday, June 20. As the tapes of his Oval Office conversations for that week show, he now attended to the Watergate matter for the first time.

Nixon quickly made a public statement about Watergate. In it, he directed the Justice Department and FBI to conduct the Watergate investigation. These two organizations were undoubtedly where the investigative responsibility belonged. Nixon must have thought it fortunate, however, that Henry Petersen, head of the Justice Department's Criminal Division, and L. Patrick Gray, whom Nixon had named acting director of the FBI after Hoover's death, were administration loyalists.

Indeed, during the early stages of the Watergate investigation, Petersen and Gray kept the Nixon White House up-to-date and involved. John Dean was allowed to sit in on interviews with prospective witnesses and to read, courtesy of Gray, dozens of confidential FBI investigative reports. Gray later testified that he even destroyed, at the unspoken but clear behest of Dean and Ehrlichman, documents found in a safe in Hunt's White House office.

Thus the Watergate conspirators were, at first, able to monitor and participate in the investigation of themselves. They could throw considerable sand in the investigative gears and change course quickly when the investigators turned up damaging new information.

Gray's cooperativeness with the White House frustrated many of his subordinates—from W. Mark Felt, Jr., acting associate director of the FBI, to the agents actually conducting the interviews and searches. In the same way, Petersen's cooperation with the White House caused resentment among his subordinates at Justice, including the three lawyers directly responsible for prosecuting Liddy, Hunt, and the Watergate burglars—Assistant U.S. Attorneys Donald Campbell, Seymour Glanzer, and Earl Silbert.

Despite the obstacle that Gray posed to the FBI efforts, the Bureau almost immediately began making headway in its investigation of the Watergate burglary. They began by—appropriately enough—following the money. In doing so, they met with an early stroke of good luck. One of the Watergate burglars, Bernard Barker, had also been doing fundraising work for Liddy. Specifically, Barker had been helping to launder certain contributions to the Nixon campaign. In April of 1972, Barker allowed $114,000 in checks, contributions to the Nixon campaign, to be deposited in a Miami bank account that he controlled. Some of the money came directly from Nixon fund-raisers Maurice Stans and Kenneth Dahlberg. But much of it had already been through one laundry cycle, reaching Barker's account via an attorney in Mexico City who was himself an intermediary.

Once the money was in Barker's account, he returned most of the $114,000 to CRP in what was intended to be untraceable cash. This cash—unfortunately for the Watergate conspirators, in sequentially numbered hundred-dollar bills—became part of the Committee's slush fund. A few weeks later, Liddy asked Hugh Sloan, treasurer of the Committee, for money from the slush fund to pay the expenses of the coming Watergate operation. Among the bills that Sloan gave Liddy were some of the hundred-dollar bills from Barker's bank account.

Liddy gave the bills to the burglars, who were carrying some of the laundered cash when they were arrested in the Watergate. The FBI, which knows how to do these things, traced the bills back to Barker's bank account, then discovered the source of the funds he held there. The money readily connected the burglars to the fundraising operations of CRP. Later, it would tie together the burglars, the break-in, and the cover-up as well.

The FBI had already begun to pursue the money trail, with disconcerting effectiveness, by the time Nixon met with Haldeman in the Oval Office on June 23, at the end of Nixon's first week back in Washington after the Watergate arrests. Bureau agents had traced the burglary cash back to Miami and Mexico. It was only a matter of time before they connected the final dots. Haldeman told Nixon, however, that

John Dean, had come up with a clever idea that could pinch off the investigation quickly.

In Dean's plan, the CIA would tell the FBI that the Watergate investigation was threatening CIA sources and therefore must be stopped. To get the CIA to play this role, Dean thought the White House could use the deputy director of Central Intelligence, Nixon's friend Vernon Walters.

Dean's turning to Walters was a revealing example of the Nixon White House's complicated relations with the federal bureaucracy. At the time of the Watergate arrests, the CIA, unlike the domestic law enforcement apparatus, was not headed by a Nixon political appointee. Instead, the Director of Central Intelligence, Richard Helms, was a career intelligence officer. The relationship between Nixon and Helms was cool. Nixon viewed the CIA in general and Helms in particular as embodying the contemptuousness and arrogance of the Eastern, liberal establishment. Nixon made no secret of his intention to bring a version of his "administrative presidency" to the national intelligence apparatus during his second term, cleaning house at the CIA and reshaping its structure and senior personnel to suit his needs.

Yet Nixon could not easily get rid of the bureaucratically skilled Helms, who had survived his own deep involvement in the Bay of Pigs disaster and was not likely to make a fatal misstep in the less treacherous task of managing Richard Nixon. Indeed, up until Watergate, Helms did not make such a misstep. Earlier, for example, when the White House first asked for cooperation from the CIA in launching Hunt, Liddy, and the White House plumbers, Helms's CIA did not refuse; it handed over the wigs, cameras, and other gewgaws of the spy trade ordered up by Hunt and Liddy.

Helms's shrewd combination of flexibility and intransigence stood in the way of White House control of the Agency. In response, Nixon installed General Vernon Walters, his long-time aide and friend, as Helms's deputy just a few weeks before the Watergate break-in.

Walters was a gifted translator; those who know about these matters say that he had an unmatched memory and a truly uncanny ability to give a precise rendition of diplomatic nuance in the several languages in which he was fluent. He had worked for Nixon on and off for some twenty-five years, and their political relationship was combat-close. In 1958, during Nixon's turbulent vice presidential tour of Latin America, Walters was his translator. Sitting beside Nixon in a motorcade in Caracas, Venezuela, then-Colonel Walters had his mouth cut by a shard of flying glass when anti-American demonstrators smashed rocks against the windows of Nixon's car.

Nixon valued Walters's capacious talent and his personal loyalty, continuing to use him as translator of choice on important foreign missions like Nixon's meeting with French president Charles de Gaulle in early 1969.

On June 23, 1972, when Nixon and Haldeman met in the Oval Office, they decided to make use of Walters to implement John Dean's idea. Helms would be told to send Walters to acting FBI Director Gray. Walters was to tell Gray that continued investigation of the Watergate money chain would compromise secret CIA sources and methods in Mexico. Upon hearing this news, Gray would order the FBI investigation stopped.

Haldeman, immediately after his June 23 meeting with the president, summoned Helms and Walters to meet with himself and Ehrlichman at the White House. There the CIA officials received the presidential instructions. Though Helms and Walters knew that the burglary investigation did not threaten any security-sensitive CIA secrets in Mexico, neither man refused to follow Haldeman's orders. Instead, Walters met with Gray later that day and delivered the message of CIA involvement. Gray did as Nixon had expected, putting the FBI's investigation of the Watergate money on hold.

Walters meticulously made a memo of his conversations with Haldeman, Ehrlichman, and Gray. It was this memo, when it later became public in May of 1973, that confirmed the existence of a White House cover-up. No one could contest the memo because no one would think of faulting Walters's memory—including, as Nixon later grudgingly noted in his memoirs, Nixon himself.

After Walters delivered his message to Gray on behalf of the White House, the CIA deputy director developed serious second thoughts. Over the next few days his doubts grew serious about the wisdom of involving the CIA in Watergate. In addition, Walters grew suspicious of the president's top aides, concluding that they were serving him badly by dragging him unknowingly into cover-up territory.

On June 26, Walters again went to the White House, this time to tell John Dean that the CIA had no interest that would be compromised by the FBI's Watergate investigation. Dean not only protested; he also took the opportunity to present Walters with the idea, devised by Mardian and approved by Mitchell, that the CIA should provide the money for the expenses of the Watergate burglars. According to J. Anthony Lukas in his Watergate history, *Nightmare*, Walters used the following words: "Mr. Dean, any attempt to involve the agency in the stifling of this affair would be a disaster. It would destroy the credibility of the agency with the Congress, with the nation." The quote is most likely from Walters himself; we can thus assume that it is accurate.

Since the CIA would not provide funds for the burglars, the money would have to come from somewhere else. Mitchell told Dean to pay the burglars through the slush fund maintained at CRP, out of which the Watergate burglaries had been financed in the first place. Dean cleared Mitchell's order with Haldeman and Ehrlichman; then, on June 28, he called Nixon's lawyer and chief fund-raiser in California, Herbert Kalmbach, and asked him to raise additional money for the burglars. He assured Kalmbach that the enterprise was legal.

As Walters was changing his mind, Gray, too, was growing anxious: His subordinates at the FBI, frustrated at not being able to pursue promising leads, were putting pressure on Gray to resume the money investigation. Gray finally told Walters that if CIA officials wanted the investigation stopped, they would have to put their request in writing. Instead, Walters told Gray that no CIA interest stood in the way of a vigorous FBI investigation. Walters further told Gray that the White House staff was endangering the president by standing in the way of the probe.

On July 6, after these events had taken place, Nixon made what he thought was going to be a routine phone call to Gray. Instead, the president heard Gray announce to him that people on the White House staff were placing him in "mortal" peril by interfering with the FBI investigation of Watergate. Nixon reacted in the only way he could, saying, "Pat, just continue to conduct your aggressive and thorough investigation." The president had thus managed both to attempt a cover-up and, almost simultaneously, insure that there would be a vigorous investigation aimed at discovering it. By the end of the first week in July, the FBI's investigation was up and running again.

On the same day as Nixon's conversation with Gray, July 6, the first payment of money was made to the Watergate burglars.

The attempt to use the CIA to deflect the FBI had been Nixon's one chance at dampening the investigation quickly and simply. When it failed, the five Watergate aides who played directing roles in the tragedy—Haldeman, Ehrlichman, Mitchell, Colson, and Dean, with Dean as the point man—had no choice but to work piecemeal, day-to-day and problem-to-problem, to delay and misdirect the investigation. Meanwhile, the White House would deny or minimize the press reports on Watergate that were appearing in some media, such as the *New York Times*, the *Los Angeles Times*, *Time* magazine, and the *Washington Post*.

And, of course, those running the cover-up had to pay. Money for the Watergate burglars ultimately came from three sources: the Committee for the Re-election of the President, a separate slush fund maintained by Haldeman, and contributions from unwitting donors through Herb Kalmbach. To help in the logistics of gathering, storing, and disbursing the money, the Committee engaged the services of Anthony Ulasewicz, a retired New York City police officer who had worked for Ehrlichman's aide Jack Caulfield on "special projects," mainly intelligence gathering. From the first payment on July 6, 1972, until the last one on March 22, 1973, almost $430,000 flowed from these sources to the Watergate burglars.

Along with the money, Nixon officials delivered hints of executive clemency for those who pled guilty without implicating higher-ups. The combination of cash and promises kept the burglars' lips sealed for some time. The enterprise required frequent attention from those responsible for keeping the scandal under wraps. During the August, 1972 Republican convention, I was sunning myself by the pool of the Doral Hotel when I noticed a group of my fellow administration members huddled together at the bar. They were talking to each other in muted tones, chain-smoking, and, unlike me, clearly not having any fun. They were, as I remember it, Gordon Strachan, Bob Mardian, Fred LaRue, John Dean, Jeb Magruder, and Dwight Chapin, with periodic visits from Chuck Colson. I knew that whatever piece of operational politics they were talking about, they would not want to share it with me. I did not know just how grateful I should have been for their attitude.

The cover-up held, however, through the November elections; all seven targets of the Watergate investigation, the five burglars plus Liddy and Hunt, refused to cooperate with the prosecutors. Even after the 1972 election, there were signs that Watergate would turn out to be politics as usual. The Miami contingent and Hunt pled guilty. Liddy and McCord went through the motions of a defense in a trial before Judge John Sirica, who until Watergate had been anathema to liberals because of his law-and-order brand of judicial activism. On January 30, 1973 Liddy and McCord were found guilty of various crimes relating to the break-in.

Upon their conviction, however, Judge Sirica postponed the sentencing of all seven Watergate operatives until March 23, 1973. As he did so, he made clear that he did not believe the two men convicted or those who had pled guilty had revealed everything the American people needed to know about Watergate. The message was quite clear: Sentences would depend upon the men's willingness to talk.

On the day of McCord's suspended sentencing, John Ehrlichman approached me with an invitation. The Senate had just formed a Select Committee on Watergate; and it was clear, Ehrlichman said, that many White House officials would be called to appear before it. Ehrlichman himself would probably be a witness and therefore could not play a lawyer's role in the proceedings. He wanted me to be the lawyer representing the White House in negotiations with the committee over the terms on which White House officials would testify. Ehrlichman also asked me to coordinate the testimony of the White House witnesses.

Before that conversation, I had not been involved in Watergate. Most of my friends in the White House were similarly detached. In retrospect, such a lack of involvement seems incomprehensible. In the course of writing this book, I have asked many of my former colleagues why, during the early days of Watergate, we did not know more about what was happening. They have said more or less the same thing, consistent with my own recollection. Watergate, we thought, was about politics. It may have involved dirty tricks on the part of the campaign organization, but dirty tricks were a time-honored part of politics. This matter had nothing to do with us.

Indeed, in later years, when I began my hunt for Deep Throat, the early ignorance about Watergate among policy types in the White House was one reason I thought I would have to look elsewhere to find someone with Deep Throat's extensive knowledge of operational politics.

By the time in January, 1973 when Ehrlichman approached me and asked me to represent the White House in Watergate matters, my early ignorance was a virtue. I was one of the few Nixon loyalists with a law degree who were not under criminal suspicion. (Some of the others—Secretary of State William Rogers, for instance—were too experienced in politics and in Nixon to go anywhere near the job.)

I did insist on talking first to Nixon himself. Nixon, in his aptly named hideaway office in the Old Executive Office Building, swore to me emotionally that he did not know about the break-in; that the burglary was a "crazy operation"; that "John" (Mitchell) had not been paying attention because of his troubles with his volubly unstable wife, Martha.

In this case, Nixon was a good liar. The job he and Ehrlichman had offered me seemed to entail defending Nixon from the consequences of bungling (on the part of CRP) and malice (on the part of the press and liberal establishment, which were using this incident to pursue their perennial anti-Nixon vendetta). I could handle that.

I accepted the assignment. All of a sudden I found myself in continuous closed sessions with Ron Ziegler and special counsel Richard Moore, trying to figure out how to keep the prosecutors, the press, Congress, and even the rest of the White House at bay. We moved with Geiger-counter caution, trying to avoid criminal contamination. We were also in pervasive denial, refusing to follow clues to their logical conclusion.

My denial was not without limits. By the time I began dealing with Watergate, in January, 1973, Mitchell and Colson had already left their official positions, though they remained involved in the cover-up. Haldeman, Ehrlichman, and Dean remained in office. I grew convinced that the president had an anchor around his neck in the continued presence of these three top aides. This damage was occurring, I thought, whether or not the three men were guilty of all the bad deeds of which they had by that time been accused.

So I pressed the president to clean house. He resisted. When he did, I thought the reason was simply denial or misplaced loyalty to his subordinates. I did not understand what Nixon himself understood fully: He was by now in no position to antagonize his closest, most steadfast assistants by ordering them out of the White House and thus making them more vulnerable to criminal prosecution. The more vulnerable they were, the less safe he was.

In between the time of McCord's conviction and the sentencing that was yet to take place, and unbeknownst to thankful me, Dean used Jack Caulfield—who, as it happened, was a friend of McCord's as well as having recommended him for the job of security chief at CRP—to deliver to McCord an explicit offer of executive clemency. It did not work. By the time of the sentencing, in March of 1973, McCord had figured out that the jig was up and decided to talk about the cover-up. He wrote Judge Sirica a letter to that effect. Sirica suspended sentencing for McCord pending their chat. At the same time, the judge handed out incredibly long sentences to the other men—a maximum of thirty-five years for Hunt, forty for the Miami burglars—but promised to review these sentences with a view to reduction if the men cooperated with Watergate investigators.

Liddy was different; Sirica believed he would not bend. The sentence the judge handed him was not provisional. Liddy would spend at least six years and eight months in prison, and possibly as much as twenty years. Sirica was right about Liddy's will. Years later, at dinner with Liddy, I asked

him why, even after Nixon's resignation, he had refused to
lighten his sentence by talking to prosecutors about his fellow
participants in Watergate. He said, "I just wouldn't give that
sonofabitch Sirica the satisfaction."

The others involved in the Watergate burglaries proceeded to talk—to Watergate prosecutors, to a reconstituted
Watergate grand jury, to the Senate Watergate committee,
and later to the House Committee on the Judiciary when it
took up the question of Nixon's impeachment in the fall of
1973. There was still some hush money left to spend but no
longer much point in spending it.

After McCord blew the cover-up in March, 1973, the Justice Department's investigation picked up speed and momen-
tum. The minor players in Watergate huddled with their
lawyers, rehearsing their lines and negotiating for immunity
in anticipation of their appearances before the Senate committee and the grand jury. The reporters at the *Washington
Post, Los Angeles Times*, and *New York Times* who had stayed
on the Watergate story since the previous June were now
joined by a cast of thousands.

By the end of April, 1973, the prosecutorial noose had
sufficiently tightened around Haldeman and Ehrlichman so
that the president was forced to accept their resignations,
along with those of Dean and Kleindienst. The pressure of
events had finally forced Nixon to take my advice, too late to
do him any good. I was at Camp David, along with Haldeman
and Ehrlichman, when the president finally took the step he
had dreaded and fired the two men. I told Nixon I was staying on; he said there would be an expanded role for me to
play. I said to him, reassuringly, "You know, I can be mean,
too."

When John Dean left the post of White House counsel, I took his place, becoming acting counsel to the president. Not long afterwards, Leonid Brezhnev visited the United States and Nixon gave him a State Dinner at the White House. I attended. As I was standing in the receiving line, Nixon pulled me aside for a private conversation. "Well, Len," he said, "have you done anything mean lately?"

To fill the position of chief of staff, left open by Haldeman's resignation, Nixon dragged Al Haig, now a four-star general, back to the White House from his post as Army vice chief of staff. Former Secretary of Defense Mel Laird, former presidential counselor Bryce Harlow, and former Secretary of the Treasury John Connally returned to lend their respectability to a White House that by that time had much too little of it. Fred Buzhardt, general counsel of the Department of Defense, came over to the White House to become my colleague, support, and friend. Secretary of Defense Elliot Richardson was moved to the Department of Justice to take Kleindienst's place as Attorney General. Richardson was confirmed by the Senate only after he promised to name an autonomous special prosecutor to handle Watergate. True to his word, he soon chose Archibald Cox—a professor at the Harvard Law School, a model of New England rectitude, and a long-time associate of the Kennedy family.

By then—mid-May of 1973—the Senate Watergate committee's public hearings had begun. Practically overnight, the revelations emerging from these hearings transformed the image of the committee's chairman, Senator Sam Ervin, Democrat of North Carolina. Ervin had formerly been known for the vigor of his defense of racial segregation and for being one of three Southern Senators who opposed to the bitter end the nomination of Thurgood Marshall to the U.S. Court of Appeals for the Second Circuit. Ervin was now described as a Cincinnatus-like defender of the Constitution and decent government. Witness after witness—McCord, Caulfield, Ulasewicz, Barker, Baldwin, Sloan, Porter, Magruder, dozens more—piled up damning testimony before him.

At one point, we, the defenders of the Alamo that the White House had become, attempted to stanch the bleeding by issuing a lengthy presidential statement answering each charge against Nixon with particularity. I worked on the statement with Buzhardt, Haig, and speechwriters Buchanan, Ray Price, and David Gergen (Safire had already left the White House). As drafts of the statement passed back and forth between us and Nixon's hideaway office, via Haig, Nixon added an impressive array of detail. Haig already knew that this recall was due not to the photographic memory of the president but to his secret Oval Office taping system. Buzhardt and I had to make do with our suspicions, which we pondered each night as we rode home in our fancy White House limousine to our neighboring homes in Virginia.

Having drawn the short straw, I presented the president's statement to the press at the White House on May 22, 1973. But the press corps, perhaps embarrassed by the fact that most of them had been so late to report in depth on the Watergate mess, had turned determined and ferocious. Journalists had concluded that all statements by or on behalf of the White House were baloney. They no longer came to the White House to learn what was going on there; instead, they came to learn the latest White House position, then went elsewhere to gather the material with which to debunk it.

Therefore, upon presenting the president's May 22 statement, I was faced with two hours of near-riot by the assembled journalists. It was all laughing, hooting, derision. Nevertheless, the detail of the rebuttal statement bought us a reprieve—for about a month.

The remission ended on June 25, when John Dean began reading his 245-page statement of testimony to the Ervin committee and a rapt national audience on live television. Dean had—and has—a truly excellent memory. He also had, it must be added, the aid of a few confidential White House documents that he took with him on his way out the door when he resigned as White House counsel in April of 1973.

Dean began testifying on a Monday and did not finish until Friday. He told about the cover-up, including the efforts to obstruct the FBI investigation by paying hush money to the Watergate burglars, Hunt, and Liddy. He accused the president of having participated in these activities from the beginning. When Dean was done with his testimony, there was no denying that attempts at cover-up and other extravagances had occurred. The remaining questions were about the depth of the president's knowledge and involvement and about what the country intended to do.

The process of finding the answers was slow, but the results were in the end straightforward. Before July of 1973, actual knowledge of the Oval Office taping system, in varying degrees, was limited to Al Haig, Ron Ziegler, Haldeman, Ehrlichman, several Haldeman assistants, and the Secret Service technicians who ran the operation. On July 10, I learned about the system when Haldeman aide Larry Higby came to ask me how much he had to disclose about it to Ervin committee investigators. I told him he was under no obligation to volunteer the information but, if asked about it, was required to tell the truth. Alex Butterfield, another Haldeman aide who knew about the system, either was getting the same advice or figured it out for himself. On July 13, 1973, asked by committee investigators whether the president had taped any conversations, Butterfield said yes. The following Monday, July 16, Butterfield repeated this information on national television in testimony to the Ervin committee.

From that day until Nixon's resignation in August, 1974, the drama of Watergate lay in the fight over the tapes—who would hear them, what was on them, and what they meant. And while we fought, Nixon's support sagged inexorably.

Both the Ervin committee and the Watergate special prosecutor, Archibald Cox, were hot in pursuit of the tapes as soon as their existence was revealed. Finally, on October 20, 1973, Nixon, feeling presidential after his triumph in resupplying Israel during the Six Day War, tried to put an end to Cox's efforts by ordering Attorney General Elliot Richardson to fire him. Richardson resigned instead; so did Richardson's deputy, William Ruckelshaus, in what came to be known as the Saturday Night Massacre. Richardson, whose conduct in this episode was not blameless, asked the Department of Justice's third-ranking official—the Solicitor General, Robert Bork—to stay in his job, carry out the presidential order, fire Cox, and keep the Justice Department running. Fifteen years later, Richardson was to testify to that effect before the Senate Judiciary Committee during its hearings on Bork's nomination to the Supreme Court. In defeating the nomination, the Senate gave credence to almost every other scurrilous charge made against Bork. At least it could not make an issue of his conduct during Watergate.

The reaction to the firing of Cox in October, 1973 was a stupendous explosion of national outrage, as Nixon's history caught up with him all at once. Telegrams poured in. Every voluntary organization in the land, it seemed, passed a resolution condemning the dismissal. *Time* magazine ran its first editorial in fifty years, calling on Nixon to resign. Dozens of Watergate-related resolutions, including calls for impeachment of the president, were introduced in the House of Representatives.

Three days after Cox's firing, Charles Alan Wright, the distinguished law professor and constitutional scholar who had joined Fred Buzhardt and me on Nixon's legal defense team, went to court and announced that the tapes would be turned over to Judge Sirica. The following week, Nixon named a new Attorney General, William Saxbe, and a new special prosecutor, Leon Jaworski, and invited them to pick up where Richardson and Cox had left off. This they proceeded to do with enthusiasm.

Because the tapes were going to be turned over, someone at the White House had to listen to them first. Fortunately for me, the person who drew that duty was Buzhardt. During the summer, fall, and winter of 1973, he spent hundreds of hours listening, smoking, and meticulously writing down what he could hear. Most of the tapes had nothing to do with Watergate, so Fred had to slog through countless conversations listening for relevant information and deciding what to make of it.

Fred was a match for the job. He had come to Washington as an aide to Senator Strom Thurmond in the late 1950s and moved quickly up the ladder of power and influence. He was thoroughly unassuming and just as thoroughly decent. He was, in fact, one of the most profoundly moral men I have known.

By November of 1973, Fred and I had concluded that in view of the sheer number of controversies to which Watergate had given rise, let alone the substantial weight of the evidence, Nixon was going to be forced to resign. We flew to Key Biscayne, Florida, where the president was staying, in an attempt to make our case to him and persuade him to prepare for the inevitable. But Nixon, knowing full well what we wanted to say, sent word through Al Haig and Ron Ziegler that he would not see us.

After the November meeting, Fred and I deliberately faded from public view. Nixon, in his memoirs, was gracious about the transition; he said he knew that he had made it impossible for us to do our jobs. We did not, however, stop working on Watergate. It was through Fred's listening in late November that we discovered the 18 $\frac{1}{2}$-minute gap on one of the tapes destined for Judge Sirica. The tape in question was made on June 20, 1972, the day Nixon returned to the White House from the Bahamas and first involved himself in Watergate. It was our job to deliver the good news to the judge.

By early January, 1974, Haig, Fred, and I had hired a new lead attorney for the president, James St. Clair, who announced that he intended to treat the case like an ordinary piece of litigation rather than political combat. Around then, things proceeded to get even worse. On January 15, 1974, a panel of experts appointed by Judge Sirica concluded that the 18 $\frac{1}{2}$-minute gap was the product of what appeared to be five separate, deliberate erasures. Nixon's secretary, Rose Woods, testified that she was responsible for one erasure:

While transcribing the tape, she said, she had inadvertently pressed the "record" button and thus created a five-minute gap. That left quite a bit to be explained and no respectable theory to explain it.

The congressional probes of Nixon metastasized, spreading to encompass non-Watergate issues such as campaign fund irregularities, Nixon's taxes, and improvements made by the government to his homes in San Clemente, California, and Key Biscayne, Florida. The House Judiciary Committee demanded more tapes. On April 18, 1974, Judge Sirica issued his own subpoena for additional tapes, at the request of the new special prosecutor, Leon Jaworski.

The battles over the tapes continued until, in late July, the Supreme Court accelerated the inevitable by ruling that the president was obliged to turn over the tapes. Nixon never considered not complying. He may have been lawless in the way and to the degree he thought his opponents had been lawless towards him; but his lawlessness, fortunately for the nation, was of a limited sort.

The House Judiciary Committee barely waited to hear the Court's opinion before taking action of its own. On July 27, 1974, the committee began voting to submit to the House articles of impeachment of President Nixon—for obstruction of justice, abuse of power, and refusing to comply with the committee's subpoenas of White House tapes.

Meanwhile, we began delivering tapes to Judge Sirica. Dissatisfied with the pace of our production, he finally ordered that all the tapes be delivered by August 7. Attempting once again to preempt bad news, Nixon released transcripts that included conversations from the tape of June 23, 1972, the day of the meeting in which Nixon had told Haldeman to order the CIA to tell the FBI to call off its investigation of the money in the possession of the Watergate burglars. Nixon accompanied the transcripts with a statement of advocacy in his own behalf. The device did not work.

The June 23 tape, though it became known as the "smoking gun" tape, added little if anything to what most Americans were by now convinced had happened. However, the tape was devastatingly, unavoidably concrete. Here was Nixon's voice impeaching him, belying his endless subsequent denials. Support for Nixon, from even his oldest political friends and staunchest allies, virtually evaporated. Everyone just wanted it over, including me. On August 1, 1974, Nixon told Haig to get Ray Price started on a resignation speech; then Nixon put the effort on hold in favor of one more presidential statement that tried to hold back Niagara. After seeing the public reaction to that effort, Ray went back to work.

On August 8, 1974, Nixon read Price's resignation speech on television. He did so partly from calculation: He knew he was out of votes. But he was also emotionally, mentally, and physically out of steam, depressed and exhausted, perhaps sensing that he would die if he did not get out. The morning after the resignation speech, Haig brought him a one-sentence letter of resignation to be delivered, according to constitutional protocol, to the Secretary of State, who was now Henry Kissinger. Nixon signed it. Later that morning, he said goodbye to his staff and left.

Nixon, exiled from public life, was later to achieve yet another of his remarkable political recoveries. The tough politicians around Nixon—Mitchell, Haldeman, and Ehrlichman—were more permanently damaged. The newcomers, like Price, Buchanan, Sears, Ellsworth, Safire, and me, kept from the center of political things, escaped harm. In fact, our reputations were enhanced by the fact that we had emerged from Watergate alive.

*   *   *

The Watergate cover-up lasted for quite some time. But for some accidents of personal temperament, it might have lasted even longer. In retrospect, however, we can see that both the thread that undid the Nixon administration—the hush money—and the unraveling of that thread began at the very start of the cover-up. By the time most parts of the cover-up were in place, it was already doomed: The investigation that would inevitably uncover it had already begun. Reporters and prosecutors did their jobs, gradually peeling away layer after layer of activities and perpetrators that Watergate had exposed.

The so-called architects of the White House cover-up were playing catch-up from the beginning. The only general tactic available to them was to portray Liddy, Hunt, and the burglars as rogue operators who had exceeded their authority and acted without their superiors' knowledge. This argument had a special vulnerability: As journalistic and official investigators discovered increasing numbers of higher-ups involved in activities related to those of the burglars, the White House had to keep expanding the definition of a rogue operator to cover the newly unveiled co-conspirators.

Finally, when Mitchell, Ehrlichman, and Haldeman were indicted all at once, the president was forced to portray himself as the only political person in the White House who did not know what was happening in the presidential reelection campaign, including the criminal lengths to which his subordinates had gone in order to conceal their earlier wrongdoing.

Even that vulnerability need not have been fatal to Nixon. The picture of a leader unaware of his subordinates' activities is not inherently implausible; the American people have accepted it on other occasions. Nixon might have drawn such a portrait and survived. But there were pieces of evidence such as Walters's irrefutable memo; and there were, of course, the tapes.

It is relevant to the issue of Deep Throat to ask, though it has been asked and re-asked, why Nixon did not do what conventional wisdom now instructs politicians to do when they get caught in a scandal—confess and ask the American people for mercy, which is usually forthcoming. In 1972, Nixon had shed his image of "Tricky Dick" for a substantial majority of voters. To them, he was a force for integrity and core values in public life. From them he might reasonably have expected sympathy and forgiveness.

Two types of theories have dominated the answers to this question. One is psychological; the other is rational.

The psychological theories have approximately the outlines you can imagine. In them, Nixon is permanently riven by the gap between his good self, the one identified with his mother, and his low, mean, finger-pointing self. He simply cannot accept the necessity for publicly identifying himself as the bad self, lest he be psychologically unable ever to don the mantle of virtue again. In the same psychological view, he cannot destroy the tapes, to which he looks for vindication in the eyes of history as a statesman and geopolitical visionary. He cannot imagine that when the tapes are released, he will sound like not a statesman but a thug.

This kind of argument does not much fit the reality of Richard Nixon. By the time of Watergate, Nixon had seen and been the object of large numbers of political scandals. In 1948, as a young congressman from California, he launched his career in national politics by investigating Alger Hiss. The most fundamental fact about the outcome of the Hiss case was that Hiss was never criminally convicted for spying; instead, he went to prison for perjury to a grand jury in a court case related to the scandal. Afterwards, Nixon told the story of the Hiss case innumerable times. The lesson of the case, he always said, was that covering up wrongdoing rather than confessing error and moving on was the surest route to disaster for a public figure.

Nixon later showed that he was capable of following this principle himself. In 1952, shortly after he was nominated as vice president, newspaper reports accused Nixon of having benefited from a "secret fund" established for him by a coterie of wealthy Southern California businessmen. The bank account was in fact small and proper, used to pay senatorial office expenses. But Nixon's running mate, presidential candidate Dwight D. Eisenhower, remained studiously aloof and ready to eject Nixon from the ticket if the younger man showed signs of going under.

Nixon responded with the Checkers speech. He arranged for the Republican National Committee to buy a half hour of national television time, which he used to provide a full public accounting of the fund and of his entire, meager financial life. Nixon made the speech in the TV studio with his wife hovering supportively in the background. His performance got the title "Checkers" from the name of a dog his little girls had received from an admirer, the one gift Nixon swore he would not return.

It was an undignified exercise, but it worked. Telegrams and phone calls backing Nixon poured in to the Republican

National Committee. Eisenhower belatedly tendered his full support. Nixon stayed on the ticket and politically alive.

It might be argued that the Checkers speech was relatively easy for Nixon, because he was in fact innocent of the charges against him. Yet in order to demonstrate his innocence, Nixon had to reveal the inadequacy of his efforts to provide for his family—an exposure more personal than any that Nixon would have had to make in admitting after-the-fact knowledge, the only kind he had, of the Watergate burglary.

President John F. Kennedy, when faced with what looked like the vastly more serious debacle of the Bay of Pigs, took responsibility even before there had been time for people to start blaming him; as a result, the recriminations never gathered the steam that might have made them politically lethal. There is not a chance in the world that Richard Nixon, who was aware of every analogy between the Kennedy presidency and his own, was unaware of this one. Indeed, the Watergate tapes reveal that as Nixon meandered in the Oval Office about the possible uses of the CIA, he thought prominently about the Kennedy administration's Bay of Pigs and the CIA's sorry connections to it.

Thus Nixon was fully capable of taking rational control of himself and doing what was necessary, even if excruciating, for his political survival. If he rejected the route of confession and apology, there was some rationally based reason. Because there was no such rational consideration connected with the Watergate burglary itself, the reason must have involved things that went beyond the burglary.

That reason now seems plain. Identifying all the people who would have to be identified in order to make an apology credible, and identifying the organizational and funding sources of the caper, would have made it possible for investigators to uncover a host of additional sleazy activities. There were the FBI wiretaps, those under a thin cover of national security and those that were clearly and uncomfortably naked. There were the wiretaps that the FBI had been unwilling to carry out, and for which the White House had found it necessary to engage other operators. There were the campaign finance illegalities in which Liddy and considerably more prominent others had participated. There were the spying and dirty tricks carried out under the direction of the White House proper, not merely by some campaign organization with a degree of deniability.

There were the illegalities connected with the Watergate operation itself. There was the cover-up that had already begun, involving the movement of impossible-to-explain hush money, not to mention Tony Ulasewicz, who had so many cover-up calls to make from pay phones that he took to wearing an old-fashioned bus conductor's coin belt. There was the random and mindless illegality, like the backdating, for tax purposes, of the deed by which Nixon gave his papers to the Library of Congress.

Thus the arrests at the Watergate would end by revealing everything. Nixon took the arguably rational course when he decided that instead of confessing to a part of these operations and seeing the rest exposed, one by one, he would attempt to paper over the entire mess.

And why didn't Nixon destroy the tapes? It was not merely ambivalence, though that played a part. In addition, I made Nixon aware of the legal hazards of destruction. Further, Haldeman told Nixon that the tapes would be helpful to him. Finally, the number of tapes was huge. The taping machines had been installed in early 1971. By the time of Watergate, there were dumpster-loads of the things, crammed into closets and other out-of-the-way places in the White House. Destroying this number of tapes in secret would have been utterly impossible. Indeed, the enterprise would have been impracticable even in public. No one wanted to perform the task for Nixon and in the process invite criminal prosecution. Nixon himself couldn't manage it; this was a man who could not even open an aspirin bottle. The only creature left to do the job was King Timahoe.

Because the investigations that would later oust Nixon from office were launched so quickly and effectively after the Watergate arrests, Nixon's cover-up strategy was from the beginning a long shot. Just as important, the operations that Nixon was trying to hide were known to more than a few people. A number of individuals in Nixon's political family were in positions that made them aware of a fairly wide range of these activities. Such individuals could speak authoritatively not just about one illegality or another but about a whole network of wrongdoing connected to the White House.

What set John Sears apart from the rest of these individuals was that he not only knew about such things but knew what to make of them and had reason to share his knowledge.

3

All the President's Men

The story of Deep Throat is not a part of the main events of the Watergate scandal itself—major milestones such as the McCord letter to Judge Sirica, Sirica's reading of the letter in open court, the testimony of Dean before the Ervin committee, Butterfield's revelation of the White House taping system, and the drama of Nixon's ultimate resignation. Instead, the Deep Throat saga illuminates one of the empty spaces in the scandal, the nine months between the Watergate break-in in June, 1972 and the collapse of the cover-up in March, 1973. During this time, White House officials were denying, by and large successfully, any high-level involvement in the burglars' enterprise. For most journalists, Watergate was still a minor issue. For most of the American public, it was not an issue at all.

Through these months, a few newspapers and magazines kept the Watergate issue alive. Seymour Hersh of the *New York Times* wrote important Watergate stories during this period. So did Jack Nelson of the *Los Angeles Times* and Sandy Smith of *Time* magazine. And, of course, so did Bob Woodward and Carl Bernstein of the *Washington Post*. The two reporters did not work alone at the *Post*. Their supervising editor, Barry Sussman, collaborated with them in their research, theorizing, and writing. The paper's executive editor, Ben Bradlee, ran interference for them when the White House applied pressure on the paper to curtail their Watergate reporting.

During this same time, as recounted in *All the President's Men*, Deep Throat was meeting with Woodward to evaluate and confirm the reporters' information and give them general guidance. During the last six months of 1972 and early 1973, with the cover-up still an apparent success, Deep Throat was helping the reporters uncover and make sense of the tangled events during Nixon's first term that led to the break-in.

*   *   *

Bob Woodward was born in 1943 and grew up in Wheaton, Illinois, then as now a bastion of conservative Republican politics within the largely liberal and Democratic Chicago area. Woodward's parents separated in a nasty divorce just before his thirteenth birthday; after the split, Woodward and his two younger siblings were raised by their father, a lawyer and later an elected state court judge. Woodward is said not to have excelled in sports or social activities in high school. But he was a very good student and citizen. He was voted the senior most likely to succeed and was elected by his class as a graduation speaker.

He attended Yale on a Navy ROTC scholarship. While there, he did not top any academic, social, or athletic ladder; but he was editor of the yearbook and was accepted for membership by Book and Snake, one of Yale's highly regarded secret societies. Woodward also wrote a novel while an undergraduate. After it was rejected by a publisher, however, he gave up on the project.

Upon graduating from Yale in 1965, Woodward was bound by the terms of his ROTC scholarship to serve four years in the Navy. For three of those years he was a circuit-control officer aboard the U.S.S. *Wright*, a military communications ship based in Norfolk, Virginia. Then he served as a communications officer aboard the U.S.S. *Fox*, roaming the Pacific from the West Coast to Vietnam.

After his obligatory term of service in the Navy ended, Woodward stayed for one more year, transferring to Washington, D.C., to serve as a communications watch officer in the Pentagon. In this capacity he briefed members of the Joint Chiefs of Staff and the National Security Council on intelligence issues.

During his year at the Pentagon, Woodward applied to Harvard Law School and was admitted. But he chose journalism instead. He applied for a reporter's job at the *Washington Post* and was hired for a probationary period. At its end, the *Post* recommended that Woodward get some journalistic experience at the smaller *Montgomery County Sentinel*. After a year at the *Sentinel*, Woodward finally landed a permanent job at the *Post*, where he started work in September of 1971 as a reporter on the City (now Metro) desk.

Carl Bernstein, twenty-eight years old at the time of the Watergate break-in, was a distinctly contrasting character. He was born in Washington in 1944 to parents who were self-professed Communists. They became public outcasts during the McCarthy era. Bernstein displayed an early writing talent.

Adrian Havill, in his biography of Woodward and Bernstein, reports that Bernstein's most notorious early writing success was a scholarly and moving history report on an important South American folk hero—who in fact existed only in Bernstein's imagination.

For a time during high school, Bernstein was active in Jewish organizational life. He was also active in billiards, poker, drinking, smoking, and general carousing. He barely graduated, and there was no hope of his going to college.

Bernstein's father found his son a job as a copy boy at the *Washington Evening Star*. Within a few years Bernstein's journalistic skill was earning him frequent bylines; but he could not become a full-fledged reporter because the *Star* demanded that its reporters have college degrees. Bernstein took classes at the University of Maryland but did not show up regularly enough to complete the program.

In 1965 the enterprising Bernstein found another route to a reporter's job: He followed one of his *Star* editors to the *Daily Journal* in Elizabeth, New Jersey, where educational requirements were not so exacting as the *Star*'s and where Bernstein rapidly built a reputation as an excellent reporter and a colorful character. A year later, Bernstein was back in Washington as a general assignment reporter for the *Washington Post*. At the time of Watergate, he was covering Virginia state election campaigns. He was himself campaigning to get reassigned to Washington, closer to what he viewed as the center of journalistic action.

*   *   *

When the Watergate burglars were arrested by the D.C. police in the early hours of June 17, 1972, they refused to say anything to police about the break-in. This silence frustrated the arresting officers. But, as Jim Hougan reported in his book *Secret Agenda*, one of those arresting officers, Carl Shoffler, knew just what to do about the burglars' intransigence:

"We couldn't get anything out of them—the 'suspects,' I mean. They wouldn't tell us who they were, what they were doing, where they were from—zero. So, I figured, what the hell, I'll put some pressure on them, get the papers interested, see what happens, y'know? So I . . . dimed the *Post* and more or less told them what we had—five mystery men."

Thus at 4:00 A.M., Officer Shoffler called in the artillery of the press.

At the more civilized hour of nine o'clock on the morning of the Watergate arrests, *Post* City editor Barry Sussman phoned Woodward at home and asked him to come in to the paper to work on a story about these five mystery men who had been arrested at the offices of the Democratic National Committee. It was a Saturday, and more senior reporters had the day off; therefore Woodward, a junior member of the City staff, got the assignment. Heretofore at the *Post* he had specialized in exposés of unsanitary conditions at local restaurants.

Sussman sent a more experienced reporter—Alfred Lewis, a thirty-five-year veteran of the police beat—to the actual scene of the crime. From the Watergate, Lewis phoned details of the story to Woodward at the *Post*. One such detail was the discovery by the police of dozens of hundred-dollar bills in the possession of the burglars. This was the money, though of course outsiders did not know it at the time, that had been laundered by Liddy through the bank account of Bernard Barker, delivered by Liddy to Hugh Sloan of the Committee for the Re-election of the President (CRP), then returned to

Liddy by Sloan and, finally, issued by Liddy to the Watergate burglars. The money would become the starting point of the trail that led from the burglars back to CRP and from the Committee to the hush money later paid to the burglars with White House approval.

Woodward received Lewis's information and made routine follow-up calls. When Lewis reported that the burglars were scheduled for arraignment in court that afternoon, Woodward marched down to the courthouse. The trip proved to be worthwhile. Woodward, after waiting in court for more than an hour, was present to hear James McCord reveal to the presiding judge that he was a security consultant who had recently retired from the CIA. That was good enough to lead off a front-page story in the next day's *Post*.

At the same time, Carl Bernstein, who had not been assigned to the story, figured out—not atypically—a way to insert himself into it. Bernstein Xeroxed notes taken by reporters who had been to the Watergate and used them as a basis for making independent follow-up calls, starting with every possible eyewitness to the Watergate arrests and moving outward from there. By the end of the day he had put together a Watergate-related story of his own, a preliminary profile of the Miami men who had been arrested at the Watergate.

The results of Woodward and Bernstein's initial reporting on Watergate were not promising. After working the story all day Saturday, they returned to the office on Sunday to learn that they had been scooped by the Associated Press. An AP reporter had discovered that one of the burglars, James McCord, was not only a CIA retiree, as Woodward had reported, but an employee of CRP. Thus the AP was able to report that there was a link between the burglary of the Democrats and the Nixon campaign.

Not only had Woodward and Bernstein been scooped on the story; shortly thereafter, no less a personage than John Mitchell, director of CRP, announced that there was no story at all. "[T]his man," he said, referring to McCord, "and the other people involved were not operating on either our behalf or with our consent."

Woodward and Bernstein kept pursuing the Watergate story in the traditional way. Indeed, the subsequent fame of Deep Throat has obscured the fact that the two reporters did not get their Watergate stories only or even primarily from a single secret source. Instead, they obtained their information through the old-fashioned, labor-intensive methods of traditional investigative journalism. And many of their best Watergate stories consisted of information from government investigators, mainly the FBI.

The reporters compiled lists of every contact they could think of and started making calls. They tried to phone McCord at his home and at the offices of his security consulting business; there was no answer. They then phoned every other business in McCord's office building. Eventually they found someone who vaguely remembered the last name of a woman who had once worked part-time for McCord. It was something like Westall. So the reporters began calling people with names that sounded like Westall. They eventually tracked down a man named Harlan Westrell, who was the father of the woman who had worked for McCord and who was himself a friend of McCord's.

Westrell gave them more names; they made more calls. So it went. They made no great breakthroughs. They were, however, able to put together a better picture than before of McCord and his substantial involvement in the worlds of law enforcement and intelligence.

Late Sunday night, Eugene Bachinski, like Alfred Lewis a *Washington Post* police reporter, phoned Woodward at home with the information that would enable Woodward and Bernstein to report the existence of a direct link between the Watergate burglary and the White House. Bachinski said that address books found by the police on two of the Watergate burglars had listed the name Howard Hunt. Next to this name in one of the books was the notation "W. H." In the other address book, a notation next to Hunt's name read "W. House."

On Monday, June 19, at a press conference in Florida, White House press secretary Ron Ziegler attempted to minimize the importance of Watergate. He described the operation as a "third-rate burglary attempt," then refused to discuss the matter any further. From that day forward, Ziegler was occupied periodically and increasingly in issuing categorical denials of press stories about Watergate. Along with the denials, he would sometimes cast aspersions on the professional skills of the reporters and editors responsible. As time went on, Ron would find himself obliged to retrench, also periodically and increasingly, when these stories were corroborated by government investigators or other media. In the spring of 1973, in the course of an especially difficult press conference, Ziegler issued his famous announcement that the most recent Watergate statement by the president was "the operative statement. The others are inoperative."

But that was in the future. On the day of Ziegler's initial denial, June 19, 1972, it sounded quite credible. Woodward sought guidance by phoning a man described in *All the President's Men* as "an old friend and sometimes source who worked for the federal government." The friend told Woodward that the Watergate case was going to "heat up" but then said he couldn't explain and hung up the phone.

This was the source who would later become the Deep Throat of *All the President's Men*. From the very beginning of Woodward's reporting on the Watergate scandal, he had the advantage of this friend's special knowledge about the significance of the break-in. Were it not for this circumstance, Woodward and Bernstein's conventional investigative reporting would probably have been less aggressive and less important. They, like other reporters, would have been overtaken by Watergate's events before they had a chance to make an independent contribution.

And, without Deep Throat, Woodward and Bernstein would not have attained the fame that they did. Movie stars—Robert Redford and Dustin Hoffman—would not have played them in a box-office hit film. People today would be focusing their curiosity about Watergate simply on the fall of Richard Nixon rather than on the transformative activities of two of the many reporters who helped do him in.

On June 19, however, Woodward's conversation with his "old friend" was less fruitful as a source of information than were a number of other calls the reporters made. Through these other calls, Woodward and Bernstein moved a few steps towards linking several key Watergate players to dirty tricks perpetrated in connection with the 1972 election. They learned, for example, that one of the burglars, Eugenio Martinez, had been involved in plans to disrupt the Democratic National Convention in Miami.

More important, Woodward learned who Howard Hunt was: a retired CIA officer working as a consultant to one Robert F. Bennett at Mullen & Co. and to Charles Colson at the White House. Woodward and Bernstein continued their phone calls. They were now trying to find out not just about McCord and his fellow burglars but about Hunt.

Watergate was still uncharted territory then. Woodward did not know what to make of the information about Hunt. The reporter's reaction to his own puzzlement was to call his "government friend" again. This time the friend told Woodward, off the record, that the FBI considered Hunt a prime suspect in Watergate for reasons beyond those facts—such as Hunt's name in the burglars' address books—that were already public. The friend assured Woodward that it would be safe to use the publicly available information to link Hunt to the burglars. But Woodward could not report either his friend's assurance or the existence of non-public information about Hunt. Woodward proceeded to write a story for the *Post* that followed his friend's rules.

Thus by the morning of June 20, everyone who had picked up a major U.S. newspaper knew the identities of the Watergate burglars. Everyone knew as well that someone named Howard Hunt was somehow involved in the burglary and somehow connected to Richard Nixon's White House.

Then Woodward and Bernstein reached the first of the many journalistic impasses they would have to overcome in their Watergate reporting. At the same time that the press started reporting Watergate, the government began its own investigation. Federal prosecutors started preparing their cases against the burglars, and the FBI started doing the actual investigative work supporting these cases. Simultaneous with these two initiatives, officials at CRP and at the White House launched their attempts to insure that neither the media nor the prosecutors and FBI could unearth any more incriminating information than they already had.

Between the stonewalling and the attempts to preserve the secrecy of the official investigation, journalists, including Woodward and Bernstein, found that leads and information had suddenly become scarce.

Woodward and Bernstein tapped every one of their contacts who could possibly have led them to more information. Their list of sources was an unusually large and well-connected one for two junior reporters. Bernstein had grown up in the Washington area and had numerous friends in the lower and middle levels of government. Woodward had contacts in defense and intelligence, as well as the White House, from his days in military service and the Ivy League.

This network would eventually help Woodward and Bernstein penetrate the various layers of the Watergate cover-up. For a long time, though, it was slow going. The two were engaged mainly in phoning every contact, knocking on every door, dialing every telephone number, and cross-checking the statements of people they managed to interview against public records and other known facts. The results were meager. During June and July, the reporters wrote about Watergate for the *Post* only occasionally. They almost never shared a byline on a Watergate piece. Instead, the story was given to other *Post* reporters to follow. Woodward and Bernstein returned to their regular beats.

In these months, news outlets other than the *Post* were breaking the big Watergate stories. Most important, in late July, 1972 the *New York Times* took the first journalistic step down the Watergate money trail with a series of stories indicating that the Miami-based Watergate burglars had been involved in more than a single break-in. On July 31, the *Times* reported that a Miami district attorney, Richard Gerstein, had discovered a suspicious $89,000 that had passed through checks in the bank account of Bernard Barker, one of the Watergate burglars.

Post editor Barry Sussman, after reading the beginning of the *Times'* coverage of the money trail, had already allowed Bernstein to go to Miami to follow up. When the *Times'* July 31 story appeared, Bernstein was in Miami and had just arrived at the office of the district attorney, who had the checks. Bernstein refused to leave until he was allowed to examine them. Among the checks, Bernstein found one that bore the name of Kenneth Dahlberg—who, research revealed, was a Republican fund-raiser. Woodward called Dahlberg, who said he had delivered the check to Maurice Stans, Nixon's 1972 campaign finance director. Dahlberg said he had no idea how his check had gotten from Stans to Barker.

Woodward and Bernstein wrote the Dahlberg story. It was their first big collaborative break in connection with Watergate. After that, they managed to keep themselves sufficiently busy with Watergate-related developments to avoid having to report any more on Virginia electoral races or the District of Columbia's rat-infested restaurants. The two reporters also convinced literary agent David Obst, for whom Bernstein had promised to write a book on an unrelated topic, that Obst could sell a book by Woodward and Bernstein about Watergate.

In the late summer, things began to change. Publicly, the reporters were still swimming against the tide. Most Americans and most journalists were indifferent to Watergate. The

White House and CRP were maintaining their silence. The FBI investigation was proceeding, but it was officially secret. More important, Pat Gray at the FBI and Henry Petersen at the Justice Department were confining their probes and prosecutions to the narrowest possible scope.

But the very intensity of these efforts at secrecy and restraint began, perversely, to contribute to Woodward and Bernstein's progress.

The best description I have read of the process that took place was written by a contemporary observer of Watergate, the late Admiral Elmo R. Zumwalt, Jr., in his memoir *On Watch*. There was a time when Zumwalt was among those mentioned as a possible Deep Throat. His motive was said to be discontent with the slow pace of Richard Nixon's disengagement from Vietnam. In fact, Zumwalt was an unlikely Deep Throat candidate. He was a man of strong views, but he was also a disciplined military officer and therefore not likely to engage in surreptitious activity of the Deep Throat type. At Zumwalt's death, there was no announcement by Woodward and Bernstein naming him as Deep Throat. It is time to strike him from the list.

Deep Throat or no, Zumwalt was an extremely keen student of the inner workings of U.S. politics and government. "[C]onscientious officials," Zumwalt wrote of the Watergate period, "when they find that the direct channels through which they are accustomed to transact their business have been blocked, inevitably and properly seek other, circuitous ones that make it possible for them to meet their responsibilities." Eventually, Zumwalt said, "late evening bull sessions proliferate, telephone conversations become portentous, photo-copying machines hum day and night, leaks appear in the press, Congressmen come into possession of papers that were presumably under lock and key, and everyone looks askance at his neighbor."

The Zumwalt effect began to be felt in the late summer of 1972, after the Watergate break-in, not only within the government but at the CRP. People in both places who knew things about Watergate were prevented from communicating their information to others in their organizations through the normal channels, as a result of both the White House–directed cover-up and the narrow scope of the official investigation. Therefore, under a kind of hydraulic pressure, they began to leak the information outward.

Because Woodward and Bernstein had followed the Watergate story so doggedly from its very beginning, they became the natural contacts for individuals who had crucial pieces of intelligence to divulge. The Watergate stories by Woodward and Bernstein in the *Washington Post* served as buoys and flags on an alternative channel of communication through which information about Watergate could flow. A critical number of knowledgeable sources decided to use this channel, spreading their information laterally to the two *Post* reporters.

In August, through a research assistant at the *Post*, Woodward and Bernstein got hold of the CRP's internal telephone directory. Throughout the autumn of 1972, the two reporters covered the District of Columbia, Maryland, and Virginia, repeatedly visiting every individual listed in the directory. At first they did not have much luck. But as they unearthed each incremental revelation and published it in the *Post*, their by-lines became better known. Potential sources became aware that talking to the two reporters could have an appreciable effect on events. Woodward and Bernstein began to receive calls from the Justice Department, the FBI, the White House, and disaffected CRP employees. When the reporters themselves initiated phone calls, fewer people hung up on them.

Yet on September 15, 1972, when indictments of the burglars, Hunt, and Liddy were handed down by the federal grand jury investigating Watergate, they contained no hint of the connections among the burglary, the burglars, and higher officials at CRP and the White House itself. If the reporters persisted, in the face of these limited indictments, in pursuing the idea that higher-ups were involved in the burglary, they were effectively accusing the Justice Department of ignoring evidence of crimes.

Woodward felt unsure enough about his information and assumptions to phone his special "source in the Executive Branch, who had access to information at CRP as well as at the White House," in order to check the story he was writing.

Woodward had been referring to the source as "my friend," in the words of *All the President's Men*. But *Post* editor Howard Simons dubbed him "Deep Throat," which was the title of a very well known pornographic movie of the time. And the name just stuck. Deep Throat, Woodward and Bernstein wrote in their book, was the same man who on June 19 had assured Woodward that Hunt was involved in the Watergate burglary.

Deep Throat's place in the Executive Branch was "extremely sensitive," Woodward wrote in introducing him; and his informant had never told Woodward "anything that was incorrect." But Deep Throat would talk to Woodward only to confirm information already found elsewhere and to add perspective.

On the telephone on September 16, 1972, Deep Throat listened to Woodward's draft story, which said that high officials of the Committee for the Re-election of the President had paid for the Watergate operation. "Too soft," Deep Throat told him. "You can go much stronger." Deep Throat then confirmed information, received by the reporters from an anonymous source, that money from the safe of Maurice Stans had financed the Watergate bugging—and, in words that Deep Throat used and Woodward considered important enough to italicize in the book, had financed *"other intelligence-gathering activities"* for the campaign. Deep Throat said that transcripts from the wiretaps placed in the Watergate during the first break-in had gone to the same Mitchell aides at CRP who had authority to disburse this money. But, Deep Throat confirmed, Mitchell's assistants were only *"among those"* with control over the funds.

Deep Throat's confirmations resulted in a dramatic story by Woodward and Bernstein contradicting the assumption in the indictments that Liddy alone had masterminded the Watergate burglaries. The story reported that Mitchell's aides had roles in administering the slush fund, that the burglars' incriminating hundred-dollar bills had been drawn from this fund, that the fund consisted of hundreds of thousands of dollars earmarked for campaign intelligence, that records of the fund had been destroyed, and that the CRP treasurer, Hugh Sloan (soon to be a key source for Woodward and Bernstein), had resigned because of his suspicions about the uses to which the fund had been put.

On the day the story ran in the *Post*, Woodward and Bernstein returned to the anonymous source who had provided much of the information in the story. She worked at the Committee for the Re-election of the President. She gave them two more names: Jeb Magruder and Bart Porter, who, like Liddy, had been issued large amounts of cash from the slush fund.

Woodward called Deep Throat once more and asked him to confirm the two new names. "They're both deeply involved in Watergate," Deep Throat answered. He confirmed that Magruder and Porter had received at least $50,000 from Stans's safe, and Woodward could be confident the $50,000 had been used for illegitimate purposes—that was "fact, not allegation."

The product of this conversation was another big story by the two reporters. But in the conversation, Deep Throat made clear that he was angry at Woodward for having used the telephone to get in touch with him. Deep Throat sounded frightened to Woodward. This unease with the telephone as a means of communication had been building. The White House, Deep Throat had told Woodward at a previous meeting, considered Watergate as something much more serious than anyone else, even the FBI, thought.

Thus Deep Throat, though he had confirmed some of Woodward's early stories by phone, wanted Woodward to make use of a more secure method of communication that the two men had devised. This was the famous signaling system. When Woodward wanted to meet with Deep Throat, he would move a flowerpot that had an old red cloth flag stuck in it, to the rear of the balcony of his apartment. During the day, Deep Throat would check and if the pot had been moved, the two would rendezvous that night at about 2 A.M. in an underground garage they had agreed on. Woodward would switch cabs frequently to be sure he wasn't followed.

There was a different procedure if Deep Throat wanted a meeting. Every morning Woodward turned to page 20 of the *New York Times*, which was delivered to his door before 7 A.M. If Deep Throat wanted to see him, the page number would be circled, and accompanied by a drawing of a clock's hands pointing to the designated time. It was a mystery to Woodward how Deep Throat got the paper and made the markings.

This procedure strains credulity, beginning with the assertion that Woodward, a meticulous investigative reporter, seems never to have asked Deep Throat how he got his hands on those newspapers. Adrian Havill, in his book *Deep Truth*, painstakingly atempted to debunk these cloak-and-dagger aspects of the Deep Throat tale. For instance, Havill argued that given the location of Woodward's apartment at the time of his early meetings with Deep Throat, it would have been impossible for Deep Throat to check the flowerpot every day without trespassing and thus drawing attention to himself, in the process defeating the whole point of having such elaborate signals in the first place.

In *Secret Agenda*, Jim Hougan, after studying the same puzzle, concluded that even if Deep Throat had somehow been able to slink undetected each day into the inner courtyard of Woodward's apartment building, he would not have been able to see the flowerpot: Woodward lived on the sixth floor, and the balconies of the lower apartments blocked the view of the magic object from the courtyard below.

Similarly, Bob Fink, who served as Woodward and Bernstein's assistant in preparing the manuscript for *All the President's Men* and who emerged from the experience doubting Deep Throat's existence, has pointed out in an unpublished paper that in order to gain access to Woodward's morning newspaper each day, Deep Throat would have been required to make arrangements with delivery people, security guards, or both. That a man wishing to remain anonymous would engage in such high-risk transactions is implausible, Fink argues. That his co-conspirators would keep quiet about it for a quarter century afterwards is more so.

The easy tack for me to take at this point would be to agree that the details are made up and go on to ask whether such camouflage is justified by the difficulty of protecting so distinctive a source under such intense scrutiny. But that would be wrong, because I remain agnostic on the issue of the details of the signaling system. After all, I was convinced for a long time that Deep Throat was a composite; then, all of a sudden, I recognized him. The same may be true, some day, of the elusive flowerpot. For instance, Hougan noted that during the time when he was talking with Deep Throat, Woodward moved to another apartment. The new apartment's balcony was more accessible, making it feasible to use the flowerpot as a signal at least during this later period.

In September of 1972, in any event, the signaling system did not get much exercise. Deep Throat's conversations with Woodward during that month were by telephone. And in the last such conversation, Deep Throat said that Woodward and Bernstein would have to do without him for a time. Then, the authors recounted, "A touch of his old good humor returned: 'Let's just say I'll be willing to put the blossoming situation in perspective for you when the time comes.' But there was disgust in the way he said it."

Woodward and Bernstein then spent several weeks doing conventional, fruitful reporting based on other sources. They managed to confirm through Department of Justice investigators that Mitchell was involved in the administration of CRP's slush fund. In late September, the reporters received an anonymous tip that led them to uncover the dirty-tricks campaign of Donald Segretti and his collaborators. Bernstein's sources at Justice confirmed this part of the Watergate story and gave the reporters their first direct indication that responsibility for the dirty tricks reached even further up the chain of command than Mitchell—which had to mean at least Haldeman or Ehrlichman, or both.

But on October 7, 1972, Bernstein was struggling to make an organized story out of the reporters' still limited, already tangled knowledge about Segretti's connections. Woodward therefore used yet another signaling method to phone Deep Throat at home without identifying himself and arrange a garage meeting. When Woodward arrived at the garage, Deep Throat was waiting, smoking a cigarette. This was, for the reporters, one of Woodward's most valuable meetings with Deep Throat; it was also the occasion for Woodward's fullest description of his friend. Their friendship was "genuine, not cultivated. Long before Watergate, they had spent many evenings talking about Washington, the government, power." They had talked about how politics pervaded the government; it was a virtual "strong-arm takeover of the agencies by the Nixon White House. Junior White House aides were giving orders on the highest levels of the bureaucracy." Deep Throat referred to it as the "switch-blade mentality"—with all the president's men fighting dirty, disregarding the effects they might have on the government and the nation. Deep Throat did not seem bitter, and had the air of resignation of one who had fought too many battles. A wise teacher to Woodward, he was "dispassionate and seemed committed to the best version of the obtainable truth."

Perhaps for this reason, Woodward noted, Deep Throat distrusted the press. "I don't like newspapers," he had said, detesting "inexactitude and shallowness." Woodward described Deep Throat as a highly atypical political operative, "an incurable gossip, . . . careful to label rumor for what it was, but fascinated by it. He knew too much literature too well and let the allurements of the past turn him away from his instincts. He could be rowdy, drink too much," and he was bad at hiding his feelings—not exactly ideal qualities for someone in his position. He was coming to "fear for the future of the Executive Branch, which he was in a unique position to observe." And the crisis was taking its toll: He looked worn out, and his eyes were bloodshot.

And Deep Throat was very knowledgeable, with information from the White House, Justice, FBI and CRP. "What he knew represented an aggregate of hard information flowing in and out of many stations."

Woodward leaned on his well-connected friend hard for more specific information about higher-up involvement in Watergate; this was a category of information that the reporters could not get through the mere exercise of persistent shoeleather. Deep Throat began by urging Woodward to be fair in reporting on the Committee for the Re-election of the President. "[P]lease be balanced and send out people to check everything," Deep Throat said, "because a lot of the [CRP] intelligence-gathering was routine. They are not brilliant guys, and it got out of hand." Deep Throat emphasized the last part of his thought: "That is the key phrase, the feeling that it all got out of hand."

Woodward asked whether Mitchell was involved. "Mitchell was involved," Deep Throat said. Woodward asked how deeply. "Only the President and Mitchell know," he answered. He would not elaborate. He told Woodward—erroneously, it turned out—that Mitchell had conducted his own investigation of Watergate for ten days after the break-in, discovering things even he hadn't known; that Howard Hunt, of all people, was briefly assigned to help Mitchell; and that John Ehrlichman had been the man who fired Hunt from this investigation and told him to leave town. Mitchell, Deep Throat said, "definitely learned some things in those ten days after Watergate":

> "He was just sick, and everyone was saying he was ruined because of what his people did, especially Mardian and LaRue, and what happened at the White House.
>
> "And Mitchell said, 'If this all comes out, it could ruin the administration. I mean, ruin it.' Mitchell realized he was personally ruined and would have to get out."

Woodward pressed for still more information about White House involvement and the larger scheme of undercover activities of which Segretti's operation was a part. Deep Throat laid out a map, albeit one with some inaccuracies:

> "There were four basic personnel groupings for undercover operations," Deep Throat said. The November Group, which handled CRP's advertising; a convention group, which handled intelligence-gathering and sabotage-planning for both the Republican and Democratic conventions; a primary group, which did the same for the primaries of

both parties; and the Howard Hunt group, which was the "really heavy operations team."

"The Howard Hunt group reported to Chuck Colson [Deep Throat went on], who maybe didn't know specifically about the bugging. There is no proof, but Colson was getting daily updates on the activities and the information. . . .

"That operation was not only to check leaks to the papers but often to manufacture items for the press. It was a Colson-Hunt operation. . . . The business of [Democratic vice-presidential candidate Tom] Eagleton's drunk-driving record or his health records, I understand, involves the White House and Hunt somehow."

Deep Throat said he knew of undercover operations by these groups in races all across the country; all were directed from high levels. "Everything was part of it—nothing was free-lance," Deep Throat said. "But," Woodward reported, "he would not talk specifically about Segretti's operation. Woodward could not understand why." Woodward angrily told Deep Throat that the reporters needed more concrete information.

"Okay," he [Deep Throat] said softly. "This is very serious. You can safely say that fifty people worked for the White House and CRP to play games and spy and sabotage and gather intelligence. Some of it is beyond belief, kicking at the opposition in every imaginable way."

Woodward listed the tactics he and Bernstein had heard were used: bugging, investigating campaign workers' private lives, following people, fake letters, false press leaks, canceling campaign rallies, stealing documents, planting spies, planting provocateurs in political demonstrations. Deep Throat nodded that it was all true. Woodward was shocked that the White House would subvert the electoral process in such pervasive ways. Had it actually hired fifty agents to do this? "'You can safely say more than fifty,' Deep Throat said. Then he turned, walked up the ramp and out. It was nearly 6:00 A.M."

Even though Deep Throat succeeded, in this lengthy meeting, in not delivering up very much in the way of specific information, he gave Woodward and Bernstein what they needed: an organizing principle. On October 10, 1972, a major story under their now customary joint byline ran in the *Post*, weaving together their research on the various elements of Watergate. The narrative they created stands as a remarkable piece of journalism. "FBI agents have established," it began, "that the Watergate bugging incident stemmed from a massive campaign of political spying and sabotage conducted on behalf of President Nixon's re-election and directed by officials of the White House and the Committee for the Re-election of the President." Woodward and Bernstein had, in a general way and with the help of Deep Throat, figured out Watergate by October of 1972.

The October 10 story considerably raised the profile of Woodward and Bernstein and of Watergate itself. In addition, around this time the reporters' planned book about Watergate took another step towards existence. They spent a weekend with their agent, David Obst, and produced a book proposal that Obst could show to potential publishers. There was no mention in the proposal of anyone called Deep Throat. Some critics have taken this absence as proof that Deep

Throat did not exist. In fact, however, it is highly unlikely that any journalist in the midst of transactions with a crucial source would produce a document offering up clues to the source's identity.

Obst used the book proposal, plus a good deal of personal pleading, to get Woodward and Bernstein a publishing contract and a $55,000 advance from Simon & Schuster.

Meanwhile, in journalistic terms Watergate was getting tougher again, for somewhat different reasons. Woodward and Bernstein were now pursuing the highest officials in the Nixon administration. These targets were much harder to crack than low-level employees at CRP had been. Hardest of all was Nixon's chief of staff and the man closest to the president, Bob Haldeman. None of the reporters' sources was willing even to talk about him. Therefore Woodward moved his flowerpot to the agreed-upon position and went to the garage to wait for Deep Throat. Deep Throat did not show up, but on October 20, he performed his trick with Woodward's *New York Times*. Woodward went to the garage that night and found Deep Throat there, smoking one of his ever-present cigarettes.

Woodward tried to get Deep Throat to confirm that Haldeman was one of those with control over disbursements from the re-election slush fund. Deep Throat resisted: "You'll have to do it on your own. . . . You cannot use me as a source. . . . I won't be a source on a Haldeman story. . . . [T]here's a lot of tension. . . . That's to put it mildly—there's tension about Haldeman. Be careful."

Woodward then asked whether Deep Throat would warn the reporters off if they presented him with erroneous information. Deep Throat stated that he would. Having said this,

Deep Throat did not issue any such cautions to Woodward during their meeting. He was confirming the story.

When Woodward and Bernstein wrote their story about Haldeman's control of the slush fund, they made a mistake on a crucial detail, one that had not been a subject of Woodward's discussion with Deep Throat. The reporters said in the *Post* that former CRP treasurer Hugh Sloan had testified before the Watergate grand jury about Haldeman's control of the fund. Though the story was right about Haldeman's control, Sloan had in fact not testified to that effect; he had not even been asked the question. The White House pounced on the error and held it up as a sign of the irresponsibility of Woodward and Bernstein's reporting.

Woodward, afraid that their mistake had taken the pressure off the White House and thus jeopardized all of their earlier work, arranged to meet with Deep Throat in the garage soon after the story ran. Deep Throat reinforced Woodward's despair:

"Well, Haldeman slipped away from you," Deep Throat stated. He kicked his heel at the garage wall, making no attempt to hide his disappointment. . . .

"Let me explain something," he said. "When you move on somebody like Haldeman, you've got to be sure you're on the most solid ground. Shit, what a royal screw-up!"

He stepped even closer, speaking in a whisper. "I'm probably not telling you anything you don't know, but your essential facts are right. From top to bottom this whole business is a Haldeman operation. He ran the money. Insulated himself through those functionaries around him. Now, how do you get at it?"

Deep Throat told Woodward that the story had been the "worst possible setback." He proceeded to explain why, in wrenching detail:

"A conspiracy like this . . . the rope has to tighten slowly around everyone's neck. You build convincingly from the outer edges in, you get ten times the evidence you need against the Hunts and Liddys. They feel hopelessly finished—they may not talk right away, but the grip is on them. Then you move up and do the same thing at the next level. If you shoot too high and miss, then everybody feels more secure. Lawyers work this way. I'm sure smart reporters must, too. You've put the investigation back months. It puts everybody on the defensive—editors, FBI agents, everybody has to go into a crouch after this."

Fortunately for Woodward and Bernstein, their editor at the *Post*, Ben Bradlee, had considerably more nerve than Deep Throat. Bradlee said, simply, "We stand by our story." The reporters were still in business.

But business remained slow. Richard Nixon won re-election to the presidency by a landslide in November. Other media frequently scooped the *Post* on Watergate news up through the time when Liddy and McCord were convicted in January of 1973 of crimes related to the Watergate burglary.

Woodward arranged another meeting with Deep Throat on January 24. In the parking garage, Woodward reviewed for Deep Throat the information the reporters had gathered for a piece they were writing on the Watergate involvement of Mitchell and Colson. This time Deep Throat did more than confirm the information:

"Colson and Mitchell were behind the Watergate operation," he said quickly. "Everyone in the FBI is convinced, including Gray. . . . Colson's role was active. Mitchell's position was more 'amoral' and less active—giving the nod but not conceiving the scheme.

"There isn't anything that would be considered as more than the weakest circumstantial evidence. But there's no doubt either. 'Insulation' is the key word to understand why the evidence can't be developed."

He outlined four factors that might lead to the "inescapable conclusion" that Mitchell and Colson were conspirators: "One, the personalities and past performance of both. This way of life wasn't new to them. Two, there are meetings and phone calls at crucial times—all of which Colson and Mitchell claim involved other matters. Three, there's the tight control of the money, especially by Mitchell, who was getting details almost to the point of how much was spent on pencils and erasers. Four, there is the indisputable fact that the seven [Watergate] defendants believe they are going to be taken care of. That could only be done convincingly by someone high up, and somehow it has been done convincingly. . . .

"What obviously makes this a Mitchell-Colson operation is the hiring of Liddy and Hunt. That's the key. Mitchell and Colson were their sponsors. And if you check you'll find that Liddy and Hunt had reputations that are the lowest. The absolute lowest. Hiring these two was immoral. They got exactly what they wanted. Liddy wanted to tap the *New York Times* and everybody knew it. And not everybody was laughing about it. Mitchell, among others, liked the idea."

Having spoken more openly about his feelings towards Mitchell than he had done before, Deep Throat added a prediction about the administration's future defense strategy. The White House, he said, was making plans to block congressional investigations; the plans included a broad claim of executive privilege to bar subpoenas of White House and Justice records.

Woodward wanted to know how firm the information was about Mitchell and Colson. "'No disagreement anywhere,' Deep Throat said. . . . 'But it's still unproven. If the FBI couldn't prove it, I don't think the *Washington Post* can.'"

And indeed, Woodward and Bernstein were unable to put their information about Mitchell and Colson in a form concrete enough for publication.

By this time, however, journalistic interest in Watergate was robust. When the White House announced the nomination of FBI acting director Pat Gray to become permanent director of the Bureau, it was widely anticipated that the hearings on his nomination, scheduled for the end of February, would be the occasion for a good number of congressional questions about Watergate. Woodward arranged for a garage meeting with Deep Throat.

When Woodward arrived at the garage, Deep Throat was not there. The two of them had agreed that on any occasion when Deep Throat could not meet Woodward, he would leave a note on a specific ledge in the garage. The note was there, and Woodward got it down with a piece of pipe. Inside it, he found instructions that the two should meet the next night at a working-class bar far from downtown Washington. "Just a sleepy, dark bar," Deep Throat remarked, perhaps ironically, when they met. "A little bit classier surroundings."

There, Deep Throat told Woodward in detail about the president's plans to punish the *Post* for its Watergate reportage: "Nixon was wild, shouting and hollering that 'we can't have it and we're going to stop it, I don't care how much it costs.'" Upon finishing his description, Deep Throat "sipped his Scotch gingerly, then wiped his mouth inelegantly with the back of his hand" and would not say much more on the subject.

Woodward went on to ask Deep Throat about the Gray nomination. The reason for it, Deep Throat said, was that Gray had gone to the White House and "implied that all hell could break loose if he wasn't able to stay in the job permanently and keep the lid on." Woodward asked whether Deep Throat meant that Gray had blackmailed the president. "'I never said that,' Deep Throat laughed. He lifted his eyes, the picture of innocence."

Then Woodward mentioned a recent story in *Time* magazine about wiretaps that had been placed on the phones of reporters and White House aides at the behest of Mitchell, Kissinger, and Haig from 1969 through 1971. Woodward asked Deep Throat whether Gray had known about these wiretaps. Deep Throat said yes: A gang of ex-FBI and ex-CIA agents hired outside normal channels did the wiretaps. Bob Mardian was involved. In a strategy session for the election, Haldeman had insisted on a wiretapping operation for the campaign, overcoming Mitchell's reluctance. Haldeman told him to shift "part of the vigilante operation from the White House to the campaign. That meant Hunt and Liddy. . . . The arrests in the Watergate sent everybody off the edge because the break-in could uncover the whole program."

This time, Deep Throat's analysis did not give Woodward and Bernstein much of an advantage over their journalistic colleagues. By the time the Gray hearings were over, everyone knew that both Gray's Watergate involvement and that of the White House were much greater than previously reported. Gray revealed White House counsel John Dean's active participation in the Watergate investigation, thus raising the possibility that the White House had taken advantage of Gray's pliability to manipulate the Bureau's Watergate investigations. Gray also submitted a statement confirming Herbert Kalmbach's role in financing and managing Donald Segretti's dirty tricks. Gray even testified that Dean had probably lied to the FBI about his knowledge of Howard Hunt's employment by the White House.

But by the time the Gray hearings wound down and Senator Sam J. Ervin, Jr.'s Watergate committee was getting started, Woodward and Bernstein were viewed as the deans of the Watergate press corps. They were in on the action in the committee from the beginning, receiving much confidential information.

Journalistic attention to Watergate had now grown by orders of magnitude; this growth meant that, for the *Post* and its two star Watergate reporters, competition was also growing exponentially. Thus in mid-April of 1973, it was the *Los Angeles Times* that reported the Nixon administration to be on the verge of a major announcement: The White House was preparing to admit that very high-level officials—though not the president himself—had been involved in dirty tricks. Woodward placed an emergency phone call to Deep Throat, following a second special phone call procedure that the two men had worked out. Deep Throat called Woodward back at a prearranged phone booth and delivered big news: "Dean and Haldeman are out—for sure. . . . They'll resign. There's no way the President can avoid it." Woodward asked if the *Post* could publish the story, and Deep Throat said, "Yes. It's solid." This time Bradlee held his reporters' story—prudently, as it turned out, since the resignations of Haldeman and Dean would not come for another two weeks, at the end of April. Ehrlichman and Kleindienst would resign at the same time. The day after the White House announced these resignations, Ron Ziegler publicly expressed regret for having cast doubt on the integrity of the *Post*'s Watergate reporting. He apologized specifically to Woodward and Bernstein.

Just before the resignations, the *New York Daily News* reported that shortly after the Watergate burglary, Gray had destroyed documents taken from Hunt's White House safe. This time, Woodward did not call Deep Throat; Deep Throat called Woodward, saying of the Gray story:

> "Well, it's true. On June 28, in a meeting with Ehrlichman and Dean, Gray was told the files were—quote—'political dynamite' and should—quote—'never see the light of day.' He was told, quote, 'they could do more damage than the Watergate bugging itself.' In fact, Ehrlichman had told Dean earlier in the day, 'You go across the river every day, John. Why don't you drop the goddamn fucking things in the river?' Gray kept the files for about a week and then he says he threw them in a burn bag in his office. He says that he was not exactly told to destroy the files, but understood it was absolutely clear what Dean and Ehrlichman wanted."

Deep Throat was not quite right about the details: Gray later testified that he actually kept Hunt's files for about six months, then burned them with his Christmas trash.

Gray resigned as acting director of the FBI on April 27, 1973, three days before the resignations of Haldeman, Ehrlichman, Kleindienst, and Dean. Gray was replaced by William Ruckelshaus, who would later become Elliot Richardson's deputy attorney general and resign with Richardson during the Saturday Night Massacre.

The day after Gray's resignation and a few days before I was named counsel to the president, I spoke with Woodward for the first time. Previously I had dealt with more established journalistic figures—Joe Kraft, Henry Brandon, Bob Semple, Jules Witcover, Ward Just, Meg Greenfield, Jack Rosenthal, Jack MacKenzie, John Osborne, Teddy White. My initial conversation with Woodward appeared in *All the President's Men*, attributed to an anonymous White House official. His account contained a good deal of his own reaction to my tremulous words and facial expressions, but it was basically accurate.

After Nixon resigned, I had repeated sessions with Woodward and Bernstein as they researched *The Final Days*. I remember late nights and Chinese restaurants. In the book, the reporters' accounts of these meetings again had the annoying habit of putting thoughts into my brain. But, again, the reporters were not far off the mark. I talked with Woodward many times after that. He never lied to me or misled me. He did display a seductive interest in everything I had to say, but that is the trick of every good journalist.

Not long after I met the yet-to-be-famous reporter, I became counsel to the president and the Ervin committee began its public hearings on Watergate. On May 14, three days before the start of the hearings, Ruckelshaus publicly disclosed that records of the administration's early wiretaps, which the Justice Department had previously declared to be missing, had been discovered in Ehrlichman's office safe.

The night before the Ervin hearings were to begin, Woodward and Deep Throat held a garage meeting. This time Deep Throat did not want to engage in extended conversation; he talked fast, then left. But he told Woodward about several major features of the Watergate cover-up—most important, the hush money, the clemency offers, and the fact that the cover-up operation had been designed less to conceal the Watergate burglary itself than to prevent disclosure of the rest of the dirty tricks.

Deep Throat also told Woodward, who later typed up the notes, "Everyone's life is in danger," and "electronic surveillance is going on and we had better watch it." This, in contrast to the information about the cover-up, was something that no one could—or ever did—confirm.

The next parts of the Watergate story followed in breathtakingly rapid succession—the witnesses testifying one after another before the Ervin committee; the appointment of Archibald Cox as special prosecutor; the escalation of media interest to the level of a feeding frenzy. In a sense, the pressure on Woodward and Bernstein was now off. Whatever the ultimate outcome of Watergate, the two reporters had won.

Now that the importance of their reporting was obvious, the two faced another kind of pressure. They had to finish a manuscript and deliver a book to Simon & Schuster, even as the Watergate story was still unfolding. Woodward and Bernstein spent a large part of the summer and fall of 1973 writing, though they did not deliver a manuscript until the spring of 1974. At Simon & Schuster, they were assigned a talented editor, Alice Mayhew, who by all accounts pressed the new

authors to make their book less of a catalogue of their significant stories and more of a narrative of how they got those
stories. Around the same time, the international film star and
budding movie mogul Robert Redford expressed interest in
turning the book into a movie.

It was in this environment of opportunities, each with its
own demands, that Woodward and Bernstein finished the
manuscript of their book.

In early November, 1973, following the Saturday Night
Massacre and the subsequent White House commitment to
turn over the Watergate tapes that Cox had demanded,
Woodward summoned the genie of the flowerpot one more
time. The reporter recorded the substance of the ensuing
meeting thus: "Deep Throat's message was short and simple:
one or more of the tapes contained deliberate erasures."

Two weeks would pass before we at the White House
screwed up our courage to notify Judge Sirica of the 18 $\frac{1}{2}$-
minute gap in the tape of June 20, 1972. There were as yet
very few people who knew about the erasures that made up
this gap. This limited number has provided the basis for elaborate speculation about who Deep Throat could and could
not have been. The speculation has not been of much use,
because knowing the identity of each person with first-hand
knowledge of the gap is not as important as knowing the
name of every person these individuals told about his or her
knowledge. Most of Deep Throat's information, almost by
definition, was second-hand; there is no reason why his
knowledge about the tapes could not have been second-hand
as well.

Would Woodward and Bernstein have persisted in their
Watergate reporting without the encouragement of Deep

Throat? There are those who say it doesn't matter. In this view, it was the official executive branch investigations, followed by the congressional investigations, that established the facts and produced the results of Watergate.

Yet nothing is that simple in American politics. What a government organization investigates, how wide it casts its net, what others will think of the often-inconclusive information it turns up—all these things are mightily influenced, in the United States, by the climate of knowledge and opinion among both the population as a whole and interested elites. This climate, in turn, is shaped in significant part by the press.

And the press cannot do this type of job of shaping unless it has an idea, apart from the particular facts it has turned up, about what is going on. That is the foundation of the power that a good source holds. An individual who can persuade journalists of his or her overall framework for viewing events can, through the press, help shape reality to fit that framework.

Deep Throat was one of those powerful sources. It was no accident that he did not want to feed Woodward specific facts, that instead he would listen to Woodward's facts and proceed to put them in "perspective." Deep Throat clearly knew the most effective way to set Woodward and Bernstein's direction and thus steer the Watergate story. His possession of this gift proved to be one of the major clues to his identity.

4

The Hunt

When I began this book, I sifted diligently through the Deep Throat candidates, picked the one for whom the evidence was most rationally persuasive, started writing about him—and realized, not before making a fool of myself, that I had reasoned my way into the wrong choice. I had to start over. It was a lucky thing I did.

In *All the President's Men*, Deep Throat was only one of a number of confidential sources for Woodward and Bernstein. The book also made clear that Deep Throat was limited and not entirely reliable as a source of specific new information. These disclaimers did not matter, because it was clear that Deep Throat had played a uniquely important role in the reporters' achievement. Speculation about Deep Throat's identity began at the moment of the book's initial success and has continued until today. Steady streams of writers, including high-level Nixon insiders and some of the country's best political journalists, have devoted huge amounts of time and energy to the hunt. They have made astute guesses supported by meticulous research.

I sorted through the Deep Throat theories, trying to figure out who were the most serious candidates. In the process, I gradually came to see that these theories were a kind of mirror of our notions about the workings of politics and government.

For instance, among the most prevalent theories of Deep Throat are those arguing that he came from somewhere in the federal law enforcement and intelligence agencies, the government organizations that were most deeply involved in the investigation of Watergate and had possession of the largest amount of pertinent information. According to these theories, Deep Throat acted partly from self-interest—to vindicate frustrated personal ambitions, protect himself from being personally burned by Watergate, or guard his agency's well-being. Yet, in these same theories, Deep Throat was also motivated by a kind of patriotism—by the sense that the Nixon White House had to be stopped from taking over the government by improper means.

In these accounts, Deep Throat was just doing his job of vindicating the law. If he had to use extraordinary tactics, it was because the president, the nation's chief law enforcement officer, had made it impossible to uphold the law by more conventional means.

The best-known Deep Throat candidate from this school of thought was Richard Helms, head of the Central Intelligence Agency. Helms had plenty of access to Watergate information and enough political sophistication to know how to use it. In addition, as an intelligence officer, he had well-cultivated habits of secrecy. Finally, Helms had particular reason to dislike Richard Nixon: He knew that Nixon, filled with mistrust of the Agency, planned to fire Helms after winning re-election in 1972.

In spite of this reciprocal distaste, the White House importuned the CIA for help when the Watergate burglars were apprehended, thus threatening to involve the Agency in dangerous lawbreaking. Nixon and his aides asked the CIA not only to provide a cover story that would cut off the FBI's investigation but to provide money to keep the Watergate burglars quiet. At this point—so the Helms theory goes—the director of central intelligence, or someone acting for him, became Deep Throat and used his pre-existing connections with the media to expose the scandal. Thus the country was saved, barely, by the power of its permanent government. The fact that Helms had to exert his influence in the dark of night showed how vulnerable this power was.

I thought this was a pretty good theory and put Helms on my short list of research subjects.

There were other candidates from the CIA. One of them, Cord Meyer, was among the handful of senior CIA officials whom Helms warned, on the Monday morning after the Watergate break-in, that the nascent scandal posed mortal dangers to the agency. Among Meyer's duties at the CIA was the guarding of the CIA's public reputation, a responsibility that he took with his accustomed seriousness of purpose. Meyer, like Helms, certainly had both access to vital Watergate information and skill in clandestine activities. He also had a special connection to the *Washington Post*: Meyer's first wife and the first wife of *Post* editor Ben Bradlee were sisters.

Unlike Helms, Meyer's personal career was not under threat from the White House. But Meyer was said to be a man capable of moral outrage on behalf of the CIA and of his country.

Worth a lunch.

A third CIA official on the Deep Throat list was Vernon Walters, deputy director of the Agency. The White House had inserted Walters into the CIA's upper reaches precisely because he was a presidential loyalist. But Walters was also a man of integrity: His loyalty to Nixon was strong, or so the theory of his candidacy went, but his loyalty to his country was stronger. He was disturbed by the White House request that the CIA involve itself in the cover-up and saw the threat it posed to the constitutional order. But his concern conflicted with his public role as a friend of the president. Therefore Walters took to the garage as Deep Throat.

Walters was also very much worth investigating.

There were also Deep Throat candidates from the FBI. Chief among them was Mark Felt, acting associate director of the Bureau at the time of Watergate. The Felt theory was a strong one. The FBI, which was investigating Watergate, had matchless access to information about the scandal. Felt, a seasoned career special agent and Bureau executive, was well acquainted with clandestine modes of operation. Further, Felt had a personal motive for acting. After the death of J. Edgar Hoover, which occurred just six weeks before the Watergate break-in, Felt thought he was a leading candidate to succeed Hoover as FBI director. But he, like other candidates from within the Bureau, was passed over in favor of L. Patrick Gray, a Nixon loyalist and a novice at law enforcement.

In addition, the Felt theory, like the Helms theory, had a powerful institutional component. The FBI had a collective reason to fear the Nixon White House. From the beginning of Nixon's presidency, relations between the Bureau and the White House were uneasy. The FBI refused to accede to some of the early White House demands for wiretaps. When the Bureau did install wiretaps, it sometimes terminated them without consulting the White House.

Nixon thought, with some reason, that Hoover was being less accommodating towards him than the director had been towards previous presidents. The Nixon White House acted to lessen its dependence on the FBI. Ehrlichman hired Jack Caulfield to do independent investigations, and the plumbers were later established to perform similar functions. After the Watergate break-in, the White House attempted once again to do an end run around the FBI by blocking the Bureau's investigation of the event. At one early stage, the Nixon men managed virtually to shut the investigation down.

It was during this period of maximum pressure by the White House, shortly after the break-in, that Deep Throat began meeting with Woodward.

Mark Felt was the prototypical career FBI man. He was, in this theory, understandably angry on behalf of not only himself but his agency. He was also believed by some of his colleagues, and therefore by Deep Throat theorists, to be a big leaker to the press. These characteristics were a good fit.

The trouble with Felt's candidacy was that Deep Throat in *All the President's Men* simply did not sound to me like a career FBI man. But I set that unease aside.

Another Deep Throat candidate from the FBI was, ironically, the same Pat Gray, acting director of the Bureau during the critical early months of Watergate, whom FBI insiders viewed as part of a White House plot to subvert the Bureau.

In the Gray theory, the Bureau's acting director, much like Vernon Walters, was an outsider who grew into his organization, coming to see that the White House attack on it was beyond the constitutional pale.

I knew that Gray was a Bob Finch–style liberal in the Nixon administration. Gray had served as Finch's counsel at the Department of Health, Education, and Welfare (HEW). It was easy to imagine Gray being repelled by both the Watergate cover-up in whose early stages he participated and the style of politics that the FBI investigation was uncovering.

In addition, Gray may have feared that because of the loyal cooperation he gave the White House in the early days of Watergate, he was vulnerable to prosecution.

I thought it was worth getting in touch with Gray, who was said to be living in Florida. I began the complicated process of trying to make contact, finding Gray's old law firm in Connecticut and asking one of his former partners to deliver a message.

There were other, more convoluted theories about Deep Throat and one government agency or another. For instance, a favored candidate of sophisticates has been Bobby Ray Inman, who at the time of Watergate was executive assistant to the chief of naval operations. Later, Inman would hold top positions in intelligence, heading the Defense Intelligence Agency and National Security Agency.

The Inman theory, as far as I could tell, was based mainly on sheer proximity. Woodward and Inman, at widely different times in their Navy careers, each did a tour of duty in Washington that included the job of giving intelligence briefings to senior government officials. After Watergate, Woodward wrote some of the key stories chronicling Inman's swift rise through the ranks of military intelligence.

As for Inman's motive, theorists argued that he, like other high-level Navy officials, was outraged at the slow pace of Nixon's exit from Vietnam and the consequent needless American deaths. This was the same argument that had led others to name Admiral Zumwalt as Deep Throat.

As I was mulling the Inman possibility, I happened to run into him in the steam room of the Marriott Health Club on the day of the annual Alfalfa Club dinner. I looked at Inman—cerebral, personally and publicly fastidious, unlikely to descend to the parking garage technique—and mentally crossed him off the list.

The most important Deep Throat candidate connected with the permanent government was not a government official during Watergate at all. In 1976, J. Anthony Lukas published a piece in the *New York Times* in which he became one of the first to make the case that Deep Throat might be Robert F. Bennett. At the time of Watergate, Bennett headed Robert R. Mullen & Co., the public relations firm and CIA front organization that had employed E. Howard Hunt. When the burglars were arrested, Woodward, who may have known Bennett before Watergate, phoned to ask Bennett what he knew about the event. Bennett spoke with Woodward at some length and remained accessible to him and to the press generally throughout the early days of Watergate.

Bennett, the son of Senator Wallace F. Bennett of Utah, served as chief congressional liaison at the Department of Transportation from 1969 to 1971, before he took over Mullen & Co. The younger Bennett had connections all over the Republican Party and the White House. For instance, Tom Korologos, who during Watergate was part of the legislative affairs operation at the White House, had served as press secretary to Senator Wallace Bennett. Bennett the younger also had political dealings with Chuck Colson from the early days of the Nixon administration onward.

As for motive, Bennett might have wanted to distance the CIA, his sponsor and source of income, from the events of Watergate. Also, as a religious Mormon, he might have felt an ethical distaste for White House misdeeds. The combination of Lukas's endorsement and Bennett's central position in Washington placed Bennett high on my list of Deep Throat candidates.

Apart from the permanent government, the major source of Deep Throat candidates was the White House itself. Virtually everyone working in the White House during the relevant time period has become the subject of Deep Throat speculation. For instance, in researching this book I more than once heard the theory, espoused at one point by Nixon himself, that Deep Throat was none other than Noble Mellencamp. Who? Well, it turns out that Mr. Mellencamp was a Department of State official seconded to the White House for a time during the Nixon administration. During this period, Mr. Mellencamp was in charge of moving all the papers from one office to another in the White House. Apart from this fact (and the additional fact of Mr. Mellencamp's memorable name), I could unearth absolutely no evidence for the theory. But it lives.

Of the more serious White House candidates, I grouped some under the "liberal virtue" theory of Deep Throat. In this view, the Nixon White House was populated mainly by con-

servative martinets, exemplified by Haldeman and Ehrlichman. Trapped among them, however, were a few liberal souls
with more humane instincts. One of these liberals, alarmed
by White House wrongdoing but afraid to speak out, perhaps
afraid even for his physical safety, dreamed up the secret
meetings and cryptic messages that so frustrated Woodward
in his dealings with Deep Throat.

The first of these exemplars of liberal virtue was—me. As
I have explained, I was then and am now constitutionally
incapable of being a Deep Throat. This did not matter to a
substantial number of Deep Throat hunters.

I first learned I was a serious Deep Throat candidate in the
middle of the night in London. It was several years after the
Watergate trauma. I was out of the White House and in
Britain in the course of my renewed attempts to earn a
respectable living at the practice of law. The phone woke me
up; it was the Associated Press calling from the United States.
(It was just like the good old days in politics, with journalists
happily oblivious to whom they awakened from deep sleep.)
The reporter informed me that I had been authoritatively
named in the *Philadelphia Inquirer* as Deep Throat. Would I
like to comment? Yes indeed, I said, denying the report as
vociferously as the time of night would allow. It was one thing
actually to *be* Deep Throat, about whom I had no fixed opinions at the time; it was quite another to be named as such
when I wasn't. The AP story ran without the denial, instead
informing readers that I had been unavailable for comment.

The reason my Deep Throat identification had seemed so
authoritative, it turned out, was that the person naming me,
Edward L. Morgan, had been assistant secretary of the Treasury in charge of the Secret Service during Watergate. It was

Secret Service personnel, Morgan said, who told him about my nighttime excursions to strange parking garages. That sounded like the actual horse's mouth.

Except that this same Ed Morgan was an incorrigible practical joker. Actually, calling Morgan a practical joker was like calling Heifetz a fiddler. In 1970, Morgan was a White House staffer working for George Shultz, me, and the committee whose task was to orchestrate the desegregation of the public schools in the Deep South. The bane of Morgan's organizational existence was the committee member from HEW, the deeply conservative, highly ideological, and extremely voluble Robert Mardian. In New Orleans one night, on the eve of Nixon's climactic desegregation address, Morgan, Mardian, and I took a nervous break from preparations by wandering down to the hotel piano bar. The pianist gave us copies of a record he had made. Mardian, leaving the bar before us, forgot his copy. Morgan picked it up.

The following ensued: Morgan penned a note to Mardian purporting to be from the pianist, who—the note said—had found his record where Mardian had discarded it, was furious at the insult, thought Nixon and his aides were creeps, and was going to raise hell. Morgan then called his buddy Ken Cole at the White House to enlist his aid; Morgan also got some friendly journalists on board. The journalists began calling Mardian asking about his offense to the people of New Orleans. Cole called Mardian to ask why Mardian was endangering the president's speech. Mardian was out of his mind, caught in a demented nightmare. We finally had to tell him. God knows what would have happened otherwise.

Morgan's involvement in Watergate, unfortunately, was anything but funny. He was the official to whom fell the duty of backdating the presidential papers Nixon donated to the Library of Congress, so that the gift would appear to qualify for an expired tax deduction. Morgan served time in prison, but, as the appearance of the *Inquirer* story told me, the years had not totally erased his sense of the ridiculous.

I got in touch with Morgan and asked him what the hell had moved him to name me as Deep Throat. He took umbrage at my umbrage, pointing out that the article had in fact been very complimentary towards me. I was not mollified. We talked some more. Finally he came up with the winning argument: "Well, Len, it *could* have been you."

Thus do someone's works of imagination become public truth.

As for whether my liberal sensibilities were sufficiently outraged by Watergate to make me into Deep Throat, the truth is that, far from being appalled by Watergate, I found it fascinating at the time. I may have been a liberal, but my primary identification in those days was as a trial lawyer. In Watergate I had lucked into one humongous case. Besides, I liked being at the White House. That is partly why I stayed there up to and beyond the bitter end, with no regrets.

A large population of Watergate buffs, however, has an unshakable sense that the person who blew the whistle had to be a humane, conscience-stricken man of the left. As a result, I am still on all the lists.

Another major candidate from the liberal theory of Deep Throat was former White House speechwriter David Gergen, to whom I was to devote serious research time. Gergen was a better candidate than I was. He had gone to Yale at the same time as Woodward, and the two men were friends. Gergen was a member of the White House speechwriting staff, a perfectly adequate base from which to acquire Watergate information. After the Nixon years, Gergen served presidents ranging ideologically from Ronald Reagan to Bill Clinton, thus demonstrating a notable amount of political heterodoxy; Gergen also became a Washington journalist, confirming that he was no hater of the press.

A third White House liberal on many Deep Throat lists was Ray Price, one of Richard Nixon's chief speechwriters in the 1968 campaign and the White House. Though not a liberal by any objective standard, Ray was often on the liberal side of internal White House policy debates, along with me. Ray's personal closeness to President Nixon and his family, both during and after the Nixon presidency, should have stricken the speechwriter from Deep Throat contention; it certainly did the trick for me. But the strength of the liberal theory of Deep Throat kept his name alive.

The liberal White House candidate who looked best on paper was Robert Finch, named early on as a possible Deep Throat. From the days of Nixon's vice presidency, Finch was his close friend and political adviser. He became secretary of health, education, and welfare in the first Nixon term, only to resign after losing a series of policy battles related to race and poverty. Finch was then named a counsel to the president and went to the White House. In 1973, Finch left government and returned home to practice law in California.

Finch was a conspicuously decent man who was liked and admired by journalists. But, as I have noted, his decency was of a straightforward kind that made him a highly unlikely participant in surreptitious meetings. In addition, by 1972 he had been associated with Nixon for decades. Becoming Deep Throat, a morally ambiguous act if undertaken by most

Nixon political allies, would have been a special treachery if committed by Finch.

In any event, Finch died five years ago. If Woodward and Bernstein are to be believed in their promise to name Deep Throat upon his death, events have removed Finch from contention.

There was also a "conservative virtue" theory of Deep Throat. In this version of things, the behavior of the Nixon White House was an affront not only to liberals but to "real" conservatives, who after all were partisans of limited government and the rule of law. One of these real conservatives, even while working strenuously against Nixon's opponents, came to recognize Nixon's threat to genuine conservative principles. This man was severely conflicted: He did not want to give public comfort to Nixon-haters but did want to purge the administration of its corruption. This was a good-enough reason to go skulking around in the famous garage.

The most important Deep Throat candidate under this theory was my colleague Fred Buzhardt, who was certainly conservative enough to fit and had more than enough information for Deep Throat purposes. If you were looking for a conservative in a position to grow disillusioned with the Nixon administration, Fred was your man.

Fred was also a highly honest man, not one to shave the truth around the edges. Near the end of Watergate, Fred and I came to suspect that the president was asking us to present to Judge Sirica, in answer to a subpoena, a recently created substitute for a missing tape. Fred was very nervous about the prospect. If Judge Sirica asked him about the tape, Fred told me, he would have to tell the truth.

This straightforwardness and sense of propriety made Fred the very opposite of a meet-you-in-the-garage type. In addition, in the summer of 1972, when Deep Throat was talking to Woodward, Fred was still serving as general counsel to the Department of Defense. He was even more clueless than I was about Watergate.

However, the idea of Buzhardt as Deep Throat was, to a liberal imagination, politically romantic. Therefore it persisted, though upon Fred's death there was no announcement by Woodward and Bernstein of his identity as Deep Throat.

The "conservative virtue" theory produced other Deep Throat candidates, within and without the White House. One "within" candidate was Richard Allen, who for a time inhabited the Old Executive Office Building as deputy to Peter Peterson in the field of foreign economic policy. Allen knew reporters and was a friend of Jack Caulfield's. But Allen left the White House around the time of the Watergate break-in, and there is no evidence that he had Deep Throat's extensive connections in the various organizations connected with the re-election campaign.

One conservative Deep Throat candidate from outside the White House was Robert Mardian, who served at HEW and later became an assistant attorney general under John Mitchell. At the Department of Justice, Mardian became known as a voluble man of conservative principles who disliked some of Nixon's top White House aides. But I did not put Mardian on the short list. He was a Nixon loyalist who participated in some of the early efforts to contain the Watergate scandal.

A variant of the conservative virtue theory was the Republican virtue theory, in which Deep Throat, a Republican Party loyalist, thought the party in grave danger from the Nixon White House but was unwilling to display disloyalty in public. The chief candidacy launched by this theory was that of Mel Laird, who left government after his tenure as Nixon's secretary of defense, only to be called back to the White House to serve as Nixon's adviser during the latter phase of Watergate. But during Watergate's early stages, when Deep Throat was talking to Woodward, Laird was not privy to Watergate information.

Finally, there were Deep Throat candidates from inside the White House whose motives their proponents simply never made clear. One was Fred Fielding, who worked for me in the White House, then became deputy counsel to the president under John Dean. Fielding was close to the center of the action and had, in theory, access to Watergate information. He had emerged from Watergate—suspiciously, some thought—unscathed.

Fred was funny, discreet, and shrewd. It seemed logical that if anyone could negotiate his way off the sinking Nixon ship, it would be Fred. It also seemed logical that someone of Fred's balanced temperament would be repelled by the men at the top of the White House heap, whose overall humorlessness was of a piece with their absence of perspective and consequently immoderate behavior.

There was one immediately apparent obstacle to Fred's candidacy. In 1980, Fielding was under consideration for the job of White House counsel in the Reagan administration. The last thing that particular administration would have welcomed into its inner midst was an individual who had been Deep Throat. Fielding, in order to qualify for the job, asked Woodward to clear him of suspicion. Woodward obliged, confirming that Fred was not Deep Throat. (In doing so, Woodward was, I thought, a rather good sport. It must produce a strange feeling when someone asks you to absolve him of the crime of having associated with you.)

Despite the public absolution, I could not let go of the Fielding candidacy; so I put the Deep Throat question directly to Fred. He denied it, of course. More important, I believed him. During the time we worked together, I had occasion to observe Fielding's manner and temperament at length. He simply did not fit. Fred was certainly shrewd enough for the role; and, let us assume for argument's sake, Watergate may have made him cynical enough. But he would not have served as point man in the enterprise of exposing his friend John Dean. And world-weariness is not Fred's style. Off the list.

Another Deep Throat candidacy from the "not sure why" school was that of White House press secretary Ron Ziegler. Ziegler's escape from Watergate was even more amazing than Fred's. From the earliest days of the Nixon administration, Ron was in the closest possible orbit around Haldeman and Nixon. During Watergate, Ron spent large parts of every day with the president, almost as much time as Haldeman and Ehrlichman did. Moreover, though Ziegler stayed with Nixon until the end and went with him into exile, Ron never came close to being in legal peril from his proximity to Watergate.

Ziegler, like Fielding, differed from most of his senior White House colleagues in having a dry, wry wit. He also had the shrewdness that would have enabled him to swim with the sharks while not quite joining them. These characteristics suggested to some theorists that Ziegler, with his information and his press contacts, must have been Deep Throat.

Ziegler was not just a lunch; the two of us had dinner at my home with our wives. At the end of the meal, though, I could see no way in which a thoroughgoing loyalist like Ziegler would have turned in his senior White House colleagues and his president.

Finally, Ken Clawson, a former *Washington Post* reporter and an aide to Nixon communications director Herb Klein, was named as Deep Throat. Clawson spent a good deal of time talking to the press. He called some of his sessions "Cocktails with Clawson" and had cocktail napkins printed to that effect. If a Nixon aide hung out with the press, the theory went, he had to be seriously alienated from his fellow members of the administration.

I was interested.

The final Deep Throat candidates were the men at the very top of the Nixon White House. One was Nixon's national security adviser and secretary of state, Henry Kissinger. Early in Nixon's first term, Kissinger had himself participated in arguably improper wiretaps of the sort that became connected with Watergate; he had reason, the theory went, to try to insure that he did not become associated with the larger scandal. In addition, no one in the White House could work the press better than Kissinger. He was precisely the sort of person whom Woodward and Bernstein would have trusted to confirm their journalists' hunches.

But Henry skulking around in the garage? Meeting Woodward in a Washington bar, even (or especially) one frequented by "truckers and construction workers"? Knowing where such a bar was in the first place? Not on your life and not on my list.

Another prominent front-runner for Deep Throat was Al Haig, Haldeman's successor as Nixon's chief of staff during the last year of Watergate. Haig, in this theory, was a military man whose regard for his country—much like Helms's or Walters's—transcended particular administrations. Haig was said to have acted to stem the political chaos into which the Nixon White House threatened to plunge the nation.

Haig was a consummately political military commander who knew how to cultivate the press in general and Bob Woodward in particular. Woodward and Bernstein's second book, *The Final Days*, bore Haig's clear imprint. Haig, like Kissinger, emerged from Watergate intact. When Haig later became secretary of state in the Reagan administration, Woodward produced favorable and exceptionally well informed reportage about him.

Maybe.

There were two more Deep Throat candidates from the highest levels of the White House: John Dean and Charles Colson. Neither of them made my short list. Their involvement in the Watergate cover-up was so deep and central that it required a serpentine calculation too deep for me to explain why either might think it personally advantageous to expose the scandal.

Those were the most serious candidates. I began winnowing the list by first pursuing those candidates who were easiest to reach. Specifically, I first lighted on my old friend David Gergen. I was not the first writer to do so. Gergen was not exactly uncharted Deep Throat territory; on the contrary, he was the most natural candidate.

Gergen and Bob Woodward had been not only undergraduate classmates at Yale but members of the same small residential college, Ezra Stiles. This coincidence seemed to satisfy the "old friend" part of Deep Throat's description in *All the President's Men*. After Yale, both men joined the Navy—Woodward straight from college, Gergen after he had completed Harvard Law School. Both men then located themselves in Washington.

In 1970, when Woodward was finishing up his stint in the Navy by doing duty as a courier and confidential briefer in Washington, Gergen's roommate from Harvard Law School, Jonathan Rose, was working in the White House. In that year, on Rose's recommendation, Gergen became one of Ray Price's speechwriters. Gergen was talented and extraordinarily energetic and rose quickly. By 1973 he was Ray Price's deputy manager of the speechwriting staff.

In 1976, just after Watergate, journalist Taylor Branch took up the hunt for Deep Throat in an article in *Esquire*. Branch was well versed in Watergate, having helped John Dean write his first book, *Blind Ambition*. Branch, in the *Esquire* article, sorted through the fourteen Deep Throat candidates who had recently been named by Hays Gorey in *Time* magazine. Branch concluded that Gergen was the "odds-on favorite" for Deep Throat, though "it wouldn't be a sure thing."

Branch interviewed both Woodward and Gergen. He noted that the two men had gotten together in Washington, well before Watergate, and talked about "Yale, journalism, and the White House." The phrase echoed the description in *All the President's Men*: "Long before Watergate, they had spent many evenings talking about Washington, the government, power."

There were more such echoes. *All the President's Men* described Deep Throat as a man "who knew too much literature too well." That characterization did not fit many people I knew at the White House; most of them were immensely pleased with themselves if they managed to get through the daily *White House Bulletin*. But Gergen, when a Yale undergraduate, had turned down membership in the prestigious Skull and Bones secret society to join Manuscript, a haven for literary types. Skull and Bones was then viewed as the passport to a glittering future; Manuscript was for bookish misfits. Choosing the latter, surely, was the act of someone who "knew too much literature too well."

Deep Throat, according to Woodward and Bernstein, was not a partisan by temperament. Instead, he was "dispassionate" and "committed to the best version of the obtainable truth." Gergen, who had come to the White House to work for Richard Nixon, was nevertheless a registered Democrat. More, Gergen had first been drawn into politics through the civil rights movement and the influence of famed activist Allard Lowenstein. David's wife, Anne, a strong and intelligent woman, supported Democratic presidential candidate George McGovern in 1972 while her husband was working to re-elect Richard Nixon.

Deep Throat's temperament, Woodward and Bernstein said in their book, was that of an "incurable gossip, careful to label rumor for what it was, but fascinated by it." This description fit Gergen—who, by his own admission, enjoyed gossip and was in the habit of talking to the press. Moreover, the Deep Throat in *All the President's Men* "was not good at concealing his feelings"; as I read those words, I remembered Gergen during Watergate days, wearing his emotions in his voice and on his furrowed brow as he talked about the latest awful revelations.

More interesting, *All the President's Men* portrayed Deep Throat as deeply concerned about the "willingness of the President's men to fight dirty and for keeps, regardless of what effect the slashing might have on the government and the nation." That description, too, recalled David in the White House during Watergate. We were all, to put it mildly, concerned—some of us because of what we did not know and some of us because of what we did. Even in this anxious company, however, David stood out. During the summer and fall of 1972, he was feverish (with good reason, it turned out). He would frequently drop by my office, which was on the same floor as his, and vent his worries about the behavior of Haldeman and Ehrlichman and their "apparatus" of young assistants.

David was particularly agitated (again, with good reason) about the dangerous mess that Chuck Colson and those associated with him had created for the president. He sensed the size of the trouble that was brewing. I remember telling him that he was probably right. At that point, however, I was not inclined to mobilize for action. I had my hands full with my own policy crises and had no inclination to jump into this particular snakepit. So I told him to cool it, keep his head down, and do the best he could; he and I were in no position to do anything about the situation.

It cannot have been very satisfying advice. Looking back on those conversations, it struck me that Gergen must have been profoundly dissatisfied with my counsel of inaction.

There was one concrete incident in *All the President's Men* that seemed to me to be a possible clincher. Deep Throat said at one point that if he was unable to make it to a requested garage meeting, he would leave a message for Woodward on a ledge in the parking garage in which the two men met. One night, when Deep Throat did not show up, Woodward went to the appointed garage ledge and found that it was too high for him to reach. He had to use a piece of broken pipe to fish the note down.

Woodward, as *All the President's Men* informed us, is 5'10". Gergen, at 6'5", could have comfortably placed the note on the ledge without giving a thought to his friend's height disadvantage. At the time, I thought this fact to be of momentous significance.

Some pieces of information that Deep Throat passed on to Woodward were flat wrong; other items were seriously off the mark. John Dean, in his book *Lost Honor*, itemized fifteen points on which Deep Throat was in error, sometimes ludicrously so. Deep Throat exaggerated the number of people involved in Donald Segretti's dirty-tricks operation. Deep Throat also charged Pat Gray with blackmailing Nixon in order to secure a formal nomination as director of the FBI. And Deep Throat said, in total error, that Attorney General John Mitchell had conducted his own investigation of Watergate, assisted by—of all inappropriate people—Howard Hunt.

This kind of distortion was wholly consistent with the idea of Gergen as Deep Throat. Specifics of the sort transmitted by Deep Throat consisted mainly of soft information, shading into gossip and rumor. In the West Wing and Old Executive Office Building, lawyers, writers, researchers, law enforcement liaisons, and even plumbers (or today's equivalent thereof) work cheek by jowl. Indeed, there is more of this talk in OEOB than in the West Wing itself; the West Wing is the bridge of the ship, but the OEOB is its working boiler room.

The denizens gab, gossip, and trade secrets by phone, in their offices, in lavatories, in halls (especially in halls), and over meals in the West Wing and OEOB messes. "Ask and you shall know almost everything, with a small amount of distortion" is the motto of all modern White House staffs.

In this environment, Gergen was Mr. Curiosity himself. But he was not directly enough involved, fortunately for him, to get the details straight on every occasion.

I was immensely proud of myself for having figured all this out. I was also impressed by the imprimatur of Taylor Branch. I phoned Branch to ask his current opinion. He said that Gergen was still at the top of his list. So I asked David to lunch, hoping that when I confronted him, either he would confess or my trial lawyer's instinct would tell me whether he was dissimulating. Once we were seated, I belabored him with my evidence and speculation.

He denied it, of course. David said he had talked to Woodward during the Watergate crisis and its aftermath, but he was not Deep Throat. His denial was emphatic and emotional. And, I realized with disappointment, it was probably the truth. Though David, like me, looked good on paper, he did not fit. Gergen did not have Deep Throat's voice and manner—that of the wearily sophisticated super-insider with the slightly sinister snarl. David also lacked Deep Throat's temperament—that of a man who could coolly weigh the ethical and strategic pros and cons of giving up White House colleagues for some abstract principle and accept the consequences.

I was back to square one.

I started roaming further afield in my search. I latched onto the idea, for instance, that Deep Throat was Ken Clawson. Clawson, like Gergen, was close enough to the action during Watergate to have picked up a lot of information and misinformation. Moreover, according to then–*Washington Post* reporter Marilyn Berger, Clawson had said he was the man who forged a letter to the *Manchester Union Leader* in which Democratic presidential candidate Edmund Muskie was accused of uttering an embarrassing ethnic slur.

Clawson knew the ambience of the White House intimately. He knew about at least some of the dirty tricks; and, a former *Washington Post* reporter, he hung out with the press. Clawson, like Gergen, was a natural. I located Clawson in the New York area. We made an appointment for dinner at a steak house in New York City. His wife and my wife would join us.

Suzi and I took the shuttle to New York just for the occasion, Suzi muttering complaints under her breath about the shlep. We arrived at La Guardia, then took a taxi directly to the restaurant in midtown Manhattan. When we walked in the door, Ken waved from the back of the room; he and his wife had been waiting for us. We waved back. It was not a big place. So as we stood at the door, Suzi had a chance to get a fairly good look at our about-to-be dinner companions. She stared for a moment. Then she turned and hissed at me through clenched teeth. "That," she said, "is not Mrs. Deep Throat."

When we got to the table, I saw what she meant. Ken's wife, Carol, was smart, open, and straightforward, a former journalist herself who was now working in press relations for a public utility company. Ken was already struggling with the chronic illness from which he subsequently died. His medical expenses were staggering. When I told him about my mission, he laughed. If he were Deep Throat, he assured me, he would have long ago—out of necessity—claimed the rewards that were sure to fall to whoever admitted being the famous source.

I also broke bread with Al Haig, mainly because he has been such an enduringly popular Deep Throat candidate. In *Lost Honor*, John Dean, after extensive analysis, named Haig as the most likely candidate. Recently a reputable historian has argued that Haig became Deep Throat because he hated Nixon's foreign policy heterodoxy—the opening to China, arms control with the Soviet Union, the messy exit from Vietnam. Haig certainly knew more than enough about Watergate for Deep Throat purposes. He even worked with Kissinger on the 1969 wiretaps. Haig has just as certainly been a source for Woodward in the reporter's subsequent journalistic endeavors.

Early in the Nixon administration, when Haig worked in the White House as Henry Kissinger's military aide, I got to know him fairly well. Then, after Haig became chief of staff and I took John Dean's place, becoming acting White House counsel, Haig and I spent a lot of time together in circumstances that were mutually revealing if not altogether joyful.

He was not my beau ideal, and vice versa: He was hardwired for combat, and I for flight. In point of fact, we nearly came to blows one night in the White House over some now-forgotten tactical dispute when the day had been especially stressful and the end-of-day booze was especially plentiful. But I respected Haig greatly then and even more now for the way he handled an unceasingly and increasingly impossible job. He had a flammable temperament (I should talk) and boundless ambition, but he also had a combat commander's sense of limits and a professional soldier's self-discipline and honor.

Haig was also, it is true, a shrewd and clear-eyed politician. But it is simply surreal to think of a career-minded Army general like Haig, not only steeped in the precepts of civilian control of the military but actually in charge of the day-to-day operations of the executive branch, putting his career on the line by leaking secrets to a cub reporter sitting on the floor in a garage in the middle of the night. Haig certainly communicated with the press at high levels when he thought it would do the White House or himself some good, but that was a far cry from the kind of systematic secret contacts in which Deep Throat engaged with Woodward.

Finally, the biggest problem with Haig as Deep Throat was that recurring issue of personal fit. I knew Haig's temperament was radically different from that of Deep Throat. Perhaps more important, Haig's manner of speech, with which the nation would later become better acquainted, often combined military jargon, bureaucratese, and deliberate obfuscation in an unintelligible mix. By contrast, Deep Throat spoke laconically and cryptically but gracefully as well.

John Dean, who made the case for Haig as Deep Throat in *Lost Honor*, has since concluded that Haig was not Deep Throat. Haig was out of town on several of the Woodward–Deep Throat meeting dates, including one on which he was in Paris conducting Vietnam peace negotiations. In addition, Woodward officially cleared Haig of being Deep Throat when Haig was considering a run for the Republican presidential nomination, an activity in which having been Deep Throat was not an advantage. In light of the problems with

Haig's candidacy, there is simply no reason not to believe Woodward's unqualified absolution.

Pat Gray's Deep Throat candidacy received a boost in 1992, when a television documentary co-produced by CBS News and the *Washington Post* named him the prime suspect. The documentary considered it significant that Gray and Woodward lived only a few blocks from one another at the time of Watergate. This proximity would have made it easy for them to meet.

Woodward had once told his fellow *Washington Post* reporter Walter Pincus that the underground parking garage in which he had met with Deep Throat looked just like the garage used in the movie version of *All the President's Men*. Pincus reacted like the investigative reporter he is, traipsing all over town to check out garages in buildings occupied by Deep Throat candidates. After his search, Pincus announced that Deep Throat's garage was Pat Gray's garage and Pat Gray was Deep Throat.

But in *All the President's Men*, Deep Throat said distinctly uncomplimentary things about Pat Gray. If the book was anything short of a hoax, this talk seemed to eliminate Gray as a candidate. More important, Gray's personality did not fit. During World War II, Gray served as a submarine commander, hardly the best training in cultivating divided loyalties or duplicity. Indeed, during his Senate confirmation hearings after he was nominated to the permanent post of FBI director, Gray essentially volunteered a confession of his role in the early stages of the Watergate cover-up.

Moreover, Gray owed his advancement very directly to Nixon, who chose him over all the FBI insiders to become acting director of the Bureau upon Hoover's death. Indeed, it was Gray's fierce loyalty to Nixon that put him in harm's way by aiding the early cover-up in the first place.

In my early efforts to get in touch with Gray, I did not have much sucess. I located a former law partner of his in Connecticut, who knew Gray's whereabouts in Florida. But the former partner, as luck would have it, had also served under Gray on a submarine and, like Gray himself, knew something about loyalty. He was not talking.

In the midst of these attempts, Woodward waved me off Gray, indicating that it was not worth my while to keep trying. Then, finally, came Woodward's public response to the theory advanced by CBS and the *Washington Post* that Gray, based on the look of his garage, was Deep Throat. Appearing on NBC's *Today Show*, Woodward announced that Gray was in fact not Deep Throat.

In 1999, I was actively considering Mark Felt as a possible Deep Throat, despite his consistent denials in the years since Watergate. So was a young man named Chase Culeman-Beckman, a high school senior, who sent me a letter announcing that he had discovered Deep Throat's identity. I opened communications with Mr. Culeman-Beckman, who initially wanted me to talk to his attorney about confidentiality agreements and co-production arrangements. But after some back and forth, he agreed to give me the paper he had written on Deep Throat. I willingly agreed to credit him if I used his theory.

Culeman-Beckman, as I learned from his paper, based his theory on a comment made to him by Carl Bernstein's son, with whom Culeman-Beckman had gone to summer camp a decade previously. Bernstein's son, then some eight years old, told Culeman-Beckman that the elder Bernstein had identified Mark Felt as Deep Throat. Culeman-Beckman also presented supporting information—some of it based on anagrams, with which, Culeman-Beckman noted, Woodward had been fascinated when an undergraduate at Yale. An example: "My Friend" (Woodward's original name for Deep Throat) = MF = Mark Felt. I had first read the information about Woodward and his love of word puzzles in Adrian Havill's *Deep Truth: The Lives of Bob Woodward and Carl Bernstein*.

I encouraged Culeman-Beckman to seek other outlets for his theory if the idea of a credit in my book did not seem enough. He took my advice. His story soon surfaced in the press and, modern times being what they are, on the Internet. Carl Bernstein was asked about the allegation. Bernstein said that his son, those many years ago, was probably parroting speculation by his mother, to whom Bernstein had in fact never imparted the secret of Deep Throat's identity.

Even before Bernstein's emphatic dismissal, I was not convinced about Felt. Woodward and Bernstein did have sources at the FBI; *All the President's Men* as much as said so. Further, the FBI—and therefore, let us assume, Mark Felt—knew many things about the Watergate investigation that it was conducting. But the investigation was not the only or even the most important subject of Deep Throat's conversations with Woodward. Instead, Deep Throat's unique contribution was to talk with Woodward about Nixon's White House. Deep Throat knew about the clockwork craziness in that place. He knew the sound of Nixon angry; he knew things about the character of various people involved in the cover-up.

This type of information was not accessible to a member of the Bureau, even one in a high position there. More, Deep

Throat's insights into people at the White House had the authority of personal experience; that was precisely why Woodward relied so heavily on him.

After concluding that Felt did not fit, I turned to the Deep Throat candidates from the CIA, thinking first of my old acquaintance Vernon Walters. He sat astride various streams of Watergate-relevant information, just as *All the President's Men* said of Deep Throat. As CIA deputy director, Walters had access to information that was held by the agency with which the burglars were most closely connected. And as a trusted Nixon insider, Walters was in the chain of political communication. Walters knew secrets. Moreover, he was a patriot who would have been highly sensitive to any threats he saw the White House posing to the constitutional order.

Over lunch, Walters and I wound up conversing about everything except Watergate. He was aging but formidably precise. As we talked, I thought about how fitting it was that Nixon should have been hoisted, in the end, on the petard that was Vernon Walters, with his considerable backbone and memo-writing accuracy.

Nixon, in most of his governing, attached immense value to competence, even as he insisted that politics was war with continuous connivance as its heavy artillery. Thus Nixon placed many smart and decent people in high places, as well as the few who were not. Nixon tried to keep the former—friendly political amateurs like Walters, Ray Price, me—out of harm's way. Sometimes he succeeded, as shown by the numbers of Nixon appointees who knew nothing of Watergate and who prospered in its aftermath. Sometimes he failed. It was Nixon's penchant for excellence that placed people like Walters in office, but people like Walters would never participate in a cover-up or hide their knowledge of one. Thus did Nixon's better self contribute to his own unmaking.

At lunch, Walters told me about a memoir he had written (he had also published a memoir some twenty years previously) of his years in public life, mainly his travels and encounters with world leaders. He asked me to read it. I eagerly agreed, and the manuscript soon arrived at my office. I wasn't far into the work when I realized that it was highly unlikely that a publisher would want it. Why? Because this fascinating man, who had met the most fascinating people and done the most fascinating work, would not tell the secrets and private things that he had learned. Walters's admirable reticence was mismatched with the current tendency of book publishing to search out scandal and startling revelation; his chances of publication were remote.

And for the same reason, I realized simultaneously, the chances that Vernon Walters was Deep Throat ranged from remote to invisible.

Cord Meyer, another on the list of CIA candidates for the honor of being Deep Throat, was a World War II hero who sported a glass eye as a result of his hand-to-hand, island-to-island combat in the Pacific campaign. Upon leaving the Marine Corps, Meyer helped launch the United Nations, then became head of the pacifist United World Federalists. In that capacity, he learned a thing or two about the Soviet Union's duplicity in general and its use of left-leaning front groups in particular. Meyer drew the logical conclusion, joined the CIA, and became one of its most ardent and effective Cold Warriors.

Meyer had at least some of Deep Throat's personal characteristics as drawn in *All the President's Men*. Cord was a

glamorous figure of the old Washington. Brilliant Yale grad-
uate, World War II hero, internationalist, convert to militant
anti-Communism, Meyer was a writer of books and doer of
deeds, like André Malraux and Arthur Koestler, though considerably more reluctant to talk about the details of his multiple careers. Meyer had a capacity for moral indignation
and for taking action on the basis of that indignation. Like
Deep Throat, Meyer was a reader of literature, a smoker, and
a man capable, by occupational definition, of being a secret
agent.

I had known Meyer casually when I worked in the White
House, but only because his wife, Starke, worked for me as an
assistant in the area of arts policy. Then it struck me: Here
was a connection between the Watergate-related information
that would have been in the hands of the CIA and the Watergate-related White House information that Deep Throat
knew. Here was Cord Meyer, near the top of the CIA; and
there, working for me during Watergate, literally next door,
sharing my secretary and, theoretically, my Watergate secrets,
was Meyer's wife. Maybe (the mind spun) some of Deep
Throat's information about the White House had come indi-
rectly from me. Maybe I was Deep Throat without knowing it.

I calmed down long enough to call Cord and ask to see
him about what I described as a private matter. He said he
was leaving for Paris that afternoon but could have a quick
lunch with me at his club—the Cosmos, Washington's hang-
out for local mavens of high culture.

Cord appeared to be the same quiet, fastidious man he
had been. However, as I described the purpose of my request
to him, he told me he did not remember any of those long-ago
events and people. He did not talk calmly about this failure of

memory, like a man who was faking it or one for whom it seemed like an insignificant lapse. Instead, he seemed agitated as he told me, after one question and then another, that he was drawing a complete blank.

As I looked past the absence of memory, however, and remembered Cord over the years, I realized that he was not Deep Throat. Institutionally, as the man in charge of the CIA's image, he had every incentive to stay as far away as possible from Watergate rather than wade into it. More important, Meyer's idealism, in all the forms it had taken during his career, and his quietly earnest manner were the polar opposite of the world-weariness of Deep Throat.

If Cord Meyer was not Deep Throat, neither was I. It was a relief.

That left the most formidable candidate from the CIA— Richard Helms, head of the agency at the time of Watergate. I began the first of several lunches with Helms in 1998 when I was in the thrall of someone else's Deep Throat candidacy and eager to try my theory out on the director. Over time, however, I became provisionally convinced that Deep Throat was none other than the director himself.

One of our lunches took place at the Sulgrave Club, a crusty private institution catering to the aging Washington elite of which Helms is a most distinguished member. The city was chilly, wet, and flu-ridden. I arrived a little late and looked around the reception area for Helms but did not see him. I inquired at the desk, where the receptionist said, "Go in and look around to the left. That's where he usually waits." She was right. As I turned the corner, there was Helms, his slender frame tucked almost invisibly into a chair, sniffling into his handkerchief, the spy who came in with a cold.

In light of my level of unsophistication about intelligence matters, I was mystified by Helms's willingness to keep on with our lunches. I found each meal delightful, but I never got a crumb of real information. When I would talk, Helms would pay close, polite attention, his fingers locked, always projecting a quality of institutional as well as personal intelligence. He would sit there, elegance itself, smiling slightly, purring gently here and there, reticent, reflective, closed as a clam. Occasionally, when I asked him what he thought, he would cast his eyes to the ceiling as if viewing a Tiepolo, his small smile widening into a genuine grin. That was the closest he ever came to communicating a point of view about Agency business.

Before long I thought I discerned his game plan: It was remotely possible, he calculated, that Garment knew something. Let the man babble on and we will find out sooner or later. Not for nothing was there a biography of Helms titled *The Man Who Kept the Secrets*.

On one occasion he ran through the story of the CIA's involvement in Watergate. By then I knew just enough to recognize that Helms was not deviating from the official version by so much as a semicolon. First came his hearing about the break-in from an Agency official. Next there was the purely tangential relationship he had maintained over the years with Howard Hunt. Then came his instruction to senior Agency officials on the Monday morning after the break-in: Hands off Watergate.

Despite the lack of concrete information from the meetings with Helms, they were strangely enlightening about the nature of the spy culture—the moments of excitement alternating with months of drudgery, the honor in duplicity. Then,

just once, this elegant, restrained man finally said something—or, rather, asked something—specific.

Helms was forced to resign as director of Central Intelligence in November, 1972. A few months later, William Colby
became head of the organization and promptly purged it.
Indeed, it was Colby himself who advised the Justice Department that Helms might have committed perjury when testifying to Congress about the CIA's role in the coup that led to the
assassination of Chilean president Salvador Allende. Colby
was right: Helms, confronted with an irresolvable conflict
between his duty to guard agency secrets and his duty to give
truthful testimony, had chosen the former. The scandal ended
with Helms pleading guilty to a choice that ended his career
but left intact his personal honor and the respect in which he
was held by his community of colleagues.

Meanwhile, within and around the CIA under Colby, the
long knives were unsheathed. The Agency was raw meat for
senators with presidential ambitions and was suspected of or
blamed for every real or imagined misadventure of American
politics, at home and abroad. Its intelligence-gathering capa-
bilities were decimated. Neither the CIA nor American intelligence in general has yet recovered from the damage that this
climate wrought.

At lunch with me, Helms said, concerning that time, "I
was the one who moved Bill Colby up the ladder. I've always
wondered: Why did he turn on me the way he did?" I mut-
tered something inadequate, something about how Colby
must have been afraid for his own political life during that
time, having himself participated in the notorious Phoenix
program in Vietnam, which included political assassination
among its tactics. Or maybe it was the young Turks within the

CIA pushing Colby to get the Agency right with the political times.

But in fact I had no idea. More than that, I was stunned: Even within an organization whose task was to know secrets, the ultimate secrets of human motivation were as unknowable as in any other, more pedestrian line of work.

Helms, I finally concluded, was not Deep Throat. Even he did not know what Deep Throat knew about the inner workings of the Nixon White House. However, I was powerfully reminded of Helms's lesson about the unknowability of human motives when I came across the CIA-connected Deep Throat candidate whose pursuit was to become the most absorbing part of my hunt.

This next phase began when I opened a document left over from my conversations with Jim Hougan—a dog-eared, rubberband-bound copy of the transcript of testimony taken in the spring and summer of 1974 by the House of Representatives' Special Subcommittee on Intelligence. It was titled *Inquiry into the Alleged Involvement of the Central Intelligence Agency in the Watergate and Ellsberg Matters.*

The House intelligence committee was then chaired by Congressman Lucien Nedzi. The proceedings of the Nedzi committee were conducted in executive session, both because of their connection to the national intelligence apparatus and because Watergate was still underway. The small print of the publication was thick with the turgid interrogatory prose characteristic of legislative hearings and stuffed with documentary excerpts in even smaller print. But, trained by the practice of law for precisely this kind of pain, I read it through. More than once.

Those who testified before the committee were mostly the usual suspects from within the CIA itself. Also among the witnesses, however, was Robert F. Bennett. This was the same Bennett who, as head of Mullen & Co., the CIA proprietary, had employed Howard Hunt while Hunt was also working as a consultant to Chuck Colson at the White House and helping Gordon Liddy run the Watergate burglars at the Committee for the Re-election of the President.

The Nedzi committee had linked Bennett to Watergate through a routine reporting memorandum written about Bennett by the CIA agent who supervised the cover work that Bennett's company did for the Agency. Committee staffers discovered the memo while reviewing documentary evidence produced by the CIA under a blanket subpoena.

Bennett, called before the committee, first described the manner in which he had come to buy Mullen & Co. after serving in government as chief congressional liaison in the Department of Transportation. Bennett knew at the time, he told the committee, that Mullen & Co. had a contractual cover relationship with the CIA. Bennett also told the committee that he knew of the background of Howard Hunt, who, at the recommendation of CIA director Richard Helms, had been employed by the firm since Hunt's retirement from the CIA.

Furthermore, Bennett said he had agreed to Hunt's simultaneously working at Mullen & Co. and consulting at the White House for Colson. Bennett was already acquainted with Colson through their mutual involvement in matters from money raising and conventional dirty tricks to Dita Beard and the ITT antitrust scandal:

I received a call from Chuck Colson in June of 1971, in which Chuck said that he had an assignment at the White House for Howard. He asked me if I would be willing to make Howard available to him on a part time basis. He said, "It would interfere somewhat with his duties for you. It would be an imposition on your time. I would appreciate it if you would accommodate yourself to this so that we at the White House can make use of his talents." I said, "Of course, Chuck. I would be happy to accommodate you."

The committee asked Bennett about the truth of a recent Jack Anderson column asserting that Bennett had known in advance about the Watergate break-in. Bennett said he did have advance knowledge, though not of the specific job the burglars were about to do, because of his connection with Hunt combined with a family-based coincidence.

Hunt, according to Bennett's testimony, had approached a young man named Tom Gregory, who happened to be the friend of a nephew of Bennett's, and proposed to pay Gregory to take a job working at McGovern headquarters. Gregory was troubled by the moral ambiguity of the double agentry Hunt was proposing and asked to talk to Bennett about it. Bennett and Gregory met, as it happened, two days before the Watergate break-in. Bennett advised Gregory about what the young man could and could not do for Hunt:

> [I]f you allow yourself to be put in a position where McGovern is depending upon you for anything significant, . . . you cannot morally discuss what you are doing with Howard Hunt and take money from him.

On the other hand, if you make it clear to the McGovern people that you are simply a college student wanting the chance to watch a Presidential campaign and you are willing to stuff envelopes and lick stamps in return for that privilege, the question of who you talk to about experiences and who pays the expenses is your own business.

Gregory, Bennett testified, then told Bennett that Hunt and his colleagues wanted the young man to do considerably more than pose as an innocent college student:

He said, "Well, they want to bug Frank Mankiewicz's office. They want me to help them." I said, "Tommy, you cannot do that. You have got to get out." He said, "I agree, but how?"

Bennett agreed to deliver a letter of resignation from Gregory to Hunt, so that the young man would not have to talk to Hunt face-to-face. The next day, Bennett placed the letter on Hunt's desk but did not see him. The day after that, the famous Friday night, the burglars broke into the Watergate.

Bennett's testimony was not quite accurate about Gregory's involvement with Howard Hunt. Beginning in March of 1972, Hunt paid Gregory $175 per month for working in the Muskie campaign and preparing intelligence reports about it. In mid-May, after the Muskie campaign had collapsed, Gregory went to work for the McGovern campaign on a similar basis. It was only when Hunt and McCord asked Gregory to provide information about McGovern headquarters in anticipation of a bugging that the young man grew morally nervous.

Bennett testified that after news of the break-in hit the papers, he asked Hunt about it and was told, "Everything is under control." Later that day, however, while Hunt was temporarily out of the office, the FBI came looking for him. When Hunt returned, Bennett gave Hunt the news. Hunt then said, according to Bennett,

> "They have nothing on me. I was nowhere near that place that night." . . . He told me that the purpose of the [Watergate] team was to photograph documents. He said that this was not the first time they had been in the Democratic National Committee, that they—the ubiquitous term, and he never gave me names—but that they were so titillated by what the team had found the first time, they had sent them back for more.

Hunt also revealed to Bennett some of the first, spasmodic steps of the cover-up, telling him, "The White House wants me to get out. . . . John Dean . . . will be in touch with you with some money for my wife." Hunt left the office and was home packing his bags when Bennett called him to relay a message just received from G. Gordon Liddy: "The powers that be . . . decided that he should stay put."

Shortly after those events, Bennett went to visit his father, Utah senator Wallace Bennett. The younger Bennett told his father he was convinced that Hunt, despite his denial, was involved in Watergate and that the White House, also despite its denials, was involved as well.

Then Howard Hunt's name hit the papers, and the press began paying heavy attention to Hunt's employer, Mullen & Co. Journalists repeatedly asked whether the company was connected with the CIA. Bennett repeatedly denied it. In the summer of 1972, Bennett had his first interview with the Justice Department officials prosecuting the Watergate burglars. He then decided to request a meeting with his CIA case officer:

> [A]fter I had my first interview with Mr. Earl Silbert, the prosecutor, and had handled the flood of press inquiries and had the specific inquiry about the CIA, which I denied, I felt that I ought to touch base with my case officer and tell him what was going on.
>
> I requested a meeting with Mr. [Martin J.] Lukoskie. We had lunch at the Marriott Hot Shoppes Cafeteria on H Street. I briefed him on what I had told the prosecutor and what I had told the newspapers also. . . . [W]hen I told him that I denied to the press that Mullen had any CIA ties, he expressed approval of that. He urged me to continue to take that posture.

And continue Bennett did. At the same time as he was endeavoring to fulfill his obligations to the CIA, he was in frequent touch with friends in the White House, warning them that the repeated denials of White House involvement in the burglary were untrue and would cause immense trouble for the White House in the long run. "I went to my friends in the White House," Bennett testified, to say, "You are lying. I don't think that you personally are lying, but I think the institution, if you will, is lying. Somebody is misleading the President. As a good Republican, I don't like this."

> I laid this whole thing out to the degree that I knew . . . [t]o Dick Cook and Tom Korologos, both of whom were

absolutely shocked. . . . I said, "I have told all this to the district attorney. I think if you don't temper your public statements pretty fast, you will have egg all over your faces when the trial comes out."

Bennett's friends at the White House countered with criticism of Bennett's friendliness towards the press:

> [A] very close friend . . . kept saying, "You are too accessible to the press. They come around. . . . They ask you questions and you answer them. You should not. You are helping to keep the story alive. If you shut up, the whole thing will die down and blow away."

Bennett explained to his White House friend why he could not just "shut up":

> I said, "I cannot shut up for two reasons. Number one is the Freedom of Information Act, because of the fact that Howard worked on the contract [that the firm had with the Department of Health, Education, and Welfare] and, number two, our firm has a relationship with the CIA. If the press gets the feeling that I have anything to hide, they are going to go over every inch of this firm with a fine tooth comb and discover the relationship to the detriment of the U.S. government. I do not want that to happen. I am perfectly willing to be personally misquoted (which I was) or misinterpreted. It is inevitable in this situation."

In other words, Bennett thought that protecting Mullen & Co.'s relationship with the CIA required two things—denying the relationship, certainly, but also remaining open enough with the press on other matters so that journalists would not suspect him of duplicity. Since he was in the public relations business, his credibility with the press was one of his stocks in trade.

It was not only Bennett's friends at the White House, however, who were leery of his methods of protecting his firm's CIA connection. The CIA itself ultimately began to question Bennett's strategy. In the spring of 1973, a senior CIA official met with Bennett to ask whether Bennett's many press contacts were necessary and beneficial. The CIA official, Bennett testified, "expressed great concern that the cover was going to be blown because of the press attention being paid to the Mullen company. I responded. I, at the time, said, 'I have gone through the most intense press scrutiny for the past year and a half and never once has the cover been blown.'"

Bennett then gave the CIA officer the particulars of his advantageous contacts with the press:

> [T]o impress the point upon him, I enumerated some of the more significant interviews to which I had been a party: "Bob Woodward of the *Washington Post* interviewed me at great length on . . . numerous occasions. I have told Woodward everything I know about the Watergate case, except the Mullen company's tie to the CIA. I never mentioned that to him. It has never appeared in any *Washington Post* story." I pointed this out to [the CIA official]. I said, "As a result, I am a good friend of Woodward." . . .
>
> I told him I considered myself a friend of Woodward; that as a result of our conversations, Woodward had some stories.

Congressman Nedzi asked Bennett, "Why did you feel compelled to tell Woodward everything that you knew about the Watergate matter?" Bennett replied that he was moved not only by a desire to protect his CIA relationship but by ethical concerns about Watergate:

> We were talking about moral scruples earlier, sir. I felt it was only through the press that the whole story could come out, having been rebuffed in an attempt to get the White House to do what I felt was the right thing, and seeing that the investigation of the District Attorney and the U.S. Attorney's Office would produce a conviction only of the seven burglars. I was satisfied there was far more to this; and, if it was going to come out, it would be because of continued pressure from the press. I had, quite frankly, what I assumed to be some of the same motivations.

The Nedzi hearings produced the picture of a man who seemed to possess the crucial Deep Throat characteristics. Bennett had the requisite relationships with the press. Through his connections with the CIA and the White House, especially Colson, he could have had access to the various types of information that Deep Throat possessed.

Moreover, Bennett, at the time of the Nedzi hearings, revealed an ambivalence about Watergate and the White House that seemed to match that of Deep Throat. Bennett, like Deep Throat, was repelled by the "switchblade mentality" of those who had taken over the White House.

True, Bennett's ambivalence was somewhat less pretty than that of most of the hypothetical Deep Throats. Bennett said that moral scruples had moved him to talk about Watergate to Woodward. In addition, however, there was the matter of Bennett's economic interests. The most obvious fact about Mullen & Co.'s relationship to the CIA was that if it were revealed, the CIA would have to discontinue it, along with the financial benefits it provided to the company. That is in fact what happened not long after Watergate, when the company's cover was finally blown.

This set of mixed motives made Bennett, to my mind, even more plausible as a Deep Throat candidate. When some writer claims that Deep Throat acted because he hated Richard Nixon's Vietnam policy, the alleged motivation is murky and uncertain. But when I thought of Deep Throat acting to keep the bread and butter coming, I had found a motivation I understood.

In addition, when I thought of Bennett as Deep Throat I remembered the one positive clue that Woodward had given me. The reason Deep Throat does not come forward even after all these years, Woodward said, is that his post-Watergate public persona is so different from the persona of Deep Throat.

There could not have been a Deep Throat candidate whom this description fit better than Robert F. Bennett. After Watergate, Bennett left Washington and made his fortune. In due course, he re-entered politics—this time electoral politics in his home state of Utah. Bennett, once an obscure public relations entrepreneur, succeeded his father as senator from Utah. The younger Senator Bennett is now a figure of considerable stature within the Senate.

Indeed, by the time I finished my Deep Throat hunt, the country as a whole was better acquainted with Bennett, because he had led the Republican side in the unsuccessful attempts to find a dignified compromise settlement in the impeachment of President Clinton.

You could hardly get more inconsistent with a garage-skulking Deep Throat than that.

Bennett even had the physique attributed to Deep Throat in *All the President's Men*. He is extremely tall. That would explain how he could, without thinking, place a message for Woodward on a garage ledge that Woodward could not reach. Finally, Bennett was the only Deep Throat candidate on record as admitting that he had provided Woodward with unacknowledged, off-the-record information. He had access, opportunity, and motivation. An evidentiary slamdunk.

At that point I did not stop to ask myself why, if everyone from the White House to the CIA knew that Bennett was talking with reporters, he had to resort to the parking garage. I did know, however, about one type of evidence that stood in the way of Bennett's being a perfect fit. Deep Throat, as portrayed in *All the President's Men*, was a chain smoker and Scotch drinker, possessor of a gift of gab and the temperament to be the self-appointed scourge of the White House tricksters and knife-wielders. Bennett, by contrast, was a living smoke- and booze-free zone—no less than an elder of the Mormon church, which condones use of neither tobacco nor alcohol—and, at the time of Watergate, despite his moral scruples, a coolly disciplined political operator happily working with the redoubtable Chuck Colson.

At first I speculated that in his younger years Bennett was more relaxed than he would later become about the strictures of his religious faith. The evidence weighed against that explanation, though. Bennett's testimony to the Nedzi committee showed him to be active in the Mormon church then as now.

When young Tom Gregory, also a Mormon, spoke to Bennett about his ethical problems with Howard Hunt's directives, Gregory addressed Bennett as "Brother Bennett." One of the significant exchanges between Gregory and Bennett took place at a gathering of church members at Bennett's home.

I could not let these small details stand in the way of an otherwise ingenious discovery. I concluded that smoking and drinking were two pieces of camouflage that Woodward and Bernstein had draped over Deep Throat in *All The President's Men* to draw attention away from the real characteristics of their source.

My wife did not like this logic. She said it violated my working hypothesis that Woodward and Bernstein, in describing Deep Throat, were telling the truth. But everything else about the Bennett candidacy was so perfect that I set aside this objection, too.

I wondered why the Bennett testimony, once declassified, had not been enough to settle the question of Deep Throat's identity once and for all. If Bennett was not literally Deep Throat, in my view at the time, he was the closest that any candidate would ever come. Bennett knew immediately about the Watergate break-in; he knew as well about the White House connections to the event, both before and after the fact. Bennett also had a powerful motive for playing the "source" card with the press: He was anxious to safeguard the existence and economic well-being of his company by protecting the secrecy of its relationship with the CIA. He had confirmed under oath that he had preserved this secret by disclosing to Woodward "everything" he knew about Watergate—which was, at the time, just about all there was to know.

My beliefs about Bennett were rapidly approaching certainty. I resolved to write a book. I acquired a serious agent, Ron Goldfarb, selling him on the idea of Bennett as Deep Throat. Ron in turn sold a publisher, Don Fehr of Basic Books. The three of us met in the Mayflower Hotel in Washington, D.C., to discuss the project. I described it with trial-lawyer force.

I started to see everything as fitting the theory. I ran into Tom Korologos, now a Washington lobbyist of great and deserved success, at a retirement dinner for General George Joulwan, head of NATO. During Watergate, Joulwan was Al Haig's military aide. As such, Joulwan was the man who saved me from physical harm on that evening when Haig and I nearly started pummeling each other. At the dinner, I told Korologos I was going to write about Deep Throat. He gripped my arm tightly, saying that my first book, *Crazy Rhythm*, had been a critical success and I should leave it at that. (Sensible as always.) I took his comment to mean that Korologos, Bennett's friend, was protecting him.

Similarly, I noted that Mullen & Co.'s chief client, apart from the CIA, was Howard Hughes. Hughes had once been Larry O'Brien's client, but O'Brien was discharged when he lost the confidence of Hughes's Mormon lieutenants. Bennett succeeded to the Hughes account. Here was more grist for the conspiratorial mill.

I ratcheted up my buttonholing of people who might have information or informed opinions about Deep Throat. I should have been more embarrassed to be bothering serious people about this hobby horse of mine so many years after Watergate; but I found that once I explained the subject of my inquiry, nobody said no to my invitation to talk. Maybe it was just that for those who had lived through the crisis of Watergate, the opportunity to revisit the scene of so much political excitement and human mystery was irresistible. The Nixon years, after all, were not merely disruptive; they were also among the most absorbing in living memory. Of the people I asked to talk with me, the losers as well as the winners, it is a safe bet that not many had had so much political fun in their lives before Watergate or since.

In addition, many of them shared my puzzlement about why this particular mystery continued to excite curiosity, even among people for whom politics in general was no longer a matter of any great interest. Some of them, again like me, were fascinated by the persistence of Deep Throat as a mystery in a community devoted to uncovering and demystifying mysteries. And they suspected or at least sensed that identifying Deep Throat would answer some important questions about the kaleidoscope of contradictions that was Richard Nixon.

Whatever it was, they sat with me and weighed my theories and questions soberly and seriously. Almost everyone added at least a grain of information and insight, even if only by telling me what I had gotten wrong or where I was wishing facts into existence. Moreover, the interest of these individuals, each with decades of experience in the heart of Washington's political darkness, fed my desire to believe that what I was doing made sense. They reinforced my determination to go on.

In most of these conversations, the main topic was my theory about Robert F. Bennett—his access to the relevant facts, his meetings with Woodward, his concrete and undeniable motive for providing Woodward with Watergate information, and the massive evidence of his long-ago testimony to the Nedzi committee. My luncheon, dinner, and drink companions did a lot of nodding and exclaiming in interest or astonishment. Only later did I realize that most of them had not given me anything like a clear statement of agreement.

My old friend Bill Safire was more forthcoming than most. Upon leaving the White House, he had become, as every politically sentient being and lover of language knows, a columnist for the *New York Times*. As such, he had spent more than twenty years becoming an unequaled judge of political evidence. He listened patiently while I presented, as straight and spin-free as I could, a summary of the evidence supporting my conclusion that Bennett was Deep Throat.

"Interesting and persuasive," Safire said when I had finished. "Is anything missing?" I asked the lawyer's catch-all question. "Yes. A confession," he said.

I do not think Bill meant that a literal confession was necessary; after a quarter century, one could hardly expect Deep Throat to come out with his hands up. What was needed, however, was something conclusive, the thing that would make any knowledgeable reader shout "Aha!" (Or words to that effect.)

I did not have that talisman of persuasiveness. I needed a clincher—at least a functional equivalent to Safire's desired confession, an intuitively obvious fit between a real-life candidate and the mythical Deep Throat.

Tom Korologos set up a breakfast meeting for me with the younger Senator Bennett in the Senate dining room. There Bennett treated me to a charming filibuster. He gave me his life story, then told me about Nixon's favorite Deep Throat candidate, the aforementioned Haldeman assistant Noble

Mellenkamp. Bennett denied being Deep Throat. He said that when he left Washington in the late 1970s, he was desperate for money. If he had been Deep Throat, he said, he would have cashed in.

I was about to start my cross-examination. I intended to ask him something relevant like, "When did you first meet Bob Woodward?" But at just that moment, Senator Bennett said he had to excuse himself. He was due to speak to a convention of urologists.

I did not have my clincher.

In this unsatisfactory situation I began to write. On the one hand, I could not make a book on Deep Throat out of a wishy-washy conclusion that he was only one voice in a chorus of informational sources; everybody already knew that Woodward and Bernstein had more than one source for their Watergate reporting.

On the other hand, I couldn't put all my eggs in the Bennett basket. There were some troubling facts that kept nagging at me. For instance, *All the President's Men* noted that Bennett, as part of his political activities, had helped organize a hundred dummy campaign committees to funnel millions of dollars in secret contributions to the president's re-election campaign. Bennett later testified to the Nedzi committee that he thought White House campaign activities transgressed the limits of acceptable campaign behavior. Did that mean Deep Throat thought the dummy campaign committees *were* acceptable campaign behavior?

So I would have to marshall the case for Bennett while continuing to explore other alternatives. For instance, I had not yet fully given up on the idea that Deep Throat might be my friend David Gergen, despite the apparent sincerity of his denials.

This absence of certainty and the pursuit of more than one thesis at the same time made for a very bad way to write a book.

I did get some cheering pieces of support. During the Clinton impeachment, I—along with every other political figure in Washington who was not himself or herself under suspicion—appeared on various talk shows. As a result of one such appearance, I got a friendly and impressive letter from a young lawyer named Tom Liddy, who was then deputy counsel to the Republican National Committee. The name, not surprisingly, rang a bell. One thing led to another. Before long, I was dining with G. Gordon Liddy himself. Liddy has been one of the truth-tellers among the Watergate survivors—both in his book, *Will*, and on the radio talk show of which he is now host. At dinner, I presented him with my theory about Robert F. Bennett as Deep Throat.

I remember the candlelight in the quiet French restaurant shining off Gordon's totally bald, shaved head. I also remember the waiters hovering around a man who had become a genuine celebrity. This was one of the strange legacies of Watergate. Liddy went to prison for a substantial amount of time, both because of his involvement in the Watergate burglary and because he refused to tell prosecutors what he knew. In other words, his life was shattered. Even more, because he did not adopt an attitude of remorse, he remained, for those who viewed Watergate as a battle between good and evil, the embodiment of the latter.

Time and character, however, had worked an immense and quite unpredictable change. As the moral certainties that once surrounded Watergate faded and became indistinct around the edges, both prosecutors and prosecuted in Watergate eventually came to share the same aura of historic importance. Some men who had played central roles in the cover-up came to seem larger figures, and hence more worthy of celebrity treatment, than those who had agonized, temporized, and cooperated with prosecutors.

Liddy, a colorful figure to begin with and one who bore his troubles with fortitude, was one of those who had undergone the magic transformation in the mind of much of the public. And, a very smart man, he knew how to use the opportunity he had made for himself.

After the dinner, I wrote Liddy a note thanking him for his time and attention. He wrote in return, "I do believe you have solved the Deep Throat riddle." I now think he was being kind. At the time, however, I felt confirmed.

I kept writing about the Bennett thesis and scurrying around investigating other possibilities. My literary output consisted of a seemingly infinite number of alternative outlines and introductions for the book. Such was the state of the work when I received a phone call in the winter of 1998 from Mike Levitas, a former op-ed page editor at the *New York Times* who is the current impresario of special events for the Century Association. The Century is an old private club in New York City, roughly the counterpart of the Cosmos Club in Washington. The Century counts among its members large numbers of artists, writers, and people in the industries associated with such activities.

Levitas asked whether I would deliver a speech at one of the club's monthly black-tie dinners. It could be on any subject—serious, whimsical, whatever—as long was it was interesting, funny, or, even better, both.

Sure, I said, agreeing to a date in February, which seemed

approximately as distant as the millennium after this one. I promptly forgot about the whole thing. A few weeks later, the conscientious Levitas called again. They were making up the program for the Century dinner at which I was to speak. How should they describe the talk I was going to give? Typically, I suggested the first smart-ass thing that popped into my Deep Throat–cluttered brain: "How I Spent My Summer Searching for Deep Throat."

I forgot all about it once again. Then, the week before the big event, Ray Price, a veteran Century Association member and a thoughtful friend, called to deliver a warning, which I recall: "This is a very tough crowd. They do not dress in black tie in the middle of the week for nothing. They come to be entertained."

I went to work, trying to patch together pieces of my Deep Throat research into an outline for a talk. In doing so, I ran smack up against the problem—though I did not realize it until too late—whose head I had been trying for months to shove permanently under water. To make the talk interesting, I had to provide lots of plot and titillating detail. But I could not come to any particular point. Even if I had been certain of a conclusion, it would hardly have done to scoop my own book in a talk to the Century Association. Besides, I didn't have a conclusion to reveal.

I thought rather vaguely that I would entertain the crowd by rambling through the various Deep Throat alternatives. Perhaps I would focus on the Watergate involvement, uncertain but suitably brooding, of the Central Intelligence Agency. Surely that would be midwinter catnip for a bunch of Centurions. I would improvise (still the jazz saxophonist at the age of seventy-plus). How bad could I be?

Well, very.

I received word that there was going to be a sell-out crowd for my Deep Throat talk. I remember thinking how nice it was that people were still interested in Deep Throat after all these years. But it wasn't until I actually arrived at the Century Association that the full import of this fact fell upon me like a mountain. By Century standards, the black-tied crowd was huge, spilling out beyond the dining room. And, since it was the Century, the audience was largely composed of "show-me" types. There they all were, the literati and media establishment of New York. I started picking them out—there was Mike Wallace, there was Andy Rooney, there were assembled editors from the *New York Times* and the *New Yorker*. There at another table were friends of mine who were associated with Yaddo, a writers' colony with which I have been associated.

Then I stopped picking, lest the exercise make me even more terrified than I already was. Yes indeed, people were still interested in Deep Throat, which meant that if I didn't deliver something substantive to this crowd, the members were going to be as cheerful as a Doberman that's arrived at his bowl for dinner and found it empty.

Wallace stopped by to say hello. "Nothing else would get us out in the middle of the week, Len, so make it good," he said in a cheery way that chilled my blood.

Realizing what trouble I was in did not, for once, make my brain work more inventively. As I canvassed the circuits for things I knew that I could offer to the discerning crowd, I came up with exactly zero. They say that when wild animals are cornered by their predators and about to be killed, they are overcome by a final, fatal moment of calm; I now knew exactly how they felt. This was the first moment, I think, when I began to get a sense of just how insubstantial and unconvincing was the work I had done up to that point on the Deep Throat saga.

Then things began to get worse. The main course ended, and it was time for the slaughter. The president began with a long, dutiful talk about club business. I was reminded of Robert Benchley's description of a similar speech: "A group under Harry Nietzsche's direction will be discussing the sex life of wallpaper in the small Marcel Proust dining room on the second floor. . . ."

Then the president introduced me to a crowd that was by now halfway to their next day's hangover. I had sent him a bio, padded in the usual way by my law firm's PR consultants, to help him in writing the introduction. He read it word for dreary, mortifying word.

I rose to speak. This was the proverbial nightmare of standing up before a waiting audience and having absolutely nothing to say, except it was a little worse. I looked around for help and instead saw, in the front row, two distinguished Centurions with their chins on their chests, already asleep. I began by telling the audience that those two gentlemen were probably the smart ones. The remark did not bespeak much confidence. The audience began to squirm. The celebratory mood was turning nasty.

From there on it got much, much worse. I heard words emerging from my mouth—but they were slow, syrupy, and wholly distant from me, like a record winding down on an old-fashioned phonograph. The horror was punctuated by my catching sight, every so often, of one of my friends, sitting in the audience with—I thought—an anguished, open-mouthed look on his face.

Afterwards, I returned to spent the night at the apartment of my friend Richard Ravitch, the most competent of attorneys and public servants, who had attended the speech. I was shaken beyond the help of booze. I talked to Dick, pouring out my anguish, hoping without hope for some reassurance. I finished. He said, "Well, it's over."

It was. I had spent several years driving myself and everyone around me crazy with the hunt for Deep Throat. After all that time, I had come up with nothing that met my own standards of evidence and nothing that I felt confident in offering to others.

I was not simply back at square one; I was at square minus ten.

5

Deep Throat

Convinced that my obsessive hobby had come to nothing, I fell into deep authorial funk. Work on the book came to a halt. One advantage of such depression, however, is that it compels you to reexamine the basic premises of your enterprise. In my case, the yawning hole where my confidence had once been forced me to think again about the characteristics of Deep Throat.

The Deep Throat of *All the President's Men* was clearly real. His unusual combination of traits did not have the sound of a literary fiction—or at least not the type of fiction one would have expected from Woodward and Bernstein. While the two of them were ingenious journalists, it would have taken not a journalist but a modern Conrad to create a persuasively living and breathing character like Deep Throat. The patent reality of Deep Throat was, in fact, precisely the reason for the power of his political and social symbolism and for the durability of public interest in the mystery of his true-life identity.

So I went through the descriptive clues in the book. Deep Throat was an old friend of Woodward's. He was someone with whom Woodward had spent many evenings, long before Watergate, talking about Washington, government, and power. Woodward had seen him drunk and rowdy. Their friendship was genuine, not cultivated. And Deep Throat had been a source for Woodward in the past, before Watergate.

This combination of characteristics meant that Deep Throat was almost certainly not far from Woodward in age. It also meant that Deep Throat was a person capable of forming a friendship with a reporter, despite the fact that he told Woodward he did not approve of American journalism.

Deep Throat was not an optimistic idealist. On the contrary, he was, as the book described him, a man "whose fight had been worn out in too many battles." And in some ways, he had the temperament one would expect of a political operative. He was, as he conceded, an "incurable gossip." He smoked incessantly and "could be rowdy, drink too much, overreach."

Yet in other ways, Deep Throat was not a typical politician. He had a sense of politics that extended beyond the partisan and manipulative. That was why he so intensely disliked the people in the White House who displayed the "switchblade mentality." In addition, as the book described him, "He knew too much literature too well" and "let the allurements of the past turn him away from his instincts." Deep Throat displayed considerable literary gifts when talking about the people and activities around the White House. In this sense, too, he clothed politics with a kind of poetry.

Finally, unlike most political operatives, Deep Throat was "not good at concealing his feelings."

All the President's Men did not—could not—specify just how much of a Nixon insider Deep Throat was. On the contrary, the book was notably vague in describing the man's position in the political world. It said merely that Deep Throat worked in the executive branch, apparently narrowing the field to some 2 million executive branch employees plus contractors, consultants, and even more tenuously connected individuals.

Other passages in the book, however, made clear that Deep Throat had far more knowledge than an ordinary bureaucrat or even political appointee. The book said Deep Throat had sources of information in the White House, the Justice Department, the FBI, and the Committee for the Re-election of the President (CRP). The book further described Deep Throat as being "in a unique position to observe" the functioning of the executive branch. Yet again, the book emphasized the unique nature of Deep Throat's knowledge: "What he knew represented an aggregate of hard information flowing in and out of many stations."

This aggregated information did not give Deep Throat any particular expertise in the mechanics of the Watergate investigation itself. On the contrary, it was when talking about these mechanics that Deep Throat was most likely to make mistakes.

By contrast, the quality of Deep Throat's information about the White House made clear that he had long, close relationships with Nixon, Haldeman, Ehrlichman, and their personal assistants. When Deep Throat described the White House players involved in the political dirty tricks operations and the Watergate cover-up, he was—I can personally attest—both accurate and psychologically acute. He memorably characterized not only Nixon and Mitchell but Colson, Haldeman, and other senior White House staffers. He described their relationships with one another, their attitudes about power and politics, and even (this was the clincher) the manner in which Nixon spoke during the climactic, tantrum-filled White House meetings about Watergate.

I knew that these pieces of information and analysis could not be whispers from the mouth of an investigator located in the FBI, no matter how high the level. Nor were they murmurs from an official who came by his information simply from access to wiretaps or moles. Deep Throat's information was much richer than what such sources could reveal.

Deep Throat was, in other words, not just some lower-level individual who happened to observe wrongdoing in high places or even a senior official observing events from the vantage of a single agency. He was a wide-ranging, high-stakes participant acting with unusual boldness in a dangerous political war.

I reminded myself that even if Woodward and Bernstein were not making things up deliberately, not every detail about Deep Throat in *All the President's Men* was necessarily correct. The reporters could have been simply mistaken in some of their information about their source.

In addition, it was possible that some Deep Throat identifiers were deliberately designed to mislead. But if it turned out, when Deep Throat's identity was finally revealed, that the picture in the book distorted the real-life Deep Throat too badly, the character in the book would seem like a hoax. And Woodward and Bernstein could not be sure about just when the day of reckoning would arrive.

I thought there would be a sliding scale for judging such false clues, a scale whose components Woodward and Bernstein knew as well as I did. For instance, if it turned out that the real Deep Throat did not smoke or drink but resembled the book's Deep Throat in other material respects, Woodward and Bernstein would probably be forgiven (though not by me). At the other end, if it turned out that the political position occupied by the real-life Deep Throat was fundamentally different from the one in the book, people who cared at all about the Deep Throat puzzle would feel scammed. The two *Post* reporters would be the main targets of the resulting fury.

Some facts—the elaborate system of signals for arranging meetings, for instance, or the shadow-shrouded garages—were probably in the middle. If they proved untrue, they would occasion cries of foul; but, as long as there were not too many of them, they would not brand Woodward and Bernstein as charlatans.

In other words, there were limits to the extent to which any rational journalists in Woodward and Bernstein's position would have tampered with the facts.

Next I reviewed Bob Woodward's early career for clues to where he and Deep Throat might have met and befriended one another.

In 1972, when the Watergate break-in occurred, Woodward may have been merely a cub reporter at the *Washington Post*. But he had graduated from Yale, where he studied literature and history. He was also a veteran of the U.S. intelligence services. He had served aboard a "floating Pentagon," a ship entrusted with the safeguarding of secret, high-level communications in event of war, and then on a guided missile frigate using experimental equipment to intercept and decode enemy communications in Vietnam. In Washington, he served as an assistant to Admiral Thomas H. Moorer, then chief of Naval Operations and later chairman of the Joint Chiefs of Staff during the Nixon years. Woodward's positions were low-level but high-access. He had the opportunity to learn a considerable amount about intelligence, its techniques and practitioners, and the habits and practices of the high-ranking military and civilian officials he briefed in Washington. The particular things he learned were not, I thought, important. Instead, what mattered was the general education in politics that Woodward's position had given him.

Finally, when Woodward left the Navy to enter journalism in 1970, he did so at a time when it was rising in influence and prestige. Woodward was smart, sophisticated, disciplined, and career-minded enough to make use of the opportunities this change presented. He was in a position, by background and employment, to become a member of Washington's new generation of the best and the brightest. He knew other members of this generation. They were his colleagues, his friends, and, when opportunity presented itself, his sources. One of them was Deep Throat.

OK, I told myself, I had reviewed the basics. The problem with the combination of characteristics that Woodward and Bernstein described in *All the President's Men* is that they simply did not add up to any identifiable human being. The jigsaw puzzle always had an ear, an eyebrow, or a nose missing. In each case an act of aesthetic faith was required to explain the discrepancies and distortions. Each time, I was looking at a Picasso (interesting enough in other circumstances), not a Norman Rockwell (preferable for present purposes).

At this point, the fact that I had been with Nixon from the beginning, and personally knew almost all the individuals who could be a credible Deep Throat, made my job more difficult. I knew that among the Deep Throat candidates who were in government at the time Deep Throat talked to Woodward, not one had a foot that could be squeezed into the glass slipper. I was doggedly confident that Woodward, Bernstein, and their editor, Ben Bradlee—Bradlee most of all—would not have put themselves and the *Washington Post* out on a long limb for a gimmick that would eventually be revealed and denounced as a journalistic fraud of historic proportions. But every possible Deep Throat suffered from major discrepancies of voice, venue, style, motive, and character.

Indeed, it was now clear to me, the major reason why I had soldiered on for so long with the Deep Throat candidacy of Robert F. Bennett was that I did not know him as well as I knew the others. Therefore I did not have the personal familiarity with his style and temperament that would have forced me, much earlier, to say to myself, "Oh, come *on*."

I had—still have—not one but two heavily annotated copies of *All the President's Men*, both of them thoroughly thumbed, eyeworn, and battered. (The paperback edition is in slightly worse shape, because I accidentally dropped it into the bathtub. Despite days of careful drying-out, the pages emerged wrinkled like papyrus, my pen-and-ink comments in the margins faded to pale blue. But I kept using it. Thus when it eventually makes its way into the Smithsonian's National Museum of American History, you will be able to see the pre-bath and post-bath comments differentiated by ink colors, akin to carbon dating.)

In the depths of my literary hopelessness, I kept going through the text, line by line, trying to transform Deep Throat from a collection of inconclusive theories into a real, recognizable human being. I once described this repetitive, seemingly fruitless process to my friend Leon Wieseltier, literary editor of the *New Republic* and author of a book, *Kaddish*, that explores the meaning of the ritual prayer that Jews say day after day for a year after the death of a close relative. Wieseltier informed me that my obsessive pursuit of a secret hidden in a text was not crazy—or at least not idiosyncratically so. He said that students of the Talmud, commentaries on the Old Testament, "would read and re-read the exceedingly small print until they solved the textual riddle—because they had to."

Well, my obsession had less divine sources and ends than those of the ancient Talmudists, but it kept me going.

In addition to forcing a reexamination of fundamentals, another advantage of depression is that you cannot concentrate on whatever it is that you are supposed to be writing and will do or read anything not directly related to the task at hand as a means of distraction and escape. One day in the fall of 1999, my collaborator Ross Davies sent me some articles from recent issues of the magazine *Brill's Content*, a fine publication that regularly skewers journalism's famous and not-so-famous. I read the articles.

The topic of these pieces was Woodward's new book, *Shadow: Five Presidents and the Legacy of Watergate*. The irony in this endeavor of Woodward's is for another time; what was relevant here was the discussion in the book of the Clinton scandals. In this discussion, Woodward made use of anonymous sources. In the September, 1999 issue of *Content*, the eponymous Steve Brill wrote a critique of Woodward's use of such unnamed sources. In the November issue, Woodward replied—and Brill, of course, answered Woodward.

The two writers waged an arcane war of words that became increasingly heated and grew intensely personalized as it wound its way through arguments, rebuttals, and sur-rebuttals right down to the final grunts of "so's your old man" at the end.

The sharpness of the exchange was not surprising. Woodward is viewed as the founder and preeminent exemplar of modern American investigative journalism. Brill is less well known but occupies a similarly lofty position in the press firmament. Brill first achieved journalistic fame as founder of *The American Lawyer*, which has become the American legal profession's major magazine of news and critical commentary. He then founded Court TV, a network through which Americans, for better or worse, can now watch marathon sessions of our real-life justice system at work. Tiring of these enterprises, Brill sold them and went on to found *Brill's Content*, designed to do for—and to—journalism what *The American Lawyer* did for attorneys.

In addition to comparable standing, the two men have similar areas of professional expertise. Both writers deal with large issues of substance and process in politics, law, and journalism, very much including the way in which language is used by participants in all these fields.

Brill's first article about *Shadow* noted that a journalist must balance conflicting obligations. His or her primary obligation is to get the historical facts right, or at least as right as imprecisions of language, memory, and self-interest permit. The journalist must also protect confidential sources, even to the extent of risking imprisonment. Finally, the journalist must create a narrative structure that enhances reader interest and comprehension. As one famed editor put it, "The first obligation of a journalist is to be read."

Brill's article—written after many interviews, including one with Woodward—argued that Woodward had struck the wrong balance, overemphasizing readability and failing in his primary duty to get the facts right.

Brill's principal example was a conversation reported in *Shadow* between President Clinton and Bob Bennett (no relation to Senator Robert F. Bennett), the attorney who defended the president in the sexual harassment suit brought against him by Paula Jones. What Woodward knew or thought he knew, said Brill,

> . . . was that Robert Bennett, President Clinton's lawyer in the Paula Jones case, had told some friends and reporters (off the record) that Clinton had told Bennett that he'd long since sworn off chasing women.
>
> What Woodward also knew from several White House reporters was that Bennett and the president had, on occasion, been seen strolling the White House grounds talking quietly, each with a cigar in hand.

In *Shadow*, according to Brill, Woodward transformed these facts into a dramatic scene in which the president announced his new chastity to Bennett while the two men walked the White House grounds with their cigars. "[I]t probably happened like that," Brill had Woodward saying to himself. Since all of Woodward's sources in this incident were clothed in anonymity, said Brill, Woodward was in effect demanding that readers take his account on faith. As Brill characterized Woodward's position,

> You have to believe me about my sources; you have to trust my assessment of the sources' reliability; and you have to trust that my instinct for filling in the information gaps isn't overwhelmed by my desire to give you . . . drama, let alone that my quest for drama hasn't led me to ignore facts that don't fit.

Brill's primary piece of evidence for these charges was an interview he had done with Bennett. This interview included, Brill said, "Bennett's denial to me that he ever had the conversation Woodward recounts during one of those cigar strolls."

Woodward wrote a reply. "I do not disclose the source for the scene in the book," Woodward said, "because these were the ground rules with the source."

More important, Woodward said, Brill had mischaracterized Bennett's denial. Here is how Woodward said he knew this: Brill had interviewed Woodward for his critique. Woodward taped the interview. In the interview, Brill told Woodward that Bennett had denied Woodward's story. Woodward then asked Brill what Bennett had actually said. According to Woodward's tape, Brill replied that Bennett had told him, "It is true they went for a stroll on the White House grounds. It is true that they walked around with cigars. It is not true that that conversation happened during one of those strolls."

In fact, Brill actually said in the same taped interview with Woodward, "Bennett indicated that the conversation took place elsewhere."

So, Woodward argued, the version of Bennett's denial that Brill gave to Woodward in the interview was quite different from the version of Bennett's denial that Brill printed in his critique of *Shadow*. In the interview, Brill had Bennett denying only that the conversation took place during a stroll around the White House. But in the version of Bennett's denial printed in *Content*, Brill made it seem as if Bennett had denied the conversation's having taken place at all.

Woodward summed up his answer to Brill thus: "[A]t most Bennett . . . seems to be denying not the quote or interchange but the venue in which it took place."

There were other examples of this type of journalistic dispute between Brill and Woodward. One of Monica Lewinsky's lawyers, Woodward reported in *Shadow*, worried that Lewinsky might be suffering from "Clara Bow syndrome," a type of female erotomania. Brill contacted the Lewinsky lawyer, named Sydney Hoffmann, who was quoted by Woodward. Hoffmann, wrote Brill in his *Content* article, maintained that the quote was "pure fiction."

In his response to Brill, Woodward explained how the quote in *Shadow* had come about. Hoffmann had worried to Woodward that her client, Lewinsky, might have "Clérambault's syndrome," a name given by the French psychiatrist G. G. de Clérambault to obsessive sexual feelings by a woman towards a man in a position of power. Woodward continued his answer to Brill by quoting from the conservative magazine *The Weekly Standard*, which had commented on the Brill-Woodward flap:

> "In flat, unaccented English—but for the barely vocalized 'm' between its second and third syllables—'Clérambault's syndrome' is, phonically, 'Clara Bow syndrome.'"

So in *Shadow* Woodward had rendered "Clérambault's syndrome" phonically rather than literally. "The substance of the [quote]," Woodward concluded in his *Brill's Content* response, "is correct. . . . It is thus misleading for Hoffmann to create the impression that the substance of the paragraph is false."

What struck me about these exchanges was the literalness, if not always the precision, of Woodward's use of language and how he could deploy fine gradations of style to protect a source. What Woodward wrote had a concrete basis in reality, but it might not always be the basis that a natural reading of his language would suggest.

After reading the exchanges between Woodward and Brill, I returned to my obsessive rereading of the text of *All the President's Men*. In particular, I reread the references not only to Deep Throat but to all of Woodward and Bernstein's anonymous sources. The references were easy to find; they were already marked in pale-blue pre-bath ink.

First there was the statement that on June 19, the Monday after the Watergate arrests, Woodward phoned an "old friend and sometimes source who worked for the federal government." Later that day, Woodward made another call to this same "government friend" for advice about the address books listing Howard Hunt's name and about an unmailed check belonging to Hunt, all of which had been found by police in the possession of the Watergate burglars.

Sometime later, *All the President's Men* formally introduced Deep Throat as a "source" of Woodward's "in the Executive Branch who had access to information at CRP as well as at the White House." Deep Throat's "identity," the book said, "was unknown to anyone else. He could be contacted only on very important occasions. . . . Their discussions would be only to confirm information that had been obtained elsewhere and to add some perspective." The book next disclosed that Deep Throat's position in the executive branch "was extremely sensitive. He had never told Woodward anything that was incorrect."

It was Deep Throat, the book continued,

> who had advised Woodward on June 19 that Howard Hunt was definitely involved in Watergate. During the summer, he had told Woodward that the FBI badly wanted to know where the *Post* was getting its information. . . . [T]he White House, he had said at the last meeting, regarded the stakes in Watergate as much higher than anyone outside perceived. Even the FBI did not understand what was happening.

The next set of clues referred to the time when the indictments in the Watergate burglary were handed down and turned out to include only the five burglars, Liddy, and Hunt. Woodward read Deep Throat the draft of a news story asserting that "federal investigators had received information from Nixon campaign workers that high officials of the Committee for the Re-election of the President had been involved in the funding of the Watergate operation. 'Too soft,' Deep Throat said. 'You can go much stronger.'" The money in the re-election committee's safe, he said with emphasis, had financed not only the Watergate bugging but "*other intelligence-gathering activities.*" John Mitchell's top assistants did not have exclusive control of the funds; they were only "*among those*" with such control.

Meanwhile, as *All the President's Men* informed its readers, Woodward was not the only member of the reporting duo with anonymous sources. Bernstein had his own contacts.

One of them was "a former official of the Nixon administration" whom Bernstein occasionally called on for information and insights about the "inner workings of the White House, of which Bernstein and Woodward were almost totally ignorant." This source, the book said, "maintained extensive contacts with his former colleagues."

On June 21, shortly after the Watergate arrests, Bernstein called his source for some biographical data about Chuck Colson. The man gave Bernstein more than that, saying,

"Whoever was responsible for the Watergate break-in would have to be somebody who doesn't know about politics but thought he did. I suppose that's why Colson's name comes up. . . . Anybody who knew anything wouldn't be looking over there for real political information. They'd be looking for something else . . . scandal, gossip."

Was it possible, Bernstein asked, that the White House could have sponsored such a stupid mission? The former official responded, "I know the president well enough to know if he needed something like this done it certainly wouldn't be a shoddy job." But it was not inconceivable, he went on, that the president would want his campaign aides to have every available piece of political intelligence and gossip. For instance, the source remembered a White House political consultant who "was always talking about walkie-talkies. You would talk about politics and he would talk about devices. There was always a great preoccupation at the White House with all this intelligence nonsense. Some of those people are dumb enough to think there would be something there."

Bernstein pursued the topic: Could Robert Odle, the young director of administration at CRP, have been the individual who had decided to hire former CIA operative James McCord as the Committee's security director? "'That's bullshit,' the former official replied. 'Mitchell wouldn't let go of a decision like that.'" One man who would certainly have been involved in hiring McCord was Mitchell's right-hand man, Fred LaRue. "[I]f any wiretaps were active up to the time of the break-in," the source said, "LaRue would have known about them."

The former government official had one final piece of information for Bernstein. He told the reporter that Murray Chotiner, Nixon's old friend and long-time political adviser from California days, was still in the business of politics. In fact, Chotiner had been put in charge of a ballot security program to prevent any theft of votes of the type that Democrats had engineered in the 1960 presidential election.

The information was authoritative, the voice that of a highly inside insider. In pre-bath pale-blue ink I had made a note of the man whose voice I recognized: "Sears."

Later in the book, Bernstein was once more on the phone with the "former administration official," who told him, "The White House is absolutely paranoid about [Senator Edward M.] Kennedy." Nixon, Haldeman, and Colson were "'obsessed' with the idea of obtaining information that could damage a Kennedy candidacy." In the margin of the book I had again noted, pre-bath, "Sears."

In another one of Bernstein's regular calls to the former administration official, the official told Bernstein that there was a large fund at CRP over which Gordon Liddy had supervisory authority: "Yeah, it's the same one," he said, as the fund that had financed the Watergate burglars. Then the former official predicted the strategy that CRP would follow in explaining the fund:

> "The present plan is for Liddy to take the fall for everyone. The story that the re-election committee will put out has nothing to do with the truth. They'll say they were deeply concerned for the security of their convention and that they had a big fund to be sure they were secure from interference. That's the word that will trickle out. Mitchell said to get the story out."

The Committee would not deny the existence of the fund altogether, said the former official: "Too many guys knew about the fund" to make that possible.

Bernstein's source was wrong about the mechanics of Liddy's relationship to the fund: Liddy did not supervise it but only received money from it. Deep Throat was right, however, about the larger and more critical issue of what the cover-up strategy would be and what reasoning lay behind it. My marginal note said, "Sears. Wrong?" Then, in post-bath ink this time, "No—correct."

Several days after this conversation, the book reported, Nixon campaign director Clark MacGregor held a press conference in which he said what Bernstein's source had predicted he would say. MacGregor expressed concern for the security of the Republican convention, said resources had been earmarked to promote such security, and told of Liddy's expenditure of the earmarked resources on his own initiative with the aim of protecting the presidential re-election effort from an attack by "crazies" at the convention.

It was clear to me that the former administration official giving Bernstein not only accurate but prescient information was John Sears. Sears had information from his friends who remained in the White House. Sears also had information from CRP. Thus I was fairly certain that Sears, after he left the White House, played almost as important a role in the reporters' Watergate coverage through his conversations with Bernstein as Deep Throat played by talking with Woodward.

Interspersed with the marked passages in the book that referred to the reporters' unnamed sources were similarly marked passages that referred to the housekeeping details of Woodward and Bernstein's investigative methods. The two reporters were classic shoe-leather, as opposed to thumb-sucking, journalists. They relied on method rather than inspiration.

For instance, the reporters "threw nothing out and kept all their notes and the early drafts of stories." These documents came to fill multiple filing cabinets. Thus it would be difficult for critics to contend, after stories appeared, that Woodward and Bernstein had invented or tampered with sources and facts. A decade after Watergate, I had a dispute with Woodward about a conversation we had held years before. He produced his old notes, as impressively detailed and accurate as one would wish of a journalist. And he was right.

In another methodical decision, each reporter kept his own separate list of sources he considered confidential, eventually running into the hundreds of names, with telephone numbers called and re-called. They maintained these separate lists and pursued their leads independently because they thought their confidential sources would feel more comfortable that way. The relationships would be more personal and seem less risky.

Woodward and Bernstein preferred this arrangement even though it sometimes led to duplication of effort. As the book reported, the two reporters, not surprisingly, crossed one another's tracks from time to time, as each of them made a separate approach to the same source.

I went over these details for the thousandth time. Once again I heard the voice of Bernstein's former administration official, which I recognized with certainty as the voice of my former protégé John Sears. Once again I heard the voice of Deep Throat—and realized that it was identical to the voice of Bernstein's former administration official. I had always assumed that if Bernstein's source was Sears, then Deep Throat must be someone else. But the two reporters' compartmentalized system of calling and record-keeping made it quite possible that the two sources were one and the same.

That possibility ran up against a large empirical stumbling block. Bernstein's source was a former administration official. Woodward's source, by contrast, was in the federal government, in the executive branch, at the time when he was talking with Woodward.

Or was he? I went back to the text yet again—specifically, to September 16, the day on which the book first mentioned Deep Throat as such. By then, the reporters, on the basis of information received from Bernstein's former White House official, believed they were onto something considerably more momentous than a third-rate burglary attempt. However, when they contacted a presumably knowledgeable source in the Justice Department about their information, he threw cold water on their theory. "There is nothing you know that we don't know," the Justice Department source said. "It can safely be said that the investigation for the present is at rest, in a state of repose. It seems highly unlikely that it will be reopened."

It was this slough of despond into which Deep Throat was called to rescue the reporters:

> Woodward had a source in the Executive Branch who had access to information at CRP as well as at the White House. His identity was unknown to anyone else. He could be contacted only on very important occasions. Woodward had promised he would never identify him or his position to anyone. Further, he had agreed never to quote the man, even as an anonymous source. Their discussions would be only to confirm information that had been obtained elsewhere and to add some perspective.
>
> In newspaper terminology, this meant the discussions were on "deep background." Woodward explained the arrangement to [*Washington Post*] managing editor Howard Simons one day. He had taken to calling the source "my friend," but Simons dubbed him "Deep Throat," the title of a celebrated pornographic movie. The name stuck.

Indeed it did.

I went back to that opening sentence. I noticed, as many times before, that it was written in the past tense, as was the whole book: Woodward "had" a source in the executive branch. But this time I had a new thought: The linguistic conventions of journalism are fairly loose. Thus the sentence did not have to mean that Woodward had a source who was employed in the executive branch at the very time he was functioning as Deep Throat. Instead, the sentence could mean merely that Woodward had a source who was in the executive branch at some point, or who performed work for the executive branch without being employed there full time. The sentence, in other words, did not necessarily mean that Woodward had a source who was working in the executive branch at the precise moment of his conversations with Woodward.

A purist would protest that if Woodward's source was no longer "in" the executive branch in the conventional sense at the time he was conversing with Woodward about Watergate, the sentence should have read thus: "Woodward had *had* a source in the executive branch," or "Woodward had a source *who had been* in the executive branch." Or some such thing. And what would Woodward say if a critic accused him of using language that misled readers about the precise time when his source served in government? He might respond as he did to Steve Brill's accusation that President Clinton and attorney Bob Bennett did not walk the White House grounds talking about sex. The dispute with Brill, said Woodward, was no more than an argument about venue. By the same token, Woodward might say, a dispute about "had" versus "had had" would be an even smaller quibble.

What went through my head at that moment, just after the business about Woodward and Brill, was the case of *People v. Dunn*. This case, as I later learned after desperate searches through Westlaw and Lexis, was not a real one. It was a piece of apocrypha invented by my evidence teacher at Brooklyn Law School, Dean Jerome Prince, who was famed for his memorable and even funny hypotheticals. Prince created this particular case to teach students why it is problematic to admit people's dying declarations into evidence at trial. In the made-up *People v. Dunn*, the murder victim declared on his deathbed (or so the jury found), "Dunn did it." Dunn was convicted. But the conviction was reversed because the court found the declaration ambiguous: For instance, it could have been part of the statement, "[Unintelligible name] done did it." In this case, Woodward done did it.

If my reading of Deep Throat's status was correct—if, that is, Deep Throat was a source of Woodward's who was at one point in the executive branch but was not necessarily there anymore—it was no longer a mystery why Deep Throat and the Bernstein source identified as a "former official" sounded so much the same. The two did not resemble one another; they were the same individual. The former official was clearly John Sears; Deep Throat, just as clearly, was John Sears as well.

And instead of Deep Throat's being composed of many real-life sources, the single real-life Sears had multiplied into two figures in *All the President's Men*.

It was one of those gratifying, mystery-unraveling moments that constitute an epiphany—what my friend Pat Moynihan, following Joyce, once described as a vision of the "whatness" of a thing. It probably did not match Enrico Fermi's flash of insight, as he took a long step across a puddle on a rainy London street, into the secret of the chain reaction; but I can't help thinking that it fell into the same general category. Ben Bradlee, executive editor of the *Washington Post* during Watergate, once predicted that when Deep Throat was finally identified, everyone would say, "Why didn't I think of that?" Which is precisely what I said to myself when I finally figured it out.

After the warm glow of relief and pleasure came the chill of uncertainty as to whether the solution would stand the test of verification. I read quickly through the rest of the well-marked references to Deep Throat and to Bernstein's former official, pre-bath and post-bath, confirming in each case that the hypothesis held—with respect to the use of past and present tenses in the Deep Throat references, the content of Deep Throat's statements, and the vivid literary portrait presented of the shared source. That confident, authoritative voice, the hauntingly familiar idiosyncratic mannerisms, the frustratingly elusive presence finally had a name and face. The pieces of the puzzle all fit. Cinderella's glass slipper had finally found its foot.

The time that passed while the long-blurred photograph turned steadily crisper and clearer was as gratifying as any in my professional life. If nothing more happened, I could die happy (intellectually, at least). But of course one more thing had to happen. My discovery had to pass the acid test, otherwise known as my wife. For years I had been presenting her with one theory after another, each one advanced with emphatic certitude. Each time she had nodded encouragingly and said, "That's interesting." This time, when I told her, she said, "Yeah. You've got it." Which from her agnostic lips was a vote of extreme confidence.

I had stumbled onto a linguistic key that enabled me to make use of something I already knew fairly well, perhaps singularly so: the history and personal dimensions of John Sears. If I had not made that connection, it may well be that no one else would have, at least during Sears's lifetime.

When Woodward called his friend John Sears about Watergate on June 19, 1972, Sears told Woodward that the investigation of the Watergate break-in was about to "heat up." Later the same day, in another call, he gave Woodward the additional information that the FBI considered Howard Hunt a "prime suspect." Sears was, it is true, generally well connected. But how did Sears come by this type of specific Watergate-related information so quickly?

One way is that Sears, after he left the White House in 1969 for the private practice of law, stayed in close touch with his many friends there. A May 3, 1976, roundup of Deep Throat candidates in *Time* magazine listed John Sears as a possibility. *Time* was impressed by the "excellent White House sources" Sears retained after his departure from the Nixon White House in 1969, and by his "cigarette-smoking and Scotch-drinking habits," which, while common enough, "correspond to those attributed to Deep Throat."

Sears's White House friends did, in fact, remain loyal to him. In a 1971 memorandum to Bob Haldeman, two years after Sears's departure, Pat Buchanan recommended that Sears, despite his unpopularity in some White House quarters, be invited to a State dinner so as to impress some of Sears's clients.

Another friend of Sears recently remembered to me that even after his departure, Sears was a frequent visitor to the Old Executive Office Building.

Upon leaving government, Sears joined the law firm of Gadsby & Hannah. This was the former firm of White House special counsel Charles Colson—though this is one Colson connection, at least, that does not seem to have figured in the Watergate story. Gadsby & Hannah was then located at 1700 Pennsylvania Avenue, next door to the White House. The firm was also located directly across the street from the law firm of Mudge Rose Guthrie & Alexander. John Mitchell, upon leaving his post as attorney general at the beginning of March, 1972, had returned to practicing law at Mudge Rose, where he kept an office, while he simultaneously managed Nixon's 1972 re-election campaign.

In a small cubbyhole office next to Mitchell's at Mudge Rose sat Jack Caulfield.

Caulfield, after serving in a security job with the Nixon presidential campaign in 1968, had wanted to become chief U.S. Marshal. John Mitchell interviewed him for the post but rejected him; Mitchell had local patronage debts for which he wanted to use such jobs. It was after this rejection that Caulfield went to work for John Ehrlichman in 1969.

There was a specific history behind Ehrlichman's belief that he needed Caulfield's services as a private investigator for the White House. The Republicans credited the intelligence gathered in 1968 by Operation Integrity in Illinois, and its counterparts in other states, with preventing vote fraud and otherwise helping Nixon win the election. That was a major reason why White House wanted a similar intelligence capability. Ehrlichman originally wanted Caulfield to perform this function from outside the White House, in a private security organization in Washington. Caulfield, however, still wanted a job within government; he wanted to be on Ehrlichman's White House staff, and Ehrlichman acquiesced. Caulfield's friend Rose Woods was instrumental in facilitating his move to the White House.

Ehrlichman's intelligence interests were catholic, and Caulfield did his best to satisfy them. Over the course of several years, Caulfield conducted an intermittent watch on Senator Edward M. Kennedy, then Nixon's prospective presidential opponent, in an effort to discover politically useful Kennedy indiscretions. Caulfield also obtained the Brookings Institution's tax returns for White House perusal and arranged for an anonymous letter to the IRS suggesting an audit of an unfriendly journalist at *Newsday*. When the FBI refused to tap the phone of columnist Joseph Kraft for the White House, Caulfield arranged an independent bugging operation. When the Secret Service tapped the phone of President Nixon's brother, Donald, to see whether criminal figures were trying to influence him, Caulfield was called in to monitor the tap. Caulfield looked for improprieties in the consulting firm through which Larry O'Brien had worked for Howard Hughes. Caulfield hunted for leaks to columnist Jack Anderson.

In a number of these enterprises, Caulfield operated with the assistance of retired New York City police officer Anthony T. Ulasewicz. Ehrlichman had hired Ulasewicz at the recommendation of Caulfield. Ulasewicz was not on the White House payroll; from the beginning, he was paid by Nixon's lawyer, Herb Kalmbach.

Caulfield's relations with the Nixon White House were complicated. In the summer of 1970, the White House tried to arrange for his appointment to a couple of different investigative positions in the Department of the Treasury. But Treasury had no interest in becoming a base of operations for such a freelancer and managed to resist the White House pressures. Not long thereafter, the flow of White House investigative assignments to Caulfield began to slow. When the Pentagon Papers were leaked in 1971, the response of the White House was not to call Caulfield but to set up the plumbers.

Caulfield's White House sponsors may have thought he was not up to the type of work assigned to the plumbers. Or it may be that Caulfield had a sense of limits that the White House found inconvenient. After all, when Chuck Colson later told Caulfield about the plumbers' intention to set a fire at Brookings, Caulfield's response was to excuse himself and find someone to whom to report the lunacy. He told John Dean, who then prevailed on Ehrlichman to turn off the plan.

Stymied in the White House, Caulfield attempted to strike out on his own in the private sector. At one point he planned to go into business with Joe Woods, who was sheriff of Cook County, Illinois, as well as Caulfield's friend and Rose Woods's brother. In the fall of 1971, Caulfield submitted to the leadership of the Nixon re-election campaign a proposal he called Operation Sandwedge. It envisioned Caulfield at the head of a private security firm and, from that base, taking charge of political intelligence for the campaign. Here, too, Caulfield struck out: The political intelligence job, as it was euphemistically called, went to Gordon Liddy and Howard Hunt. Deep Throat was later to tell Woodward that the choice of Liddy and Hunt was not accidental. The Nixon campaign knew what it was getting.

Caulfield did get a job with the 1972 Nixon campaign, working for John Mitchell—though it was a less important job than the one the former police detective had envisioned. His office was near Mitchell's at Mudge Rose, and the former police officer served as Mitchell's bodyguard and general assistant.

At the end of April, 1972, Caulfield finally got his government job. He went to the Treasury Department, and in July, he settled in as acting assistant director for enforcement at the Bureau of Alcohol, Tobacco and Firearms. But Caulfield remained very much in the White House and campaign loops. His erstwhile assistant, Tony Ulasewicz, continued to do work for the Nixon organization. Caulfield quickly knew about the arrest of the Watergate burglars and immediately appreciated the scale of the problem, phoning Ehrlichman on the day of the arrests to express his concern. When the White House wanted to make an explicit offer of executive clemency to Watergate burglar James McCord, it was McCord's friend Caulfield who delivered the message and talked with McCord about the latter's doubts.

Partly because he had been squeezed out of a central role at the White House and CRP, Caulfield, when Watergate burst open, escaped the worst type of personal consequences. But Caulfield had been involved deeply enough in White House intelligence gathering and damage control efforts to find himself in need of a lawyer. He turned to his friend John Sears. When Caulfield testified publicly to the Ervin committee in May of 1973, newspaper pictures of the event showed him accompanied by Sears, his attorney.

Caulfield was, of course, not Sears's only source of information about Watergate. For instance, Sears remained close to Rose Woods, a highly political and extremely smart woman who had unparalleled access to information about the Nixon inner circle and harbored her own long-standing resentments of Haldeman and his allies.

In addition, Sears may well have had a source in Nixon himself. A 1976 article in the *Washington Post* about that year's presidential campaign managers stated—probably on the basis of an interview with Sears—that Nixon, even during his Watergate troubles, continued to call Sears for advice. Monica Crowley, who served as Nixon's assistant after his presidency, says in her book about that time that Nixon and Sears were still in touch.

By the time Caulfield was called to testify to the Ervin committee, Sears was at political loose ends. During his brief stint in the White House, he had been close to Vice President Agnew, with whom he had traveled during the 1968 campaign. Sears considered Agnew the individual most likely to become the Republican nominee for president when Nixon's second term ended in 1976. In 1969, this was not an outlandish thought. Then came Watergate and Agnew's resignation (because of an unrelated scandal) in 1973, forcing a political operative like Sears to recalculate his future.

Nixon had not yet resigned in 1974 when Robert Walker, a political adviser to California Governor Ronald Reagan and an old friend of Sears from the 1968 Nixon campaign, asked Sears to consider becoming campaign manager for a possible Reagan run for the presidency in 1976. Sears had, deservedly, received much of the credit for Nixon's brilliantly successful delegate operation in the 1968 campaign. He also enjoyed a reputation for having unparalleled access to and influence with the Eastern press.

By this time, Sears's hair had turned prematurely gray. During one oft-reported 1974 meeting during the negotiations between Sears and Reagan, Sears told the governor— contrary to the opinion of almost everyone else at the meeting—that President Nixon would be out of office within six months (it turned out to be three). Sears further said that Vice President Gerald Ford, who would succeed Nixon, would prove not to be up to the task of governing the nation and would thus be vulnerable in 1976. These on-the-money predictions impressed all who attended; they could not have known how uniquely placed Sears was to make such an assessment and what a role he had played in bringing the events to pass.

Sears proceeded to put his career where his mouth was. Even before he was offered the job of Reagan's campaign manager for 1976, he turned down an early offer of a job with the Ford re-election campaign. After finally becoming Reagan's campaign manager, Sears both enhanced his reputation for great political creativity and made enemies among Reagan's more ideologically conservative supporters.

The enmity arose because Sears's strategy for Reagan, unlike Barry Goldwater's strategy in 1964, was not to run against the conventional politicians of the Republican Party but instead to allow them to elect their delegate slates in the major states. Sears's plan was then to persuade these political managers that President Ford was a sure loser and that delegates pledged to Ford through the first convention ballot should, if Ford failed on that ballot, be allowed to abandon him on the second vote. This strategy required that Reagan not run as a right-wing ideologue but move towards the center. The plan displeased those conservatives who wanted Reagan to be just like Goldwater, only more electable.

Strategy was not the only issue that separated Sears from the traditional Reaganites. In addition, Sears raised their hackles as a man who was not properly respectful towards the candidate. The California Reaganites thought Sears too dismissive of the governor and too ready to manipulate him. According to one typical story, a reporter complained to Sears that Governor Reagan hadn't said anything new in months; Sears is said to have replied, "I certainly hope he hasn't."

In the pull and haul of contending factions in the campaign, Reagan emerged on the eve of the 1976 Republican

convention without enough votes to prevent Ford from tri-
umphing on the first ballot. In order to prevent what was
apparently inevitable, Sears hit upon the device that would
make him famous for political ingenuity. He did not even
notify the candidate himself until the last moment; then Reagan approved the plan. Following Sears's advice, Reagan
announced his choice for vice presidential running mate in
advance of the convention.

The choice—shocking to many of Reagan's long-time
supporters—was liberal Senator Richard Schweiker of Pennsylvania. After Schweiker was announced, Sears set about
trying through procedural votes to force Ford to announce his
own vice presidential choice, calculating that if Ford were
compelled to do so, whoever he chose would almost surely
alienate one wing or another of the president's fragile delegate
coalition.

The move did not succeed; Reagan's troops might have
gone to the Republican convention ready to do battle, but
they were not prepared for the battle over procedural rules
that was necessary to make Sears's tactic succeed. Still,
Sears's plan kept Ford from being able to claim overwhelming victory. And Sears came close enough to actual success so
that in later years, even Reagan insiders who came to dislike
Sears did not fault him for his attempt to pair the conservative Reagan with the liberal Schweiker.

Some of these Reaganites were brought along with the
Schweiker plan by old-fashioned personal politicking: Nancy
Reagan persuaded Sears to call a meeting of Reagan's Califor-
nia supporters to ratify the choice. Others simply saw the logic
of Sears's tactic. For instance, Reagan's long-time friend Paul
Laxalt, then Republican Senator from Nevada, approved of

Sears's plan: When Sears devised it, Laxalt later remembered to journalists Rowland Evans and Robert Novak, the only Republican delegates truly up for grabs were from the Northeast, the area most likely to approve of Schweiker. Sears did what he had to do.

Also of note is what Sears did not do: He did not throw Reagan and Reagan's delegates into a frontal attack on Ford's foreign policy, which is what many Reagan supporters wanted. Reagan loyalists do not seem to have faulted Sears for this decision, either, perhaps because the candidate himself was also disinclined to split the party by an all-out battle.

Thus Sears emerged from the 1976 campaign with a reputation for technical brilliance. In the run-up to the convention, he was the *New York Times'* Man in the News, described as a man "widely acknowledged to be one of the best political operatives in either party." Sears was no longer obscure. His public persona, just as Woodward had suggested to me, had undergone a large change.

Sears, despite his last-minute convention heroics, also emerged from the convention deeply mistrusted by many of Reagan's core supporters. In the years between 1976 and 1980, some of these supporters told the candidate they would not support him if he hired Sears again. Reagan told them Sears would not be his campaign manager in 1980.

But by 1979, Sears was once more managing a Reagan presidential campaign. Gary Wills has speculated that Reagan, more determined to run in 1980 than he had been in 1976, saw the importance of setting his campaign in early, visible motion. Sears had the advantage of being already on the scene and familiar with the mechanics of running this particular candidate.

Sears brought Reagan to the brink of victory in 1980, then got himself fired by the candidate and the candidate's wife. The story of how this happened has been told and retold by now in dozens of books of political reportage, usually as a tale of how Sears's megalomania did him in. The truth was probably more complex.

A candidate for high office is usually surrounded by an entourage of friends and advisers who view the candidate as a kind of proprietary right to be guarded against encroachers. Ronald Reagan, for reasons of ideology and temperament, had an entourage that was more possessive than most. In the 1976 campaign, Reagan was, for an extended period of time, hesitant about running. Therefore the entourage was not so heavily mobilized as it might have been. And even in 1976, Sears had to share his power in Washington with a control center based in the offices of Michael Deaver's public relations firm, Deaver and Hannaford, in Los Angeles.

In preparation for the 1980 campaign, by contrast, Reagan let it be known early that he was determined to run. Reagan's long-time associates were more attentive. Sears's two most notable supporters among this group, at the beginning, were Nancy Reagan and Michael Deaver, who remembered Sears's shrewdness from the 1976 campaign. But most of the pre-existing Reaganites disliked Sears from the outset.

This is not wholly a matter of speculation. At the beginning of the 1980 campaign, Republican political operative David Keene, who had worked with Sears in the past and whom Sears hoped would join him in the Reagan effort, decided not to do so. Keene looked at the array of forces in the Reagan campaign—Sears versus the entrenched Reaganites—and judged, correctly, that Sears could not successfully fight them for control of the candidate. Therefore Sears would not be able to determine the direction of the campaign and would be unable to protect his people within the campaign. Keene signed on with candidate George H. W. Bush.

Keene probably did not predict, however, the ugliness that accompanied Sears's defeat. Some of the clashes that Sears had with other members of the campaign were over matters of campaign strategy. For instance, Sears was struck by the fact that Jack Kemp, a Republican congressman from New York who was the first public official to introduce supply-side economics into national politics, was one of the few Republicans whose economics and general outlook could appeal to the blue-collar vote. Sears became engaged in an effort to court and neutralize Kemp and to persuade Reagan to adopt elements of the supply-side approach.

In doing so, Sears clashed with Reagan's issues adviser, Martin Anderson. Anderson finally left the campaign over these disagreements. In addition, in an attempt to bind Kemp to the Reagan campaign, Sears told Kemp that he could take the place of Reagan's old friend Senator Paul Laxalt of Nevada as campaign chairman. Laxalt, upon learning of the offer, was not amused.

Some of the clashes had to do less with ideology than with power. Sears and Deaver pushed veteran Reaganite Lynn Nofziger out of the campaign. Then, at the end of November, 1979, Sears pushed out Deaver, forcing him to resign under circumstances that left the candidate angry at Sears.

Meanwhile, Sears had devised a front-runner strategy for Reagan in Iowa, with only limited appearances by the candidate. Reagan's daughter Maureen was miffed that the campaign organization did not call upon her to campaign in Iowa.

Reagan's son Michael was annoyed by the fact that Sears took on press appearances in place of the candidate, with Sears always smoking, in Michael's words, his "stupid cigarette."

When Reagan lost the Iowa caucuses to Bush, Sears lost the protections of victory. The Reagan campaign moved to New Hampshire. Sears supervised a new round of television advertising. Sears was also instrumental in the ploy that gained Reagan the most publicity in New Hampshire. Seeing that the poll numbers looked good for Reagan, and that Reagan therefore did not need the exposure of a one-on-one debate with his closest competitor, George Bush, Sears arranged for Reagan to invite the other Republican candidates into the planned debate, for which Reagan and Bush were footing the bill. At the debate, the organizers tried to keep these other candidates from speaking. Reagan defended them, with his now-famous line, "*I am paying* for this microphone."

Along the way, Sears tried to force out of the campaign the last high-placed old Reaganite, Edwin Meese III. In retrospect, I know firsthand how foolhardy this attempt was. Meese is a man of extraordinary affability and equanimity. He is therefore both easy and dangerous to underestimate. When Ronald Reagan finally became president in 1981, Meese first went to work for him in the White House; then Reagan nominated Meese to be Attorney General. Meese's opponents were quite sure that they could derail his nomination with charges—some two dozen of them—about Meese's ethics. I represented Meese in this controversy. When his attorneys became agitated over one accusation or another against him, Meese would calmly, smilingly insist that there was nothing to it. "No problem," he said each time.

And he was right; his nomination succeeded. It must have been easy for Sears, back in 1980, to misjudge Meese's power and influence.

Thus in trying to unseat Meese, Sears instead got himself fired by Reagan on the day of the New Hampshire primary. Sears's strategy for recovery in New Hampshire proved correct; Reagan won in New Hampshire and was on the way to victory in the 1980 election.

Sears was back in private life. I saw him from time to time. At one point I tried to bring him back to work with me at Mudge Rose, to which I had returned. It did not happen. Sears did well in the law and politics. He became a television commentator for NBC. In the mid-1980s, when most viewed South Africa as nothing but a pariah, Sears, as a consultant, worked on the development of a democratic politics there. He told me a transition to democracy was coming; he was right.

In 1992, the excellent and enterprising Allison Silver, opinion page editor of the *Los Angeles Times*, persuaded Sears to join the newspaper's stable of outside political writers. Sears wrote for the paper for a little over four years, during which he revealed more about his political views than a political operative usually does or is able to do. The time during which he wrote was not an inspiring one for the Republican Party. President Ronald Reagan had been replaced by President George Bush, whose first term set no political houses afire. Moreover, as the Republicans readied their re-election effort in 1992, there was a third major candidate in the wings—Ross Perot.

Sears flirted seriously with the idea of Perot in 1992, saying in print that if Bush could not come up with a positive reason to vote for him, Sears might desert the party of his

GOP ancestors and vote for Perot. By October of 1992, Sears had concluded that he would not in fact jump ship and that Americans would not elect Perot president—in no small part because of the disloyalty Perot had shown his own supporters by temporarily dropping out of the race. Sears observed, however, that Perot, while not understanding much about politics, understood power. Specifically, he understood how to demonstrate and increase his power by forcing the Republican and Democratic candidates to send delegations to him to curry favor and gain the votes of his supporters. In this clear-eyed understanding of power, Sears said, Perot was like Richard Nixon.

Repeatedly in his *Los Angeles Times* pieces Sears returned to Richard Nixon as the gold standard for political leaders. When talking about the paucity of both principle and loyalty in modern politics, Sears referred by contrast to Nixon's decision not to contest the results of the presidential election of 1960. After Bill Clinton took office as president and quickly convened an economic summit, at which the president listened to advice from all and sundry, Sears explained to his readers the danger of such a ploy. He quoted Nixon's remark that presidents should be very careful about whom they allow to give them advice: Taking advice from someone looks very much like sharing power with him.

As the 1996 presidential race approached, Sears saw the political paradox of a Democratic candidate who could be beaten and a Republican Party that lacked an idea to beat him with. Sears expressed contempt for Republican front-runner Robert Dole's reported remark to a group of supporters that he would be "anything you want." Sears explained that when Nixon talked about running to the right in the primaries, then running to the center in the general election, he meant in each case emphasizing the issues on which one agreed with the voters in the target constituency. He most definitely did not mean, Sears said, the kind of pandering in which Dole was engaged.

However, in August of 1996, at the time of the Republican convention, Sears changed his opinion of the Republicans' presidential prospects. The reason was that Dole had chosen as his vice presidential running mate the man whom Sears had tried to bring into the 1980 Reagan campaign, Jack Kemp. The Republican ticket, Sears thought, now had a chance. In fact, in the op-ed piece in which he voiced this opinion, Sears announced that he would no longer be writing commentary on the election for the *Los Angeles Times*. Instead, he was going to work on Kemp's campaign. "You see," he explained, "this is why politics is not a science; it can make cynical old men like me believers again."

The revival was only temporary, of course: The Dole-Kemp ticket went down to defeat in 1996.

Around this time, the filmmaker Oliver Stone was producing his much-heralded film on Richard Nixon. As part of his research, Stone arranged meetings for himself with various Nixon associates. I attended one such meeting, a lunch at the very same Brookings Institution that Chuck Colson had once planned to firebomb. Sears and Ziegler were also there. Sears was by far the most authoritative presence at the table. Certainly Stone thought so; he made Sears one of his chief consultants on the project.

On the basis of Stone's politics and past productions, conservatives and friends of Nixon anticipated the film with distaste. Yet when it appeared, though there was plenty for a pro-Nixon viewer to dislike, actor Anthony Hopkins's portrayal of Nixon was distinctly sympathetic. Stone even had Nixon standing up to a fictional conspiracy of rich men who had helped put him in office. Sears had shaped the movie much as he had shaped the reporting of Woodward and Bernstein.

The release of the film was accompanied by a book comprised of the screenplay and some essays, one of them by Sears. Nixon, Sears said, was the loner produced by a nation of loners. That was the reason the country could not forgive Nixon for his illegal acts, even though others had done the same: "We are a land of loners and our only protection is the law." "Did I want him to escape at the time?" Sears asked rhetorically. "Yes. Did I think he would? No."

But was Nixon, on balance, worth it for the country? "I would submit," Sears said,

> that if the world survives for a million years, perhaps its finest hour may be that in the last half of the 20th century, when the power to blow up the world rested in the hands of a few men in two very unsophisticated and suspicious countries, we didn't do it, and one American, Richard Nixon, moved the Cold War away from permanent confrontation toward victory. How can any wrong that he did compare with that?

The last time I saw Sears, a couple of years ago, we dined together and both manifested our Deep Throat–like tendency to drink too much and be rowdy. In the course of preparing this book, I phoned Pat Buchanan to ask him various things about Deep Throat and times past. When I called him, he was in good humor. It was apparent that he was going to be the presidential candidate of the Reform Party for the year 2000, which meant that he was due to receive some $12 million in campaign funds from the federal government. I mentioned John Sears. Pat laughed and said he had just had breakfast with him. If Sears is back in action, the campaign is sure to be more than usually interesting.

People have said that Sears used to describe himself as a political jockey looking for a horse. Yet in reading Sears, I was struck by how little he fit the mold of a political "gun for hire." Instead, his writing took me back to the pictures I have of Sears in my mind, from the days when we met and first worked together to our more sporadic meetings through the years.

In those pictures, he is always dressed in a suit, a white shirt, and a subdued tie. I know he must have gone swimming and played tennis and golf. Yet in the pictures, he is never holding a golf club or tennis racket or wearing a bathing suit.

I remember that the eye contact John made was nervous and broken; as often as not, he would be looking down not at me but at a point somewhere in the space between his eyes and my tie. At the end of a confident-sounding declaration about this or that political phenomenon, he would let out a nervous chuckle—not a laugh, more like a vocal grimace.

His gift was for taking mundane facts, putting them together, and infusing them with meaning. As a result, each comment of his, even about something trivial, sounded portentous. Every shift of the wind, as described by John, was the sign of a coming storm. You paid attention to what he was saying. We had long conversations; given my own temperament, I know that I must have talked as well as he. But what

I remember are his soliloquies—meant to be listened to, as indeed they were.

When I first met Sears he was a young lawyer working for me; but when I listened, I felt like a younger brother or a kind of acolyte in the new devotion of politics. There was something priestly about him. He believed, so you believed (or maybe it was the other way around). What he said rang bells like the sounds of some song you were happy to hear and remember.

Among my clients during the years when Sears worked for me at Mudge Rose were the Sisters of Charity of St. Vincent de Paul. The firm's work for them was surprisingly varied, ranging from matters of finance to, unfortunately, a case of gang rape committed by some of the sisters' young wards. Sears did a good deal of work for the sisters. Part of the reason was that they and the priests that managed their affairs felt very much at home with him. They seemed to recognize him as one of their own.

Sears's political career was not so inconsistent with this slightly otherworldly air, despite his designation as a political technician. He was always looking for the center, not as a matter of uninspired political compromise but as a way of finding what was deepest in the American political psyche. First came his support of John F. Kennedy, the type of early attachment from which few break completely. Next came the Nixon campaign, with Sears among those of us who thought that Nixon could be the avatar of that centrist, everyman politics abandoned by the Democrats.

Ronald Reagan's early supporters viewed Sears as an enemy of conservative ideological integrity. They were not quite right. Sears did not like the raw right-wing version of

conservatism that he found in some of Reagan's original supporters. This dislike of his was not inconsistent with his support of Reagan, whom he saw—correctly, I think—as a man
with conservative positions but a non-ideological temperament. And when Sears found a new, more broadly appealing
conservative ideology, based on supply-side economics, he
went to work to try to build it into the Reagan campaign. To
an appreciable extent Sears succeeded. Reagan's embrace of
tax cuts, rather than traditional Republican budget balancing, was a significant factor in his victory over President
Jimmy Carter in 1980.

In 1996, when Sears saw another chance at a political
campaign for something other than establishment Republi-
canism, he took it, despite the long odds. For someone with
the reputation of being a political calculator, he did not
behave like a man maximizing his self-interest.

When, after the Watergate break-in, Sears decided to continue talking to Woodward and Bernstein, the odds must also
have seemed long. Sears was gone from the Nixon administration, and he had always liked to talk to the press. His private livelihood, however, depended on his contacts inside the
administration; and his political future lay with the Republican Party. Perhaps he thought he could manage his juggling
act. But, Washington being what it is, he must have known
that he could not count on his role as Woodward and Bernstein's source remaining secret for any length of time. Sears
was and is one of the best calculators in politics, but at some
point the calculus must have eluded even him. His plunging
ahead must have been an act of faith.

Conclusion

The story of Deep Throat holds enduring interest for more than one reason. First, Deep Throat's actions, like Watergate itself, had momentous consequences for American politics and government. Only now are we coming to see the size and reach of those consequences. Next, beyond issues of governance, Deep Throat's decisions haunt us as a fascinating morality play on the theme of divided loyalties. Finally, we continue to pursue the puzzle of Deep Throat because we sense that somewhere in it lies a crucial and previously unavailable key to the enduring mystery of Richard Nixon.

An assessment of Deep Throat's significance for this country's politics must begin by noting both what Deep Throat was, politically speaking, and what he was not.

Deep Throat strongly disapproved of some of the conduct of the Nixon White House. He was not, however, an individual who had resigned from the government in protest against that conduct. The Nixon administration had officials who did resign in protest, openly or quietly. For instance, John

Andrews, a White House speechwriter, left the premises over the invasion of Cambodia and wrote publicly about the reasons for his departure. People such as Bob Finch and Commissioner of Internal Revenue Randolph Thrower resigned out of a general distaste for the politics they saw taking over the White House. Some officials resigned citing thin pretexts, like an irresistible employment opportunity or pressing family considerations, in order to remove themselves from what they saw as moral unpleasantness or personal risks.

By contrast, *All the President's Men* gave the impression that Deep Throat was still working in the government—either in the permanent government, where the demands of loyalty to the incumbent administration were less exigent, or within the Nixon political family itself.

In addition to presenting a Deep Throat who had not resigned in protest, *All the President's Men* gave no indication that Deep Throat was telling his colleagues within government about his objections to current policy or waging a private fight to get things changed. The Nixon administration had these internal protesters. Many of us took this route at one time or another, especially in the administration's last turbulent months. Woodward and Bernstein's book did not depict Deep Throat as one of these internal warriors. The book portrayed him as worn out from past battles, not engaged in present ones.

Deep Throat protested in a very specific way against the practices to which he objected. He delivered his criticisms to outsiders, not insiders; and he did so not publicly but secretly. Even more specifically, he talked in secret only to the press. In this way he procured an additional layer of protection for the secrecy of his communications. Journalists, after all, not only have a professional obligation to protect their anonymous sources but actually fulfill that obligation to a substantial extent. Deep Throat selected the method of protest that provided him with the best chance of being able to maintain his secret, dual role over time.

Why these walls within walls? To judge by the book, it was not simply some rational calculation that kept Deep Throat allied with the Nixon administration. Instead, the only explicit descriptions in the book suggested that Deep Throat acted in secret because he was afraid. The book described Deep Throat as a politically sophisticated man, not susceptible to hysteria. If Deep Throat was afraid of something, therefore, it was probably something to be afraid of. And Deep Throat did indeed think that the White House had power to do him great harm. What kind of harm was never concretely specified, but at one point the book's Deep Throat was actually afraid for his life and for the lives of Woodward and Bernstein.

In drawing this picture of Deep Throat, *All the President's Men* drew, by implication, a picture of the way American government works. In this picture, the most important thing about government is the secret knowledge held by those near the center of power. Access to these secrets is the most important ingredient in the ability to do political good or evil.

Thus while Woodward and Bernstein gathered a great deal of concrete information from many sources and Deep Throat rarely gave the reporters any such information, Deep Throat gave the reporters something more important. Because of his place at the center of power, he knew the secrets of which items of information were true, which were significant, and how they were related to one another. It was this secret knowledge that enabled the *Post* reporters to pursue their quarry persistently enough and aim accurately enough to expose Watergate.

In this same picture of how politics and government work, people in power know the unique value of secrets like the ones Deep Throat knew. Precisely for this reason, they are willing to impose terrifying costs on anyone who reveals the secret information. That is why it was reasonable for Deep Throat to be afraid.

If we accept these two assumptions—about both the unequaled value of secrets to the public and the high costs of revealing them—then someone like Deep Throat is clearly justified in acting secretly to reveal information while retaining his position on the inside of a corrupt political effort. By protecting himself, he remains in a position to reveal still more of the crucial secrets. In this view, Deep Throat's tactics were justified, even if one ethical price he paid was that he had to keep working at his day job somewhere in the evil empire.

This was the picture of Deep Throat that developed during and after Watergate. The image came to be seen as an emblem of the lessons of Watergate as a whole. The most important of these lessons—or so opinion leaders and legislators thought at the time—was that government was unacceptably corrupted by secret money and secret influence. In this view, the well-being of the country demanded a change in the balance of political power so as to weaken any organization devoted to keeping secrets, like the CIA, and put more force in the hands of individuals dedicated to exposing secrets. These individuals included journalists, public interest activists, and crusading Congressmen and their staffs. They also included whistleblowers who delivered up the embarrassing secrets of their own organizations.

The political and cultural effects of this picture were profound. For instance, the post-Watergate Congress came to think it axiomatic that the Attorney General, because he was appointed by the president, had a private, personal loyalty to the president—a kind of secret loyalty in conflict with his public duty. Therefore the Department of Justice headed by this Attorney General could not be trusted to investigate high-level presidential appointees accused of wrongdoing.

In fact, Watergate taught the opposite lesson. When Nixon tried to fire the special prosecutor appointed by Nixon's own Attorney General, the resulting outcry eventually toppled Nixon from office. But post-Watergate reformers did not want to rely on extraordinary political outcry to do the job of insuring prosecutorial independence. They wanted a permanent change in the day-in, day-out power balance. Therefore Congress passed legislation establishing the Office of the Independent Counsel, designed to insure that investigations of high administration officials were thoroughly independent of Justice Department and presidential control.

The design worked wonderfully. Twenty years would pass before we were able to rid ourselves of this experiment.

There were other such apparent Watergate lessons. One was the idea that government officials, instead of acting in the public interest, were routinely motivated by secret, private considerations such as financial holdings, receipt of gifts, promises of future employment, and connections with family and friends. Out of this belief came post-Watergate legislation. It subjected high-level government officials to unprecedentedly stringent financial reporting requirements. It also severely limited the professional contacts that these ex-government officials could have with their old agencies and government colleagues.

This same post-Watergate picture of how American government worked, or did not work, led to the establishment of an Office of Government Ethics to insure agency compliance with ethics-related regulations and began an entire movement in government agencies to crack down on improper influence. Agencies acquired larger ethics bureaucracies, increased their capacity for internal investigations, and became more rigorous in policing the practices of the government contractors under their control.

The Watergate-bred, Deep Throat–fed notion of how American public life functioned and malfunctioned led to a reallocation of resources in the private sector as well. The growth in public interest organizations, parts of a phenomenon that began in the 1960s, accelerated after Watergate as increased numbers of people became convinced that public and private bureaucracies needed sustained criticism from the outside to perform properly. The purpose of many of these public groups was precisely to reveal secrets that the agencies and corporations in their policy fields did not want revealed. An agency's desire for secrecy, conversely, was taken as proof of dishonesty.

These changes in the public and private sectors both encouraged and were encouraged by the vigorous post-Watergate growth in the phenomenon of investigative reporting.

Investigative reporting was not a creature of Watergate. This type of journalism has existed in some form or other since the beginning of the republic, when newspapers were avowedly partisan and journalists made no pretense of being disinterested fact finders. The roots of American investigative journalism may not be pure, but they run deep.

In the late nineteenth and early twentieth centuries, a new type of investigative journalism emerged in the work of writers such as Lincoln Steffens, Upton Sinclair, and Ida Tarbell, who attacked political and industrial corruption with passion. Theodore Roosevelt, speaking for politicians universally, named them muckrakers. They used their share of unnamed sources. They helped fix the image of the irreverent news reporter in the public mind. But there were not very many of them; and the journalists who succeeded them in subsequent decades were, by and large, considerably more sedate.

In the late 1960s and early 1970s, the cultural currents that produced public interest groups also gave rise to a more adversarial culture in journalism. Woodward and Bernstein were a product of this movement. Their doggedness in pursuing figures of authority did not spring full-blown from two idiosyncratic souls.

Still, when Woodward and Bernstein performed their feats of relentlessness in 1972 and early 1973, they were slightly ahead of their time. Their colleagues in the press did not rush to join the train and beat down the doors of the Committee for the Re-election of the President. For months, the two reporters were close to alone in their quest. Most media were more skeptical than the *Post* about stories based on a theory of rampant official corruption. Other media organizations were also more fearful of the consequences of making possibly false accusations against very powerful political figures. Woodward and Bernstein's isolation during those months was unlike anything they would experience today.

In due course, government investigators began to confirm that Woodward and Bernstein's stories in the *Post* had been, if not wholly correct, at least largely so. The audience of journalists upon whom this revelation fell had already been prepared by the new adversary culture of journalism for the idea of thoroughgoing official corruption. Journalists therefore absorbed the news quickly and started to play catch-up.

In the wake of Woodward and Bernstein's success, a particular theory of news, heavily influenced by the symbol of Deep Throat, became prevalent. It assumed that the most important—and thus most newsworthy—things that happen in public and corporate life are kept secret because, if known, they would damage powerful people. Thus what is newsworthy about an organization, almost by definition, is whatever the organization wants to hide. It follows, in this view, that a good reporter is one who has an adversarial relationship with whatever people or organizations he or she is covering. In other words, a good reporter is an investigative reporter, adept at the techniques needed to pry information out of hostile targets.

Persuaded by this theory, news organizations undertook more investigative reporting. Investigative reporters grew in numbers and skill. They gave us, predictably enough, ever more news about the failings of institutions and leaders. They directed sunlight to some places that surely needed it. They also fed an unjustified and dangerous disenchantment with public life. Even as post-Watergate politics sought to cleanse government, the steady stream of scandal news led people in and out of office to believe that government is almost necessarily corrupt—and to act accordingly.

As a result of all these changes, the federal government today is without doubt superficially cleaner than it was before Watergate. But government service has become a much less attractive proposition than it once was, and people of a mind to evade the new rules still find ways to do so.

Indeed, the ironic aftermath of the changes that Watergate and Deep Throat set in train is that politics and government are in substance distinctly meaner and dirtier than they were when Deep Throat decried the "switchblade mentality" in the White House. The process of governing in the Nixon White House—or in Lyndon Johnson's or John F. Kennedy's White House—was considerably more serious and sophisticated than it is today. The caliber of political appointees was, with some distinguished exceptions, higher. The tone of politics was cleaner.

I do not think the above comparisons are the result of misplaced nostalgia. As for the influence of money in politics, there is virtually no one, even among those who oppose campaign finance reform, who thinks there has been a material improvement since Watergate. You no longer have to hang out in a garage in the middle of the night to know that you have to follow the money.

Why all this has happened is a matter for the political scientists. I know only that somehow, as a result of Watergate, the idea of politics as inherently corrupt has led to its becoming more so. John Sears, as I remember him, did not think of politics as evil. I sometimes wonder what he thinks of the changes to which Deep Throat so crucially contributed.

To the post-Watergate changes we should add the ironic saga of what has happened to the whistleblower himself, the figure glamorized by Deep Throat in *All the President's Men.* We have seen that Deep Throat was no ordinary whistle-blower. While he told of others' secrets, he knew how to keep his own from being revealed. He was an individual of unusual access to information and had the power that comes with it. Deep Throat was—like his successors on television's *X-Files,* the omniscient, endlessly smoking Mr. Cancer and the shadowy Mr. X—too wily to be in real danger of reprisal.

Yet despite these advantages, Woodward concluded that Deep Throat was afraid; and that was the way the book depicted him. As a result, people took from the Deep Throat story the lesson that there must be public action to protect whistleblowers. This conviction led to the formation of private organizations devoted to whistleblower advocacy. It also led inexorably to legislation.

Like the drunk looking for his keys under the lamppost because that's where the light is, Congress first tried to protect whistleblowers who worked for government agencies because those were the organizations over which Congress had most control. Thus the Civil Service Reform Act of 1978 included measures to prevent agencies from firing whistleblowers. Yet five years after passage of the act, surveys found that more employees than before feared reprisals for blowing the whistle. From this fact reformers concluded, of course, that the 1978 act had not gone far enough. The result was more protective legislation in 1989. After five years under the new and improved system, Congress concluded that reprisals against whistleblowers were occurring at a greater rate than before. Critics said the Reagan administration had failed to enforce the law and complained that federal courts had interpreted it improperly. Therefore in 1994 Congress amended the law again. Now critics are writing about the inadequacies of the re-amended law.

There is something grimly inevitable about this legislative dynamic. Most whistleblowers do not much resemble Deep Throat, who brought such formidable skills to his battle with his political adversaries. Most whistleblowers do not enjoy great power in their organizations. They are not working in secret; they need protection precisely because, unlike Deep Throat, they have voluntarily or involuntarily been publicly identified as whistleblowers. The law may keep them from being fired. But unless they have revealed unambiguously shocking abuses, they will become the targets of resentment from their colleagues. No law can protect them from this resentment, no matter how many loopholes it closes.

Thus lawmakers and the press have failed to create a forest of Deep Throats to stand where Deep Throat once stood. If the attempt has fallen short, it is largely because these well-meaning reformers have been beguiled by the Deep Throat myth and misled about the complex reality of Deep Throat and Watergate.

This connection between the idea of Deep Throat and this country's post-Watergate politics, though it is important, is not the primary reason why interest in Deep Throat's true identity has persisted. Far more intriguing has been the complex nature of the figure's loyalties and motives, a complexity that echoes recurring ethical dilemmas in public life.

The Deep Throat in *All the President's Men* was a distinctively political man. He was, Woodward and Bernstein said explicitly, experienced in political battles. Deep Throat was rowdy, as political operatives often are and corporate citizens are not. He was a gossip, indulging in the vice that is, as much as money, the mother's milk of politics. Deep Throat was also a constant smoker and a drinker, sometimes to excess. Though these two habits were considerably more common in those days than in our own, they had a special connection to the smoke-filled rooms of politics.

Deep Throat was generally fond of talk. That was how he came to be a "marshaling yard" of many types of political information from many sources. More distinctively, Deep Throat knew literature. He was given to conversing about large and conceptual things. He was not good at concealing his feelings. Though Woodward and Bernstein portrayed these traits as being unusual in a political operator, they are in fact quite consistent with the practice of politics, at least with a certain type of politics. Political life is, after all, based on elevated talk. Irish-American politicians, in particular, were for many years heirs to a political tradition in which the ability to make a kind of poetry out of public issues was a foundation of political power. The tradition was not just Irish. "With words," Disraeli put it, "we govern men." That might have been Deep Throat's motto.

So Deep Throat, while a distinctive character, was not an unfamiliar type to readers who knew about or had participated in American politics. Woodward and Bernstein's readers could picture themselves in Deep Throat's shoes, facing his dilemma.

This dilemma, as primal as anything gets in politics, was the dilemma of loyalty. Politics is based on loyalty. That is one of its glories. Even today, after the reaction to Watergate created a political climate denigrating loyalty, that remains true. As I write this conclusion, James Carville, the political operative who took Bill Clinton to the White House and defended him publicly and colorfully throughout the president's scandals, has just published a book titled *Stickin': The Case for Loyalty*. I do not think there are many political people, even among those who disagree vehemently with almost every position Carville takes, who do not give him many points for the loyalty he has shown.

Well, then, what about Deep Throat's loyalty? Why did he talk? What was he after? What would the reader have done in his position? Did Deep Throat have sufficient provocation to do what he did?

For those who were partisans in the Watergate wars, pro- or anti-Nixon, the answers were relatively simple. Pro-Nixon advocates had no trouble deciding that Deep Throat was a snitch, pure and simple. They were sure he had acted from some motive—saving his own skin, currying favor with the press, venting personal resentment—that was totally unacceptable as a justification for the disloyalty he showed.

For staunch anti-Nixon types, the answer to the question of Deep Throat's motive was similarly simple. Deep Throat was a patriot who exposed abuses that threatened the constitutional order. Conventional political loyalty had to bow before the demands of a larger loyalty to the nation.

But for most readers, those in the great skeptical middle, it was not so clear. They did not have a ready *a priori* answer to the questions of what political loyalty required and where the bounds of such loyalty had to be drawn. Therefore they did not think, based on the information provided in *All the President's Men*, that they could answer the question of whether Deep Throat did the right thing.

If you were one of these agnostics, you wanted to know more—about Deep Throat's position in government, the nature of his personal ambition, his relationships with the people about whom he talked to Woodward, the nature and credibility of the threats to which he referred. Deep Throat's identity was more than a matter of curiosity: It was necessary to an assessment of the moral quality of Deep Throat's actions.

If indeed John Sears was Deep Throat, as I am convinced, we can begin supplying answers to these questions—begin, but not end. The ambiguities in the description of Deep Throat in *All the President's Men* were also present, in more elaborate version, in the real-life Deep Throat.

Was Sears loyal to his president, President Nixon? Well, in a sense Sears remained loyal to the Richard Nixon he knew. This was the Nixon that John first met in 1963. Many years after that meeting, Sears remembered that Nixon was the one who was nervous. Nixon knew what a prize he had in Sears. Nixon also placed a high enough value on sheer mental capacity to take the young man under his political wing and give him an extraordinary political education. This Nixon, despite his personal tics, was not so different from a conventional, old-time machine politician—guarded by his Irish secretary Rose Woods, his tough Irish wordsmith Pat Buchanan, and Irish New York City cop Jack Caulfield, all of whom became Sears's friends in the campaign and the administration.

This Nixon with whom Sears signed on was both an expert counter of votes and a man capable of understanding and championing great policies. Even years after Watergate, and after running two presidential campaigns for Ronald Reagan, Sears returned repeatedly in his *Los Angeles Times* pieces to that Nixon—the one who knew what the presidency meant and how to use it.

That Nixon was not, needless to say, the Nixon that Sears encountered via the persons of John Mitchell, Bob Haldeman, and John Ehrlichman. Sears was no less a political calculator than they. Anyone who could conceive of pairing Ronald Reagan with Richard Schweiker, as Sears did in 1976, has earned a permanent place in the political calculators' Hall of Fame. But Sears's three nemeses displayed—to him, certainly—only calculation, without compensating larger notions of politics and public service. Sears was a skilled political operator who also stirred something in Nixon's larger, more poetic nature. This was precisely the part of Nixon's nature that Mitchell, Haldeman, and Ehrlichman took it to be their job to suppress, encouraging instead Nixon's implacable toughness. They succeeded.

Having spent too much of my spare time on shrinks' couches, I generally do not like to impose psychological explanations on other people's actions. I remember, however, Sears's saying to me that his father died in a fire when John was young. When Nixon, Haldeman, Ehrlichman, and the young Sears entered the White House, Nixon's two lieutenants pushed Sears ever farther from the president. Sears's resentment of them, justified on its face, probably went considerably deeper.

Sears was loyal to his friends in the administration, with whom he kept in close touch even after he left the White House. He was loyal to his friend Jack Caulfield, who undertook large numbers of missions for the White House only to be passed over for what Haldeman, Ehrlichman, and Mitchell considered the big intelligence jobs. As the Watergate scandal deepened, and the White House tried to dump one operative after another over the side to lighten the boat, Caulfield was one of those from whom the men at the top tried to distance themselves. Sears became Caulfield's lawyer. Though I have no firsthand knowledge on the subject, I will bet that Sears did not become rich off this representation.

Sears's famous propensity to talk to the press was not inconsistent with this type of politics and this type of loyalty. Difficult as it may be to imagine, there was a time when politicians and journalists lived together in something slightly more civilized than today's atmosphere of thorough mistrust and mutual manipulation. It was thus possible for politicians to like reporters, at least some reporters, and for the two breeds to talk with one another.

Was Sears pursuing self-advancement at the expense of the institutions to which he owed allegiance? When Sears spoke with Woodward, he had already left government— although there is a sense in which Sears had not left at all. True, he was out of office, in the private practice of law. But his career, present and future, was still bound up in his relationships with the Nixon White House and Republican politics. Sears had not resigned from these connections. Until 1973, when Vice President Agnew was found to have accepted bribes and was forced to resign his office, it was not unreasonable to think that Sears might be running an Agnew presidential campaign in 1976. Agnew would become the Republican candidate only if Nixon lasted out his term in tolerably good repute. It was not in Sears's immediate interest to imperil this prospect by talking to Woodward.

It is possible that Sears viewed his conversations with Woodward as a kind of Hail Mary pass, similar to the Schweiker selection he would later engineer for Ronald Reagan, that was the only hope of saving the Nixon presidency. In any event, conventional careerism was probably not Deep Throat's motive.

But if Sears was not conventionally disloyal, why the extreme secrecy? One reason would have been that Sears believed in the old politics. He himself would have been put off by not just disloyalty but the appearance of disloyalty. He would have assumed that other politicians, candidates and operatives, would react the same way. Even if Sears did not think he was acting disloyally towards Nixon, he would have been aware of the appearance created by his consorting with the *Post*.

True, by the time of Watergate, some Republican Party officials were openly resentful of the Nixon White House for building its own political power at the party's expense. Still, in 1972, an individual who wanted a future in Republican politics would not wish to be seen publicly fingering his president's campaign organization. For the sake of his general political well-being, he would have wanted to avoid such an impression. In addition, because of his own beliefs about loyalty, he would have felt uncomfortable about what he was doing. These were reasons to prefer nighttime and the interior of a garage.

Was Sears also afraid? It is easy enough to dismiss the dramatic expressions of fear with which Woodward and Bernstein peppered *All the President's Men*. Sears, however, had had a certain amount of personal experience with Haldeman, Ehrlichman, Mitchell, and some of the less savory operatives at the White House and CRP. More particularly, Sears was among the first Nixon staffers wiretapped by the FBI. By 1972 Sears may have known of the wiretap; his sources were good. Sears had also been under 24-hour, ten-agent FBI surveillance. There is not much way he could have avoided knowing about that, too.

With or without such specific knowledge, Sears knew enough through Caulfield about White House intelligence so that he was certainly not crazy in his reluctance to talk to Woodward by telephone. As for the rest of the elaborate secrecy, it is hard to re-create, from today's distance, the atmosphere of Washington in the days after the Watergate arrests. After a decade of social revolutions, Vietnam, assassinations, and the political intelligence operations that lay behind Watergate itself, there was a widespread feeling that politics had entered uncharted waters and that the unprecedented was not only possible but likely. Much of what sounds melodramatic in Sears's statements to Woodward would not have sounded so unrealistic back then.

So Sears as Deep Throat was loyal and not loyal in unique proportions. What is striking is the extent to which these proportions fit tightly into the equally unusual puzzle pieces that had come to constitute Richard Nixon's personality by the time Sears met him.

I thought, at one time, that I knew a lot of things about Nixon. Only later did I understand that I knew only what he wanted me to know.

Nixon arrived in New York in 1963 fully formed as to his large political goals. His ambitions were precisely defined and unconditional—to gain the presidency in particular and, more generally, to play a significant role on the American public stage for the rest of his life.

Nixon's political techniques were also well developed. He had absorbed the lessons of his victories and defeats. He knew the political landscape and, in detail, the characteristics of its inhabitants. He had figured out the alternate paths to his ends and knew where the escape routes lay. His key sherpas were identified, his supplies already stocked.

Within this framework, Nixon improvised, in a process that varied according to the news of the day and the nature of his audience. The extent and type of this improvisation can be heard on many of the Nixon tapes. Similarly, Nixon was flexible in tactical matters. For instance, he mapped out tentative roles for his various followers; but he stood prepared to abandon both the role and the follower as circumstances dictated.

Finally, Nixon arrived in New York on the eve of his presidency with his psychological masks already in place. The outlines of the Nixon biography—the angry, populist father; the saintly, sweetly judgmental mother; the two dead brothers, beloved and haunting for all of Nixon's life; the accidental candidacy for Congress; the act of daring ambition in the Hiss case; the escape from failure in the Checkers speech; the humiliating collapse in the 1960 and 1962 campaigns—are signposts along the road by which Nixon became a deeply secretive man. These facts do not explain Nixon, but they at least cast light into some corners of his psyche.

Not long after Nixon left office, he gave an interview to his former aide Ken Clawson. In it, Nixon himself provided a clue to the process that had produced him: "What starts the process, really, are laughs and slights and snubs when you are a kid. But if you are reasonably intelligent and if your anger is deep enough and strong enough, you learn that you can change those attitudes by excellence. . . ."

Nixon had what all truly successful politicians have—the gift (which is in fact its Greek meaning) of charisma. It took different forms at different stages in his life. When he was young, he was handsome. His black-Irish coloring and intense eyes made him so, in spite of the oversized head and the ski-jump nose that would later help to give definition to his caricature.

As Nixon grew older, the latter features grew more dominant. As his hair receded, the Nixonian widow's peak became more pronounced. His face became, when at rest, dark-lined and jowly. Yet as these changes took place, Nixon somehow became more, not less, compelling, his face as commanding of attention as a red light. Years after Nixon left the presidency, I attended a meeting at the Wye Plantation in Virginia during which Nixon addressed a conclave of television executives. As the former president rose to speak, the TV type sitting next to me turned and said in wonderment, "He really *looks* like Nixon!"

Even as Nixon's face aged, his smile remained sunny—startlingly so when it appeared in the midst of the otherwise stern Nixon face. When people like Sears and me first met Nixon, the former vice president was a loser, a funny-looking man, a Californian fish out of water in New York; yet his presence was utterly commanding, and he got what he wanted from each of us.

He presented himself to me—and, I think, to Sears—as thoughtful, knowledgeable, and sophisticated. We accepted him as such, seeing him very much as the "new" Nixon of his press releases. That was silly; Nixon had not changed, and this thoughtful, knowledgeable, and sophisticated self had always been there, just one of his many selves.

During his Navy days in the Pacific theater, Nixon had been a famously poker-faced poker player. In his politics, he never showed his hand. He told no one the whole of his real plans or how he intended to proceed to realize them. Indeed, he kept his internal calculus so hidden that even now we can only guess at it.

Because he knew a great deal about himself, his strengths, and his weaknesses, he also knew how to manage those who worked for him. He did so by communicating with us, in the main, one-to-one. He also divided us into groups, each of which got a different picture of Nixon. In the 1968 campaign, Haldeman and Ehrlichman belonged in one group. Ray Price and his writers were in another. Still a different group was composed of Rose Woods and Pat Buchanan. Sears and I, in addition to Tom Evans, constituted our own bunch.

In his skillful practice of manipulation, Nixon had just a few weaknesses; but they were significant ones. First, he perspired. Time after time, before a camera, under studio lights, or before a hostile audience, I could see the beads breaking out first on his upper lip, then on his forehead. A sweater myself, though not to Nixon's extent, I suffered with him empathetically.

Also, Nixon was not good at eye contact. He seemed to know that it is impossible really to see another person without being seen. This knowledge, like his sweating, kept him from being good at doing the lying that a politician has to do. A politician who is truly skillful at the practice can do it so well that even if you know he is lying, you simultaneously forgive him. Nixon, by contrast, may have been competent at lying; but he was usually quite bad at concealing the fact.

Nixon's eye contact problem, however, extended beyond lying; it was more general. Nixon was adept at looking at your tie, your mouth, a spot on your forehead—anywhere but your eyes. In relatively informal political settings, Nixon would sit behind his desk, feet up, and talk. This posture gave the impression of ease. It had the added virtue, from Nixon's point of view, of keeping his companions in conversation at a distance and making it unnecessary to look straight into their eyes.

The failure to make eye contact was a habit he shared with Sears. So was the posture. I remember repeatedly seeing Sears, during the campaign, on the telephone, feet up, adopting the classic Nixonian pose.

Nixon's formula for managing others and his own psyche seemed brilliant. In 1968, we used the slogan "Nixon's the One" because it seemed like shorthand for so many pieces of Nixon's history and the country's history. It comprehended Nixon's long experience in national politics, his having done battle for the country on the world stage, his knowledge of foreign leaders, his surmounting of crises, his anti-Communism, his sheer persistence through victory and defeat.

Then there was the Nixon campaign bromide, "The man and the times have come together." This slogan was meant to bring to mind world-class historical figures like Winston Churchill—once dismissed by British politics as a crank, then called to office to save the nation during World War II—or Charles de Gaulle, another political phoenix. In Nixon's case, the slogan was true. The frightening politics of the 1960s, not just Vietnam but more general upheavals in the emotionally freighted areas of race and sex, came together with the man,

Nixon, whose quality of unchanging durability promised that he could navigate a way through the chaos for the rest of us.

Yet the same formula that produced Nixon's success also produced his failure. Nixon, perhaps the last pure example of early twentieth-century political man, found his techniques and psychological postures, then stuck with them. As Nixon put it in his interview with Clawson, "You find you can't stop playing the game the way you've always played it. . . ."

Thus Nixon, though capable of liking individuals of almost any demographic description, from Chief Newman to Elvis Presley, had self-destructively infallible antennae for detecting whether people hated him; and he was incapable of not hating them back. Nixon shut down R & D, as it were, and went with what he had. What he had, as we have seen, was not good enough. Practicing the same politics that had gotten him to the presidency, and much the same politics that had been practiced by presidents before him, was not good enough for the roiling Vietnam-bred politics that he faced once he took office.

The unchanging character of Nixon's responses to political threat produced the intelligence operations at the White House and CRP. In the same way, the unchanging character of Nixon's responses after the arrest of the Watergate burglars led inescapably to the end of his presidency. On the White House tapes, as Nixon improvises endlessly, he is often inventive; but he is always working off the same limited script.

This is only a partial explanation, both of Watergate and of that part of Watergate that stemmed from the nature of Nixon's psyche. The great physicist Murray Gell-Mann, in trying to explain the scientific process to laypersons, said that it is relatively easy—only relatively, mind you—for physicists to dig ever deeper into the nature of matter, discover smaller and smaller particles and forces, and specify their characteristics and behavior. This process he called going downward. It is more difficult, he said, to go upward—to aggregate what is known about small things and use it to explain the behavior of larger things.

Explaining leaders who shape history is like that. When we are dealing with a figure of large proportions, a Luther or a Lincoln, the many pieces we can unearth about their lives and times will not fully explain them. So it is with Nixon. You can dig endlessly and profitably into the details of his history; they are indeed illuminating. But in the end you cannot explain him with any certainty. In particular, the details do not fully explain why he lived his life, personal and political, by giving so little of himself in such small, separate packets to different people.

He gave to John Sears, as he gave to me, a packet that was in many ways the best of Nixon. But it was only a packet. In my case, the packet sufficed. I was in the White House from almost the beginning to beyond the end. I am a conventional loyalist by nature. While I worked in the White House, evidence began to roll in that was inconsistent with the Nixon I knew. But by that time, a combination of accrued loyalty, denial, and sheer excitement were enough to keep me on the job.

John, having left the White House early, did not have the chance to develop those ties that bind. Nixon did not intend to cast Sears out of his political life. Nixon's correspondence with Haldeman just after the inauguration shows that he wanted John and me to get busy on the 1972 re-election campaign. But Nixon was dependent on Haldeman, Ehrlichman, and Mitchell in a profound sense, as part of a pact that Nixon had made with himself long ago and was incapable of re-examining. All of them, Nixon included, booted Sears out of office precisely because Sears had access to a Nixon who was different from and, they thought, more dangerous than theirs.

One consequence of this pact of Nixon's was that the balance barely maintained in the 1968 campaign was seriously upset by the time of the 1972 campaign. Nixon still had people around him of high character and purpose. However, most of them were largely concerned with public policy. The political side of the White House and the re-election campaign fell to other types. Nixon's political counselor became not John Sears but Chuck Colson.

Another consequence of this choice of Nixon's was that when Watergate occurred, Sears, though still in touch with Nixon, was out of the White House and thus without the obligations of institutional allegiance that fell on those of us still working for the president. Sears's obligations of loyalty were of a more amorphous sort. He was certainly not a snitch or even a whistleblower in any strict sense of either word; by 1972 he had long been on the outside looking in. In the 1960s, Sears had gone to work for and devoted himself to the politician that he thought Richard Nixon was. By the time of Watergate, thanks to the radical compartmentalization with which Nixon conducted his public life, that politician was extremely hard to recognize.

This change, the paradoxical product of Nixon's inability to change, is in the end not the stuff of political science, even though Deep Throat had effects on our politics that political science does well to study. Instead, it is part of those facets of human character that are beyond reduction to universal laws. Thus, like the old men at the funeral, we solve the riddle of Deep Throat only to stand face-to-face with this deeper mystery.

Epilogue

When I finished writing the manuscript of this book, I phoned John Sears and asked to see him. We met for drinks on April 16, 2000, at the Four Seasons Hotel in Georgetown. I told him about the book and that I believed that he was Deep Throat. As I expected, he denied this. However, as an old friend, and in the interests of "full disclosure," as he put it, he did admit to me that the conversations reported in *All the President's Men* between Carl Bernstein and a "former official of the Nixon administration" were in fact conversations between Bernstein and himself. So the voice I had recognized as Sears's did in fact belong to Sears. The first major step in my analysis was confirmed. We continued to talk some about Richard Nixon, but we had been around that track too many times for much in the way of fresh revelation or insight to emerge. We reminisced in a friendly way, then parted company, promising to be in touch again soon. I was surprised at just how soon.

Meanwhile, a major television news program had become interested in the book and began making phone calls to its *dramatis personae.* I gave Sears's private phone number to their chief correspondent so that he could hear Sears's side of the story. The correspondent reported back that Sears had adamantly denied (unsurprisingly) that he was Deep Throat, even volunteering to take a lie detector test. Sears then argued (surprisingly) that Deep Throat was in fact Charles Colson. I told the correspondent that in *All the President's Men*, Deep Throat had talked about Colson on a number of occasions, not only in the third person but in an uncomplimentary fashion. The correspondent then reached Colson, who contended that Deep Throat, though something of a composite, was primarily John Sears. It was striking to me that, almost thirty years after Colson had replaced Sears as Nixon's political counselor, the animosity between the two men was as fierce as ever.

The next day I received a letter from Sears threatening a lawsuit and including the sort of unpleasant language that typically accompanies such threats. I telephoned him. We debated my belief that he was Deep Throat heatedly and inconclusively. At the end he said he was glad that I had called, and he asked to receive a copy of the book as soon as it was published. I was happy to promise the book and a lunch on me.

The evidentiary uproar did not send me back to the state of abject uncertainty that had beset me after the collapse of Robert F. Bennett's candidacy as Deep Throat. This time it was different. The evidence was still circumstantial, and, in the absence of a smoking gun or a confession, it remains so. Yet in this case, the evidence was so strong that I was and remain convinced that of all the candidates seriously mentioned for the role of Deep Throat, Sears was the only one with the requisite access to the press, range of knowledge, opportunity, motive, and characteristics of psychology and temperament. Furthermore, Sears was the one with the best reason to believe that he could expose the Watergate cover-up and enable Nixon to avoid the destruction of his presidency.

But the pre-publication back-and-forth illustrates the fact that absolute knowledge on matters of history is rare. More often than not—much more often, in fact—there will be a degree of uncertainty. In this case, we cannot know Deep Throat's identity with certainty unless or until one of the four holders of the secret—Woodward, Bernstein, Ben Bradlee, or Deep Throat himself—chooses to reveal it. And each of them may have reasons at which we can only guess for not wanting the details of the story, like Deep Throat's reality-defying access to Woodward's copy of the *New York Times*, to be known and reexamined, even after twenty-five years.

For me, the search for Deep Throat has ended. I do not think I will wonder about him anymore. I am sure, however, that I will return from time to time to the larger puzzle of Richard Nixon, one of the last century's great mysteries. And that, after all, may have been what my search was really about in the first place.

Cast of Characters

Robert Abplanalp—*Then:* Aerosol tycoon and friend on whose private Bahamaian island Nixon was vacationing when the burglars were arrested at the Watergate. *Now:* Still a tycoon, and a successful vintner as well.

Spiro T. Agnew—*Then:* Nixon's Vice President. *Now:* Died 1996.

Richard V. Allen—*Then:* Deputy Assistant to the President, specializing in foreign economic policy. *Now:* International business consultant; former National Security Adviser to President Reagan.

Martin C. Anderson—*Then:* Special Assistant to the President. *Now:* Senior Fellow at the Hoover Institution, Stanford University.

Alfred C. Baldwin III—*Then:* Security guard employed by the Committee for the Re-election of the President; Assistant to James McCord monitoring wiretaps placed by the Watergate burglars. *Now:* Unknown.

Bernard L. Barker—*Then:* Watergate burglar. *Now:* Retired municipal employee.

Robert F. Bennett—*Then:* Howard Hunt's employer at the Robert R. Mullen & Co. public relations firm. *Now:* United States Senator from Utah.

Carl Bernstein—*Then:* Reporter at the *Washington Post. Now:* Contributing Editor for *Vanity Fair.*

Robert H. Bork—*Then:* Solicitor General. *Now:* Lawyer; author; John M. Olin Scholar in Legal Studies at the American Enterprise Institute; former federal judge.

Benjamin C. Bradlee—*Then:* Executive Editor of the *Washington Post.* *Now:* Vice President of the *Washington Post.*

Patrick J. Buchanan—*Then:* Special Assistant to the President, specializing in speechwriting. *Now:* Presidential candidate; author, political commentator.

Alexander P. Butterfield—*Then:* Deputy Assistant to the President; aide to Bob Haldeman. *Now:* Retired management consultant.

J. Fred Buzhardt—*Then:* Deputy Counsel to the President. *Now:* Died 1978.

John ("Jack") Caulfield—*Then:* Aide to John Ehrlichman. *Now:* Executive in one of Bob Abplanalp's businesses.

Murray Chotiner—*Then:* Political advisor to Nixon. *Now:* Died 1974.

Kenneth Clawson—*Then:* Deputy Director of Communications at the White House. *Now:* Died 1999.

Kenneth R. Cole, Jr.—*Then:* John Ehrlichman's assistant and successor on the Domestic Policy Council. *Now:* Investment company executive.

Charles W. Colson—*Then:* Special Counsel to the President, specializing in political affairs. *Now:* Prison evangelist; founder of Prison Fellowship.

John B. Connally—*Then:* Secretary of the Treasury. *Now:* Died 1993.

Richard K. Cook—*Then:* Deputy Assistant to the President. *Now:* Aerospace industry executive.

Archibald Cox—*Then:* Watergate special prosecutor. *Now:* Law professor at Harvard University.

Kenneth H. Dahlberg—*Then:* Midwest Finance Chairman of the Committee for the Re-election of the President. *Now:* Retired industrialist.

John W. Dean, III—*Then:* Counsel to the President. *Now:* Investment banker.

Harry Dent—*Then:* Deputy Counsel to the President, specializing in political affairs. *Now:* Semi-retired.

John Ehrlichman—*Then:* Assistant to the President for Domestic Affairs. *Now:* Died 1999.

Daniel Ellsberg—*Then:* Former Department of Defense official who gave the *New York Times* the Pentagon Papers in 1971. *Now:* Retired.

Robert F. Ellsworth—*Then:* U.S. Ambassador to NATO. *Now:* Investment executive.

Sam J. Ervin, Jr.—*Then:* U.S. Senator from North Carolina and chairman of Senate Watergate committee. *Now:* Died 1985.

Thomas W. Evans—*Then:* Managing partner of Nixon Mudge law firm. *Now:* Lawyer in private practice.

W. Mark Felt, Jr.—*Then:* Acting Associate Director of the FBI. *Now:* Retired.

Fred F. Fielding—*Then:* Deputy Counsel to the President. *Now:* Lawyer in private practice; former Counsel to President Reagan.

Robert H. Finch—*Then:* Secretary of Health, Education, and Welfare. *Now:* Died 1995.

Peter M. Flanigan—*Then:* Deputy Assistant to the President, specializing in economic issues. *Now:* Investment banker.

David Gergen—*Then:* Deputy Assistant to the President, specializing in speechwriting. *Now:* Professor at the John F. Kennedy School of Government, Harvard University; former adviser to Presidents Ford, Reagan, and Clinton.

Seymour Glanzer—*Then:* Assistant U.S. Attorney on the team prosecuting the Watergate burglars. *Now:* Lawyer in private practice.

Virgilio R. Gonzalez—*Then:* Watergate burglar. *Now:* Unknown.

L. Patrick Gray—*Then:* Acting Director of the FBI after J. Edgar Hoover. *Now:* Retired, living in Florida.

Alan Greenspan—*Then:* Member of the Council of Economic Advisers. *Now:* Chairman of the Board of Governors of the Federal Reserve System.

Alexander M. Haig, Jr.—*Then:* Assistant to the President, Chief of Staff after Bob Haldeman. *Now:* Business executive and investor; former Secretary of State and Supreme Commander of NATO.

H. R. "Bob" Haldeman—*Then:* Assistant to the President, Chief of Staff. *Now:* Died 1993.

Bryce N. Harlow—*Then:* Special Assistant to the President, specializing in congressional relations. *Now:* Died 1987.

Richard M. Helms—*Then:* Director of the Central Intelligence Agency. *Now:* International consultant; former Ambassador to Iran.

Lawrence M. Higby—*Then:* Deputy Assistant to the President. *Now:* Health care executive.

Alger Hiss—*Then:* Former State Department official who had been convicted of perjury following an investigation into his Communist connections by then-Congressman Nixon. *Now:* Died 1996.

J. Edgar Hoover—*Then:* Director of the FBI. *Now:* Died 1972.

Howard Hughes—*Then:* Billionaire recluse, and generous and ecumenical campaign contributor. *Now:* Died 1976.

Hubert H. Humphrey—*Then:* Lyndon Johnson's Vice President and the Democratic presidential candidate in 1968. *Now:* Died 1978.

E. Howard Hunt, Jr. (a.k.a. Eduardo)—*Then:* White House consultant working for Charles Colson; employee of Mullen & Co.; White House Plumber; leader of the Watergate burglars. *Now:* Author.

Bobby Ray Inman—*Then:* Executive Assistant to the Vice Chief of Naval Operations. *Now:* Investor; former electronics executive.

Leon Jaworski—*Then:* Watergate special prosecutor after Archibald Cox. *Now:* Died 1982.

Herbert Kalmbach—*Then:* Deputy Finance Chairman of the Committee for the Re-election of the President; Nixon's personal lawyer and chief fund-raiser in California. *Now:* Lawyer in private practice.

Henry A. Kissinger—*Then:* Assistant to the President for National Security Affairs; Secretary of State after William P. Rogers. *Now:* International consulting company executive.

Herbert G. Klein—*Then:* Director of Communications in the Nixon White House. *Now:* Editor-in-chief of newspaper chain.

Richard G. Kleindienst—*Then:* Attorney General after John Mitchell. *Now:* Died 2000.

Tom C. Korologos—*Then:* Deputy Assistant to the President, specializing in legislative affairs. *Now:* Government affairs consultant.

Egil ("Bud") Krogh, Jr.—*Then:* Deputy Assistant to the President for Domestic Affairs; White House Plumber. *Now:* Lawyer in private practice.

Melvin R. Laird—*Then:* Secretary of Defense; Senior Counselor to the President, specializing in international affairs. *Now:* Executive, Reader's Digest Association.

Frederick C. LaRue—*Then:* Deputy Director, Committee for the Re-election of the President; John Mitchell's right-hand man. *Now:* Retired.

G. Gordon Liddy—*Then:* White House Plumber; Finance Counsel to the Committee for the Re-election of the President; leader of the Watergate burglars. *Now:* Radio talk show host.

Clark MacGregor—*Then:* Director, Committee for the Re-election of the President after John Mitchell. *Now:* Retired.

Jeb Stuart Magruder—*Then:* Deputy Director, Committee for the Re-election of the President. *Now:* Presbyterian minister.

Robert C. Mardian—*Then:* Assistant Attorney General; political coordinator, Committee for the Re-election of the President. *Now:* Corporate lawyer.

Eugenio R. Martinez—*Then:* Watergate burglar. *Now:* Car sales manager.

Alice Mayhew—*Then:* Editor of *All the President's Men*. *Now:* Editor of books by Bob Woodward, John Dean, Steven Brill, and many others.

James W. McCord, Jr.—*Then:* Chief of Security for the Committee for the Re-election of the President. *Now:* Retired.

George S. McGovern—*Then:* U.S. Senator from South Dakota; Democratic presidential candidate in 1972. *Now:* U.S. Ambassador to the United Nations Food and Agriculture Organization.

Jamie McLane—*Then:* Staff Assistant to the President, heading the White House's Council on Aging. *Now:* Health care executive.

Cord Meyer—*Then:* Assistant Deputy Director for Operations, Central Intelligence Agency. *Now:* Newspaper columnist.

Starke Meyer—*Then:* Assistant to Leonard Garment, specializing in arts policy. *Now:* Artist.

John N. Mitchell—*Then:* Attorney General; Director, Committee for the Re-election of the President. *Now:* Died 1988.

Edward L. Morgan—*Then:* Assistant Secretary of the Treasury in charge of the Secret Service. *Now:* Died 1999.

Richard Nixon—*Then:* Thirty-seventh President of the United States. *Now:* Died 1994.

Lawrence F. O'Brien—*Then:* Chairman, Democratic National Committee. *Now:* Died 1990.

David Obst—*Then:* Book agent for Woodward and Bernstein. *Now:* Author.

Robert C. Odle, Jr.—*Then:* Director of Administration, Committee for the Re-election of the President. *Now:* Lawyer in private practice; former Assistant Secretary, Department of Energy.

R. Spencer Oliver—*Then:* Executive Director, Association of State Democratic Chairmen. *Now:* Secretary General of the Organization for Security and Cooperation in Europe, Parliamentary Assembly.

Henry E. Petersen—*Then:* Assistant Attorney General, Criminal Division. *Now:* Died 1991.

Raymond K. Price, Jr.—*Then:* Special Assistant to the President, specializing in speechwriting. *Now:* President of the Economic Club of New York.

Elliot L. Richardson—*Then:* Attorney General after Richard Kleindienst. *Now:* Died 2000.

William P. Rogers—*Then:* Secretary of State. *Now:* Lawyer in private practice.

William D. Ruckelshaus—*Then:* Acting Director of the FBI after Pat Gray; Deputy Attorney General. *Now:* Investment group executive; former Administrator, Environmental Protection Agency.

Donald H. Rumsfeld—*Then:* Counselor to the President and Director, Economic Stabilization Program. *Now:* Retired corporate executive; former Secretary of Defense.

William Safire—*Then:* Special Assistant to the President, specializing in speechwriting. *Now:* Newspaper columnist; author.

James D. St. Clair—*Then:* Special Counsel to the President. *Now:* Retired lawyer; Trustee of numerous charitable organizations; Director of Boston Opera Association.

William B. Saxbe—*Then:* Attorney General after Elliot Richardson. *Now:* Lawyer in private practice.

John P. Sears III—*Then:* Deputy Counsel to the President; lawyer in private practice. *Now:* Lawyer in private practice.

Donald H. Segretti—*Then:* Political trickster employed by Nixon White House. *Now:* Lawyer in private practice.

George P. Shultz—*Then:* Secretary of Labor; Secretary of the Treasury. *Now:* Emeritus professor, Stanford University.

Earl Silbert—*Then:* Assistant U.S. Attorney on the team prosecuting the Watergate burglars. *Now:* Lawyer in private practice.

Howard Simons—*Then:* Managing Editor of the *Washington Post*. *Now:* Died 1989.

John J. Sirica—*Then:* Federal judge conducting Watergate burglars' trial. *Now:* Died 1992.

Hugh W. Sloan, Jr.—*Then:* Treasurer, Committee for the Re-election of the President. *Now:* Automotive industry executive.

Maurice H. Stans—*Then:* Secretary of Commerce; Finance Chairman, Committee for the Re-election of the President. *Now:* Died 1998.

Gordon C. Strachan—*Then:* Deputy Assistant to the President; Bob Haldeman's right-hand man. *Now:* Lawyer in private practice.

Frank A. Sturgis—*Then:* Watergate burglar. *Now:* Died 1993.

Barry Sussman—*Then:* City Editor of the *Washington Post. Now:* Author; public analyst and pollster; journalist.

Anthony T. Ulasewicz—*Then:* Independent investigator employed by the White House and supervised by Jack Caulfield. *Now:* Died 1997.

Vernon A. Walters—*Then:* Deputy Director of the Central Intelligence Agency. *Now:* Retired U.S. Army lieutenant general; former Ambassador to Germany and the United Nations.

Richard J. Whalen—*Then:* Special Assistant to the President. *Now:* Retired.

Joe Woods—*Then:* Sheriff of Cook County, Illinois. *Now:* Retired.

Rose Mary Woods—*Then:* Secretary to the President. *Now:* Retired.

Robert U. Woodward—*Then:* Reporter at the *Washington Post. Now:* Author; Assistant Managing Editor of the *Post.*

Charles Alan Wright—*Then:* Professor of law at the University of Texas; consulting counsel to the President. *Now:* Professor of law at the University of Texas.

David R. Young—*Then:* Assistant to National Security Adviser; White House Plumber. *Now:* Founder and head of international management consulting firm.

Ronald L. Ziegler—*Then:* Press Secretary to the President. *Now:* Association executive.

Elmo R. Zumwalt, Jr.—*Then:* Chief of Naval Operations. *Now:* Died 2000.

Index